Taking care
of Dad

Taking care
of Dad

John B. Reynolds

SunCreek
B O O K S
Allen, Texas

Send all inquiries to:
SunCreek Books
An RCL Company
200 East Bethany Drive
Allen, Texas 75002-3804

Telephone: 800-264-0368 / 972-390-6400
Fax: 800-688-8356 / 972-390-6560

E-mail: cservice@rcl-enterprises.com

Website: **www.ThomasMore.com**

Printed in the United States of America

Library of Congress Catalog Number: 2003102338

5707   ISBN 1-932057-07-2

1 2 3 4 5   07 06 05 04 03

To Jean and Jim.
Together again,
and still fitting each other like gloves.

Acknowledgments

I WISH TO ACKNOWLEDGE and thank Debra Hampton and John Sprague of Thomas More Publishing—the former for believing in this book, and the latter for editing the work and bringing the vision home. I wish to acknowledge and thank Ruth McGugan and John Riddle for talking me down. I wish to acknowledge and thank Sarah and Paul, my children; Mary, my sister; and everyone mentioned upon these pages for helping me in their own ways to tell this story. I wish to acknowledge and thank each person who lingers over the words that follow for treading the path with me. And I wish to especially acknowledge and thank Gail, my friend and my wife, for believing not only in the book, but also—and from the very beginning—in its author.

Contents

Introduction

This book is a collection of letters. They have been written to a friend—you the reader are that friend! The events and emotions described are very real. I know this to be true because I wrote them about my father, and I am my father's son.

I NEVER GAVE MUCH THOUGHT to eldercare, even as my mother was caring for Dad. Busy with my own life, I thought that eldercare was somebody else's business—Mom's, in this particular instance. Perhaps you know the feeling from the outside looking in, or perhaps you are knee-deep in your own eldercare situation. If so, I hold you immediately as a friend, and I want you to know that you are not alone in the work you do. According to surveys conducted by the American Association of Retired Persons and the National Alliance for Caregiving, an estimated 22.4 million U.S. households—nearly one in four—are "sandwich generation" households.

The individuals heading these households are defined as baby boomers (adults born between 1946 and 1965) who are caring for children at home and who have at least one living parent. Additional surveys suggest that collectively today's boomers likely will spend more time caring for a parent than for their children.

While the time frame didn't come to pass in my case, I put in a rather intensive five years on the front lines of eldercare while caring for my children at the same time. The "average" caregiver in the United States is said to be mid-forty-something and female. I didn't make this cut either but that's okay. We men are an adapting bunch.

The fifty "letters" which follow tell my father's story and, of a certain necessity, my own. While they are personal in nature, I pray that they are universal in scope. One letter at a time, Dad and I thank you for entering into our world, and for welcoming us into yours.

Part One

Getting the News

When I picked up my teenage daughter last year on her final day of school before summer vacation kicked in, she slid into the front seat next to me with a smile and an agenda.

SHE TOLD ME that she was going to go home, change into something cool (a T-shirt and maybe some shorts), get something to eat (preferably something cold, like ice cream), plop back on the couch with her latest teen magazine, and paint her nails. I've never been a fifteen-year-old girl, but I remember summer vacations, and I envied her.

Everything worked out for Sarah that afternoon, and she gloried in the moment. But life doesn't always go according to plan. As Forrest Gump pronounces so deliberately, life is like a box of chocolates, and as we all have learned, we never know what we're going to get. But we can hope, can't we? We can dream. And after working hard year after year for decades, aren't we entitled to our days in the sun? Unfortunately, if my father was expecting an age-appropriate modification of Sarah's plan—retirement, travel, hobbies, . . . a chocolate-covered cherry, if you will—he ended up with something much, much different. He didn't get a chocolate-covered cherry. He got a rock.

Shifting to a baseball analogy, let's just say that Dad was looking for a fastball high and inside as he entered into his golden years but life threw him a curveball low and away. I hate curve-balls. And as the truth about his condition comes out, curveballs are flying all over the place. My mother, perhaps, is being affected most by all of this, but I was expecting a fastball for Dad, too, as were my brother and sister. Today's news about Dad, and tomorrow's news about Mom, will come to affect us all.

A friend of mine once told me that the problems we have an opportunity to ponder over for days and weeks and even months never really develop into much. Most of these just go away on their own. The real problems, he said, are the ones that hit us like giant waves on a clear day, knocking us backward as they pour over us, giving us no chance to catch our breaths or regain our feet. Wise words. Depending on circumstance, getting the news that someone we love is failing can come to us in either fashion. Depending on circumstance, what we do with the news can define us for a lifetime.

1

Dad is slowing down. This is how I see it, anyway. He's retired, after all, and he worked at that bank for over thirty years.

A MAN HAS A RIGHT to slow down after thirty years, no? Mom says so, too. Actually, I'm buying into the whole slowing down thing because of her. It's easier for me to say his decline is age related than to listen to the talk coming from the relatives and the in-laws. Talk always gets back to you, you know? The word on the street is that Dad's sick. Mom says no to all of this, and I want to believe her. Still. She's been married to the guy for thirty-five years, and I sense she knows more than she's saying. Dad's definitely lost a step or two, and as much as I don't want to admit it, the reason behind his fading may be something more—and something worse—than just the years taking their toll.

For one thing, Dad has stopped walking with Mom to Mass in the morning. Those two have walked together to 6:30 A.M. Mass for years. Mom used to tell me that people would always stop and offer them rides before they realized that my folks were out there because they enjoyed it. That's the nice thing about growing up—and in Mom and Dad's case, old—in a small town. Streator people know each other. And they not only know each other, they care about each other, too. I love my brother and sister, but I remember them saying when they were preparing to graduate from college that they were ready to leave town. When I graduated, I hated the thought of leaving Streator behind. And I wouldn't have, I don't think, if I thought I could have found a job there. Anyway, I digress.

Like I was saying, nothing stopped Mom and Dad from their daily walk to Mass. They weren't fanatic about it or anything, but a little rain, sleet, or dark of morning never slowed them down. They could have been mail carriers. But on some of my visits home over the past several months, Mom's been telling me that it was too much for Dad to go with her in the mornings. "It's okay, Johnny," she says. "Dad's just slowing down a little." I can see it too, like I said. I can see it in the way he moves around the kitchen and has to hold on to things. And he sits a lot more, as well—there on the little love seat in the kitchen. Nine times out of ten when I go home these days to say hello, that's where I find him.

Home. I've been living and working up here in Chicago for years, and I still call Streator home. I catch grief about it from my coworkers, Barbara especially. She always corrects me when I say I'm going home for the weekend. She tells me that Chicago *is* my home. She says it's where my house is, where my wife is, where I sleep each night, where I park my car. She's a smart lady, Barbara. Of course, she's right, and if she had heard what I said to my wife a few days ago, she would have fallen out of her chair.

Gail and I were talking about grocery store chains for some reason. Kroger's, I think. That's when I asked Gail, "Do you have those stores up here in Chicago?" It was as if I had forgotten everything about where I live and work and have a home with my wife. It was as if I had forgotten that I've been in Chicago all these years. I think that for an instant, I actually thought I still lived in Streator and was just visiting my wife up in the big city. Maybe I was time-warping or something. It worked in the *Rocky Horror Picture Show,* anyway. All I know for sure is that Gail looked at me stunned. *Stunned!* And I think I was a little stunned, myself.

Another thing about Dad. He's stopped clerking the auction sales back home. I don't know how he and Mom got that job, but it had something to do with Dad's work at the bank. You ever been to a small-town sale? One man's junk is another man's treasure, and there's a lot of junk out there. There's good stuff, too, of course. Gail and I bought our dining room chairs at a sale in Streator recently. And Dad bought his pick-up truck at a sale. It's a red Ford F150, '76, I think. Every time I go home, I ask Dad if I can take it around town. It's got a stick shift on the column, a firm clutch, and beat up interior, but not too beat up. I love that truck. Dad does, too. And even though he kept his car, he took to driving the pick-up to all of the sales. In case he and Mom bought more stuff.

Mom would call me and tell me about the chair or the sofa or the painting they got at the latest sale. Now they're tripping over the stuff, but they had a great time accumulating all of it. And I must admit that they got it at some really terrific prices. It's like the furniture that Gail and I bought. If you happen to want something that nobody else wants, you can get it for a song. Every time I go home, it's apparent to me that Mom and Dad were doing more than just clerking those sales. They were buying, too! But now those happy auction days are gone, and Dad doesn't drive the F150 much anymore.

Beyond all of the auction clutter, the house itself is a problem, too. I read a great slogan once. Maybe I saw it in the yellow pages, or on a billboard somewhere. Regardless, it promoted an appliance repair business, and it said, "If we can't fix it, it isn't broken!" Dad could have written that. The man is the original Mr. Fix-It! At least he used to be. You know, before he started slowing down.

I can still remember helping him replace some shingles on Grandma's house over on Illinois Street back home when I was a kid. I didn't do much other than schlep his tools for him up and down the ladder. It was cold that day. And windy—the kind of wind that cuts right through you. Dad said he needed some help so I volunteered, even though I didn't really want to. I felt bad for him going off to do the work alone. He replaced the shingles just fine, and seemed to have a good time doing it. That was the crazy part. He always seemed to enjoy this household maintenance stuff.

I remember another time, too. Clear as a bell. We had a backed up sewer line and the most disgusting liquid on earth was backing up into our bathtub. Dad said we needed to rod the line. He put on his old brown cover-alls and his boots, and he climbed into the tub. Yecch! Then he started feeding a coiled, metal snake—the rodder—down the drain. I didn't do much that time either. I just watched and, I suppose, tried to offer Dad moral support by being there.

And I'm glad I stayed, because I watched in amazement as Dad kept feeding the line into the drain. It must have gone out thirty to forty feet when Dad started struggling with it. He pulled it back and sent it through a few times, as I remember, and each time he found chunks of tree roots at the end of the rodder. Dad said some roots from the big old oak tree outside the house on Uncle Russ's side were blocking the line. Dad removed the chunks from the end of the rodder and said that it shouldn't take long now.

He sent the rodder through one last time, and this time, it punched its way through the roots and whatever else was blocking the line. And just like that, all of the black, stinking water that Dad had been hunkered down in for that previous hour started to move down the drain. Dad reeled the rod back in as the water churned away, and just before it was all gone, it formed a tiny whirlpool and started making that sucking sound that water makes when it has somewhere to go. That's when Dad told me that there was no better sound in the world than the sound of water rushing down a cleaned-out drainpipe. I've thought about that a lot, because he said it like he meant it. All of this happened over twenty years ago, and the memory is still fresh.

Now that Dad's slowing down, he can't get so much of the work done. I catch Mom doing it sometimes when I go home to visit. She hasn't rodded out the sewer line lately—at least not that she's told me about—but she's doing lots of other things. Besides taking care of Dad, she does the grocery shopping, cuts the grass in the summer, shovels snow in the winter, washes the clothes, cleans the house, and pays the bills. She probably shouldn't be doing all of this stuff because she's no spring chicken, as she often tells me. She's plenty strong, though, and she says somebody's got to do it. I suppose.

She could hire somebody, but that's not my parents' way. They'll probably have to someday, though. In the meantime, I do what I can. I was home just a few weekends ago, took down all of their screens, and put up their storm windows. And it was no small job. My folks have the old-fashioned storms and screens—the big wood-encased ones that have to be entirely removed from the window and hung somewhere else during the off-season. Mom and Dad hang theirs on top of the garage, which is really just an old barn with an attic. It was hard work for me. There's no way Mom or Dad could have done it.

And so it goes. Little repairs that need tending to aren't tended to. I should do more, but I'm not very good at this stuff for one thing. Didn't watch Dad enough when I was small, maybe. He loved puttering around the house then, like I was saying. But me? I preferred playing baseball or bike-riding or golfing or playing tennis or swimming. I bet I could have learned a lot from Dad about puttering if I had hung around at his side a little more. Often, I regret not doing this. Not so much for the household maintenance lessons as for the whole father-son thing.

Mom and Dad never took us on vacation when my brother and sister and I were growing up. Dad always took his two weeks off in October when Jim and Mary and I were in school. Mom said he took time off in October so he could putter around the house and get it ready for winter, and rarely did I join him in the work. It's like he was too busy for us in the summer with the bank, and we were too busy for him in the fall with school and everything. This doesn't keep me up at night. Still, I think of it from time to time, and wonder how things might have been between us if I had paid Dad a little more attention. Or vice versa.

But the bigger reason I don't head down to Streator more often now to help out is just the time availability at this end. It's a two-hour drive for one thing, and with my work and all, it's hard to get away. It's always great when we make it home, though. Last weekend, Gail and I paid a surprise visit and found Mom and Dad eating at Weaver's Fried Chicken on North Bloomington Street. It's one of their usual Saturday night dates. Gail and I knocked hello to them through the restaurant window. Mom was just tickled to see us, and I think Dad was, too. I cut the grass the next day, and I'll shovel snow when I'm home in the winter. Beyond that, Mom will be doing all the work. Or at least most of it. Like she keeps saying, she has to. Dad is slowing down.

It's pushing 7:00 A.M., and I had better start getting ready for work.

2

Dad has Parkinson's disease. That's what the doctor in Streator is saying, so I guess all that talk on the street was right.

MY SISTER MARY got the news first, but she uncovered it on her own. She's good! Mary was home for a visit with her husband and her two small boys when she found the Sinemet in Mom and Dad's medicine cabinet. Apparently, Mom took Dad to the doctor and this is what he prescribed. Mary called a friend of hers who is a nurse, and learned that Sinemet is one of the commonly used medications for Parkinson's. Mom didn't want to admit any of this, and she downplayed it quite a bit according to Mary. But my sister has long been the clearinghouse of information within the Reynolds household, and once again, she ferreted out the truth.

When I first got the news from Mary and then from Mom, I didn't know what to think. Still don't. I've heard of Parkinson's, but I don't think you die from it. I mean, it's not like cancer or a heart attack or anything. It just gives the people the shakes. That's Parkinson's. At least that's what I think of as Parkinson's. Having the shakes isn't a good thing, but these people still get around, so how bad can it be? Don't get me wrong. I mean, it's terrible that Dad has it and all, but if you *have* to contract a disease when you grow old, Parkinson's is probably as good as any, right?

These were my first thoughts, like I said, but thinking more about it, I remember that Gloria's dad had it, too. Gloria is a girl I knew down at Champaign, at the University of Illinois. We played racquetball and tennis over at the intramural sports building. We went ice skating on a beautiful snowy Friday night, and she made me spaghetti back at her place afterward. We even drank some green beer at Second Chance once after a chemistry exam on St. Patrick's Day. We shared a few beers lots of times, in fact.

Actually, the only reason I'm around to write this letter to you now is because when Gloria and I were walking back from the White Horse one night after sharing a pitcher, she saved me from being hit by a car. I was strolling across Green Street like I owned it and I didn't even look for the car coming from campus town. The driver was probably speeding besides. Next thing I knew, Gloria had me by the shoulders and was yanking me onto the sidewalk and out of harm's way. Sometimes when I went running down at school after the homework was done, I would sing her name in my head. "And her name is G–L–O–R–I–A. . . ." The Shadows of Knight version. What a great song.

Anyway, Gloria's dad had Parkinson's disease. I met him a few times when I was picking up Gloria at her home or dropping her off. Her mom was a live wire and I think she liked me, but her dad. . . . Her dad didn't do much. He just kind of sat off by himself. I remember picking up Gloria once and seeing him—I think his name was Tom—sitting by himself at the other side of the room. I can't recall if it was daytime or nighttime, but he looked like a shadow sitting there, like the black silhouette of a man just wasting away. I always felt a little awkward with her dad around. It was like he was there, but he wasn't there. Weird. He had Parkinson's disease, and now Dad has it too.

I'm sure he was an active man before this thing got hold of him. I don't know what he did, but he was probably busy all of the time like Dad. Before he started slowing down, I mean. But Gloria's dad seemed to be way beyond the slowing down phase. Gloria's dad was essentially stopped. So now I'm asking myself, *Is this what my own father has to look forward to?* Thinking about all of this and knowing what I know, I've come to a much different conclusion on Dad's diagnosis. Parkinson's disease seems a lot scarier all of a sudden, so I've been reading up on it. I don't want to bore you with the technical stuff, but let me tell you what I've found out.

First of all, it's a progressive disorder of the central nervous system. Seems like every article, pamphlet, and book I've read recently has opened up with those words, or similar ones. Progressive. It's funny, the word actually has some good connotations, doesn't it? Progressive schools offer their students innovative learning techniques. Progressive companies give their employees sabbatical time every few years to pursue community work. My wife and I are part of a progressive dinner each Christmas season with some friends, and everybody has a great time going from home to home for appetizers, the main course, and dessert. In Dad's case, though, progressive is a bad thing. It means that nobody really gets better from the disease, beyond the short-term benefits brought about by medication and in some cases surgery. Mostly with Parkinson's, the symptoms of the disease just keep getting worse and worse.

An English physician, Dr. James Parkinson, originally described the disease in the early 1800s. He called it "Shaking Palsy." Fitting, and nearly two hundred years later, Dad's in good company. At least by the numbers. I read somewhere that PD currently affects a million people in the United States alone. A million people! But nobody ever asked Dad about it, and probably nobody asked Gloria's dad, so let's call it a million and two.

Typical onset of the disease comes between the ages of forty and seventy, although there have been exceptions, particularly at the younger end of the scale. Both men and women are afflicted. The classic symptoms—in their totality—are a decrease in spontaneous movements due to muscle rigidity, shuffle-like steps, mask-like facial features, postural instability, and tremor. But all patients don't develop all symptoms to the same degree, if at all. Dad doesn't have the shakes, for example, but he has shown signs of everything else. And don't forget the whole progressive thing. Eventually, the physical limitations can become severe, and some degree of dementia may kick in as well. I keep thinking of Gloria's dad sitting there in the shadows.

"Parkinson's disease is caused by the degeneration of the pigmented neurons in the Substantia Nigra of the brain, resulting in decreased dopamine availability." Impressive, no? It should be, because I quote it directly from some American Parkinson's Disease Association literature. But for all the ten dollar medical words, the bottom line is this: (1) Dopamine is a chemical produced in the brain which is necessary for normal muscle movement and control; (2) lack of this chemical causes the onset of the Parkinson's symptoms. The APDA's motto is "Ease the Burden and Find the Cure." If it's too late for Gloria's father, maybe it's not too late for Dad.

Apparently, doctors can't do what seems to me to be the obvious. They can't administer dopamine directly to their patients because dopamine itself cannot cross the blood-brain barrier. It's never easy. Instead, PD patients are often treated by the oral administration of levadopa, a dopamine precursor. Once the levadopa reaches the brain, it is converted to dopamine and the process is complete. Theoretically, at least. Unfortunately, levadopa doesn't prevent the progressive nature of the disease in general, and it has its own side effects in some people. Hallucinations, for example. Other drugs are being developed which, when given with levadopa, can enhance the effect of the precursor drug and decrease its side effects as well. Better living through chemistry.

All of this stuff, at least as I see it right now, is pretty much out of my control. But I keep hanging on to one thing that maybe wasn't, and that maybe I should have seized upon and done something with. A few of the articles I read have indicated that certain chemicals can induce Parkinson's disease, suggesting that it might have an environmental origin. One article even said that Parkinson's can be triggered by environmental trauma. Environmental trauma? My God, I thought they just had the flu. . . .

Years ago, I called Mom to say hello and to see how she and Dad were doing. She said they were doing okay, but that they were both feeling a bit under the weather. She said she didn't know if it was a cold or what, but that they were tired and run down. They couldn't have been real bad, though, because Mom said they were still walking to church in the morning. So, I probably said something stupid like, "Maybe it's just the weather." We're a healthy family, after all. Always have been. In fact, I got a perfect attendance award when I graduated high school and I only missed a few days in grade school. "You come from good stock," Mom and Dad often told me when I was growing up. They still tell me this today sometimes. Mom and Dad never get sick. They're always up and moving. Yea, it must have just been the weather.

But I spoke with Mom again a few days later, and she said they were doing worse. Said they were real tired, and all of the time. Mom may have mentioned the possibility of them having the flu, or maybe I dreamed it up on my own. Either way, I was sure they would ride out the storm and feel better soon, so I sent them flowers and wished them well. What I didn't know as I was placing the order was that their lives were in danger, and maybe had been for quite a while. What I didn't know as I was speaking with the florist over the phone and thinking well of myself for being such a thoughtful and caring son was that Mom and Dad's furnace was malfunctioning, belching carbon monoxide gas into the air that they were breathing.

My sister Mary may have suspected this all along. I can't say that I ever got sick going home to visit Mom and Dad, and I went home quite a bit. Mary, though, and her kids—I think Jeff was about two at the time, and Chris maybe four—seemed to get sick almost every time they went to Streator for a visit. Mary's husband—my brother-in-law John—even went to the hospital in Streator once complaining of nausea and dizziness. They told him he had an inner-ear infection. Maybe. But along with mild headaches and shortness of breath, nausea and dizziness are symptoms of carbon monoxide poisoning.

Like I said, Mary and John's children were small, and this may have explained a lot. Mom and Dad always kept their house plenty cool. Gail and I joked about it and threw on extra sweaters before making a Streator swing in the fall or winter. We adapted to the chilly environment accordingly. Mary and John would have too, I'm sure, but my folks cranked the heat up whenever they came home to visit to keep Chris and Jeff comfortable. In hindsight, Mary thinks they got sick because of the increased carbon monoxide in the air. She's probably right.

And this particular time, she may have saved Mom and Dad's life. She had been home for a visit which she actually cut short because Jeff and Chris got sick again. But by the time Mary reached Ottawa on her trip back up to Chicago, her kids were doing fine—as they often were by that time, Mary told me—so she was convinced it was something in the house. She called Mom and Dad when she reached Chicago, and suggested that they have the furnace checked out. Coincidentally, Aunt Marge stopped by the house a day or so later, and Dad was so sick by then, he had to crawl to the door. And I send them flowers from one hundred miles away. Yes, such a thoughtful and caring son.

Because Mom and Dad were sick, they never turned the heat down after Mary left. Maybe they were too mentally unaware to do anything about it. More heat, more carbon monoxide in the air. The crawling thing must have finally hit home, though, because that's when they called the furnace repair guy. He confirmed the malfunction and took care of it. As Mom said later, he told them that they were lucky to be alive. Good job, Mary! Good job, Marge! And good job, Mr. Furnace Man, wherever you may be all these years later.

Personally, I attribute their survival to their daily Mass routine. All the while a faulty furnace was filling up their lungs with carbon monoxide, Mom and Dad kept walking to Mass every morning at dawn until they got too sick to do it. By my theory, most of the carbon monoxide they breathed in, they breathed right back out again by walking two miles each way to and from St. Anthony's. One of the best treatments after exposure to carbon monoxide, after all, is fresh air. Well, Streator has plenty of fresh air. I sucked it in by the gallon when I was growing up there, and every morning to and from St. Anthony's, Mom and Dad sucked in a few gallons, too.

Now, my father has been diagnosed with Parkinson's disease, and experts say that environmental trauma can be causative in its onset. We'll never know for sure if this is what triggered the "degeneration of the pigmented neurons in the Substantia Nigra" of Dad's brain, but I think about it often. Then again, maybe Dad was exposed to something while serving with the Navy in Guam during World War II. I don't know, but somewhere in his past, I suspect, is an unseen enemy. And it looks like it's finally taking him down.

Now, it's time to head off to work. My quality assurance job at Topco is a good gig, taste-testing food and hitting the road to inspect pickle and peanut butter factories, but I'd rather sit here and keep the conversation going. There's plenty of time for that, though, I guess, and many more letters to write. "Sir, more than kisses, letters mingle souls / For, thus friends absent speak" (John Donne, 1598).

[3]

*Gail was right. She's almost always right, in
fact. That's not why I married her, of course.*

I MARRIED HER because she's creative, caring, daring, and beautiful. Not to mention a great kisser. I think I also figured that she'd be a terrific mother for our children, and after Sarah and Paul came along over these past few years, she's proven herself accordingly. "She's a good woman." That's what Dad always says about Mom, and now I say it about my wife. Without question, marrying Gail was the single greatest thing I've ever done, and I'm sure that'll stand until the end. I'm still not sure why she said yes when I asked her, but I know that I got the better end of the deal.

Anyway, she was right when she said that we should find a Parkinson's disease specialist for Dad in addition to his doctor back in Streator. She was the one who came up with Dr. Michael Rezak. She said she made some phone calls to various chapters of the Parkinson's Association, and ended up with him. He's out of Glenbrook Hospital. It's in suburban Chicago, not too far from Skokie, where I work. Mom and Dad hated driving to Chicago long before Dad even got sick, and I'm sure neither of them was too crazy about the notion of having to drive two hours to see a new doctor. But that's exactly what we asked them to do, and it's all working out. In truth, I think they like the guy.

He's pretty young. Good-looking, too. You know, in a firm-featured, squared-jawed, easy smile kind of way. He looks like a doctor, this one. At least as much as I look like a food technologist. And it turns out that he's a hotshot in the Parkinson's world, as well. Medical director of the local chapter or something. Mom and Dad came here from Streator to keep the appointment. Mom drove. I'm sure that pissed Dad off plenty, but we all knew it was coming. Mom says that Dad still drives around Streator some. She says he is good most of the time, but sometimes he stiffens up behind the wheel. Or "has a spell," as she puts it. Great!

They stopped at our house first, and I helped Dad out of the car and up the stairs. Actually, Dad did pretty well with the stairs, but I felt better being at his side than letting him tackle them alone. Just as I felt better helping him with the shingles at Grandma's house or with the bathtub drain at our place so long ago, I guess. Of course, he has to go up and down the stairs back in Streator by himself, or with Mom's help. Fortunately, they have only two steps leading up to their back door. Dad built those steps himself, in fact. But that was years ago. Before he started to slow down.

Going down the stairs was actually harder, but he did it. And when we got to the hospital, Dr. Rezak put Mom and Dad at ease. Being put at ease was no problem with Dad, because he's always been easygoing and laid-back. Mom's easygoing and laid-back, too, I guess. In her own tightly strung way. But, no question, she can get riled up when provoked. My sister and I still talk about the time some guy stole Mom's parking space back in Streator. Mom had been driving around town looking for a place, and when she finally found one, she had to pull past the spot to back into it. That's when some guy in a little car came out of nowhere from behind her, pulling into Mom's spot going forward. She left her car running right there on Main Street in front of Van Loon's Sporting Goods store, jumped out, and absolutely nailed this guy! You don't know what road rage is until you've seen my mom in action.

And another time—years later—she told me to go to hell. It was near the end of my freshman year of college, I think. I had come home for a visit, and, as usual, Mom and Dad couldn't have been any nicer to me. Their kindness and love always blew me away. Still does. Anyway, Mom went out that weekend and bought me some clothes at J.C. Penney's. I didn't really need anything, and Mom knew it, but she said they were on sale and she couldn't pass them up. Auction mentality. Then Dad gave me some spending money for no reason. Mom even made one of my favorite meals—machonka—for dinner. It's a ground beef and noodles casserole, and it's good.

Everything was going along just fine, but before heading back to Champaign on Sunday, I was showing Mom how I had learned to juggle tennis balls from some of my dorm mates on Taft I. I wasn't great, but I was above average. Still, I knocked over one of her lamps in the little room off the back porch. Broke the thing, in fact. I told Mom I was sorry, but she wasn't in a forgiving mood. She was in a hellacious mood, in fact.

But Dr. Rezak got on Mom's good side just fine. Which is not to say that he had it easy getting there. Mom was fighting him early on in the visit. Not openly. Not viciously. But I could tell. For starters, like I said, she didn't want to be there. And beyond this resentment was the real heart of the problem: She wanted to take care of Dad on her own, just like she'd always done. Even before he got sick, I might add. One thing about Dr. Rezak, though. He's a good listener. And he says the right things at the right times. And the thing he said to Mom that won her over—probably forever—was a sympathetic, "This has got to be hard on you, too. . . ."

Bingo! Mom opened up like a morning glory. She told Dr. Rezak how hard it was when Dad was doing poorly and how nobody knew what it was like. In truth, I thought she was whining a little, but Dr. Rezak nodded his head and said things like, "Yes. . ." and "I see. . ." and just like that, Mom had found a friend. She evened mentioned something about her pies to him. Mom makes the greatest pies in the world, and by the end of the day, Dr. Rezak and his nurse—without ever tasting one—knew it.

Something else about that first visit that made me smile was the handshake that Dad and the doctor shared. My Dad has a killer grip. Always has. I know he taught me many, many years ago to shake hands with a firm grip, and I've never forgotten the lesson. But Dad is the master, and I think that his Parkinson's rigidity makes his grip even firmer. Even before he got sick, I saw more than one person cringe when Dad extended his hand to say hello, and Dr. Rezak, jokingly—but not totally so—did the same when, after shaking Dad's hand to say hello, we were preparing to leave. I shake Dad's hand often. Every time I see him. And something in that firm grip of his tells me that even though he's sick—even though he has a hard time walking and he takes medicine for Parkinson's disease and he's only going to get worse, not better—he's still okay. As I see it, as the firm handshake goes, so goes my father.

Dr. Rezak kept Dad on the medicine prescribed by Dad's doctor back home, the Sinemet, the "little yellow one" as Mom calls it. Dr. Rezak said he didn't want to change Dad's current medication schedule until he had a chance to see how he was doing on it. This made sense to me. And he said something else that made sense to me, and to Mom and my sister, too, who met us there for the initial visit. Dr. Rezak talked about Dad's "on" and "off" times. He said that when the Sinemet kicks in—when the levadopa in the drug gets into Dad's system and is converted to dopamine, which is the stuff Dad needs to move—he moves, or, he's "on."

Conversely, he said that between medication doses, especially near the next med time, Dad's dopamine levels get low, and rigidity kicks in, or, he's "off." I've seen it. And it can come on pretty quickly. Dad'll be shuffling along without too much problem, and all of a sudden, he'll stop, unable to go another step. It's not always that dramatic, but it can be. It must be tough when you tell your leg to move—or your arm or your neck or whatever—and your body won't respond. I've heard Mom yell at Dad sometimes to move quicker, or, when he freezes up, to move at all. But Dad doesn't have the chemical guns inside to move like he's supposed to. Like Mom does. Or like I do, and take for granted.

There was something else Rezak mentioned in that first visit that's got me thinking. I didn't pick up on it at the time, but it was a fancy word he used—dyskinesis. Essentially, he said, it's a body's uncontrolled movement. The shakes, I guess. But with Dad, it's not shaking per se but just a general flailing of his arms. And this doesn't happen all the time. We usually see it at the beginning of Dad's "on" time, when the Sinemet is kicking in. Mom sees it most of all, of course, because she's the one that makes sure Dad gets his meds on time each day. Damned Parkinson's disease. One minute it freezes you up so you can't walk, and the next minute it's shaking you around so you can't sit still.

Anyway, when Dr. Rezak saw this, he said that my father might be overmedicated. He said that if he's getting loose like this often, it might mean that he's on too much Sinemet. I know Mom and Dad, and I'm sure they were thinking the less medicine, the better. Dr. Rezak told Mom to keep a log of Dad's progress over the next several weeks. He asked her to mark down how Dad was doing from day to day, keeping track especially of how he did before and after med times. He said he'd then decide if Dad should be changed to a different medication schedule, and he mentioned something about a "drug holiday" as a possibility. Poor Dad. He could use a holiday, and Mom could, too.

Speaking of holidays, it's time for me to give this letter a rest. It was a rough night last night. Sarah is four now and Paul is barely two, and how can such tiny people tire you out so much? Rough day at work yesterday, too. I don't know. I gave myself five years at Topco when I started, and I'm already there more than ten. It's a good gig, like I said, but lately I've been sensing more and more that grading product and inspecting food factories isn't my calling in life. I've told my bosses this lots of times—Howard first and then Bob and now Howard again. Mostly, they just look at me funny.

In truth, I sense that my calling in life isn't food-related at all. I sense that it's word-related. Maybe teaching. Maybe writing. When I was a kid, I never pictured myself as a food technologist. I pictured myself as a writer for *Sports Illustrated*. *SI* is a great magazine. I read it cover to cover—even the swimsuit issue—every week for years, and often, I'd flip to the inside front pages where they have the staff listed, and I'd imagine seeing my name there.

I wrote the act for our grade-school variety show. Sent a long story off to *Reader's Digest* once when I was a kid, too. Nothing came of it, but Mom said it was terrific. I've been sending stuff to editors off and on ever since, and I've even gotten a few things published. The pay was never much, but it was all pretty exciting. And every time I sit down to a writing project, it just feels right, you know? Maybe even these letters are part of my specific fit in the cosmic scheme of things. I sense that they are.

[4]

*A drug holiday is no holiday. Seeing how Dad
was doing after monitoring Mom's hand-
scribbled chart on Dad's progress, . . .*

D<small>R. REZAK SAID</small> that he was going to take Dad off his
Parkinson's medication then start him up again in a more
controlled fashion. He covered the whole idea with the family.
Conceptually, it sounded good. I've read that people who buy into
the macro-diet thing—no processed foods—sometimes don't eat
anything for days first to purge whatever toxins they may have
accumulated in their system before starting fresh. A drug holiday
wasn't the same thing, of course, but I could draw a parallel. We
said okay. Dad, too. And the nontreatment treatment began.

Unfortunately, it didn't have the desired effect. Dad rebounded
a little, but not much, and for a while there I thought it was the end
for him. We all did, I think. Even at least a few of the doctors.
Everybody but Mom, that is. Mom saw beyond the hospitals and
the nursing homes. She saw beyond the drugs and swallowing
therapy. She even saw beyond the feeding tube, which the doctors
eventually put directly into Pop's stomach. When everybody was
looking at the trees, Mom was looking at the forest.

The doctors said the feeding tube was necessary because Dad's
swallowing had shut down altogether and the flexible tube which

they had snaked down his throat was just a temporary fix. It seems to me that someone said that the feeding tube in the stomach—the peg, the doctors called it—could be used on a temporary basis, too, but not "temporary" in that it could be taken out later. They meant more that if Pop was doing particularly well on some days, he could take a little food by mouth. Mostly though, he was to take liquid nutriment through the tube inserted directly into his stomach. The doctors said that he really needed to do this in order to get some substantial nutrients into him, not to mention the Parkinson's medications. We said okay to this as well.

Dad hated that tube, and Mom did, too. Dad hated it because he loves to eat, and what pleasure can there be with that kind of sustenance? I remember reading a restaurant critic's review somewhere about a meal that left him "filled, yet unfulfilled." So it certainly went with Pop. Mom hated the feeding tube for another reason. Planning to take Pop home and care for him there on her own, Mom hated it because she had to be trained how to hook it up and unhook it and flush it with water and give Pop his medications through it and everything else associated with the whole set-up. My mother is not a patient woman anyway, and the tube was taking her over the edge.

But for everyone's disdain of the thing, it worked. Dad got a little stronger and a little stronger still. From the hospital, he was sent to a nursing home for therapy and rehabilitation. A place called Brentwood. The poor guy was on his back for so long, it must have felt great for him to actually get up and move around. Mom essentially moved in with Mary and her family so that she could be with Dad every day. I love my mother, but I'm not sure I'd want her living with us. Hats off to my sister and her entire family for welcoming Mom into their household.

I made it to Brentwood often to see Pop, usually at night after work. He always seemed happy to see me, and for some reason, I began reading him stories from some of the books that we had gotten for Sarah and Paul. They were simple passages for the most part, but Pop took to them, and Mom liked the idea, too. This is how we passed many evenings in each other's company. All the while, Dad grew stronger, and all the while, Mom said he'd do even better when she got him back to Streator where she could take care of him on her own.

Eventually, she got her wish. The doctors and the therapists said Dad could go, and Mom jumped at the chance. She was originally resistant to the notion of having a home health aide come in to help her a few times a week, but as the weeks fell away, Mom came to appreciate them more and more. They gave Pop sponge baths and walked with him and such, freeing up Mom to do the laundry and maybe run to the store for a few things. We went home to visit once or twice and, in truth, Mom and Dad seemed to be getting along just fine.

It was on one such visit home when I came to learn that the peg tube was gone. Mom said she tried to work with it, but Pop was always sneaking food anyway. She said, too, that it always got jammed or leaked and that she was spending a lot of time on it. She said Dad never liked it anyway, so eventually he just pulled the cursed thing out. I don't know if they saw their doctor at home through any of this ordeal. All I know is that when I saw Pop a few weeks later, he looked better than ever. He had gained some weight. He seemed to be walking a little better. And all Mom could say was "I told you so."

It's still hard on her, no question. Sometimes when I'm home for a visit, she'll cry when she tells me what her days are like. Pop is doing okay, but the general slowdown that began years ago is still going on. He falls sometimes, Mom says. He wants to drive, but he can't. She's crushing the medicines for him. He has bowel movement or urine accidents sometimes. Mom says I don't know what it's like. She's right, of course, but sometimes she wearies me with her complaining. I try to be sympathetic to her in person, but in my head, I'm thinking, "C'mon, Mom. Just deal with it!"

Anyway, that's the day-to-day of it for now. Pop's home. Mom's in charge. And to a certain degree, things are back to normal. In his *Lettres Provincales* back in the mid-1600s, Blaise Pascal wrote, "I have made this letter longer than usual, because I lack the time to make it short." I've liked the notion ever since I came across it. Paraphrased, I have neither the time nor the talent to write you a short letter, but I'm hoping you don't mind.

[5]

*Mom's dead! I can't believe it, even as
I write the words to you. What's going to
happen now?*

GAIL CALLED ME AT WORK with the news last week. It was
Thursday morning. Seems Mom died earlier that day of a massive
heart attack, or an "acute cardiac infarction," as the death certifi-
cate would later say. I told Gail I would be right home, but beyond
the shock, I had two immediate thoughts when I got the word, the
first of which I'm not especially proud of. "Why couldn't it have
been my dad?"

By some people's standards—I guess even by my own—Dad
doesn't have much of a life. He has advanced Parkinson's disease
which keeps him on a medication schedule of twelve pills a day.
He's prone to falling, he floats mentally at times, and his compro-
mised swallowing has already landed him in the hospital twice
with aspiration pneumonia. By comparison, Mom was as healthy
as you and me. And just as strong. Even though she was seventy-
eight—four years older than Dad—the concept of her dying was
absolutely foreign to me. The concept of her dying was like the
idea of the sun not coming up in the east tomorrow morning or not
setting in the west tomorrow night. It was a given. I know people
die, and I think I've been preparing myself mentally for my father's
passing, but Mom? Not Mom.

Gail and I had just been home for a visit two weekends prior. We all had a great time. Mom and Dad came out into the backyard to watch as Gail and I played wiffle ball with Sarah and Paul. Eventually, Mom and Dad became second base. They weren't playing second base—they *were* second base. When Sarah or Paul hit the ball, they had to run and actually touch their grandparents to be safe. A nice thought, yes? For all of us.

Mom loved those kids, and they loved their Grandma. Sarah and Paul love Dad, too—or Pop, as we all started to call him following my sister's son's lead a few years earlier—but they never knew the Dad I knew. They've just gotten to know him recently, after he began to slow down. Still, Dad lights up whenever we come home, and I still remember him sitting on the love seat in the kitchen with Sarah next to him, looking up to him, and smiling. Sarah was tiny and Dad was slowing down even then, but they both recognized love when they saw it. They saw it in each other, and I saw it there, too.

I had one more immediate thought when Gail called me with the news about Mom. It came right after the question about why couldn't it have been my dad—it was the unmistakable notion that my life was about to change in a profound and dramatic way.

These thoughts swirled through my head as I stood at my desk for a few moments and organized my work into piles for no real reason, like it was important or something. It had been, of course—very important—just moments before, but things can change in a heartbeat. Or with the final heartbeat of someone you love. Calm and shaking at the same time, I went straight into Howard's office. Howard's my boss. He hired me at Topco over seventeen years ago after Oscar Mayer had fired me from my first job out of college. I had only been at Oscar Mayer's for a couple of months, and the guy letting me go said I didn't have a corporate personality, or words to that effect. I was crushed. None of this seemed to matter to Howard though. Howard took me in when I was sure no one else would.

And he couldn't have been more supportive when Mom died. I had barely gotten the words out when he pulled a handkerchief to his mouth and I saw the tears well up in his eyes. He can be hotheaded at times, and having worked for him for so long, I know his moods well. Once, we were traveling together somewhere out east and he got agitated at the rental car window because the paperwork flow wasn't going his way. The clerk behind the counter told him to not get upset. Getting even more agitated to hear this affront, Howard responded, "I am not upset." The clerk didn't believe him, for she asked, "Then what are you like when you *are* upset?" Howard paused as he collected himself for the perfect response, and I think he hit it when he turned around, pointed at me waiting over by the window, and said, "Ask him!" I smiled. Yea, I've seen Howard upset, but I was hurting last Thursday morning, and he gave me all the comfort and support I needed.

The details of Mom's sudden and unexpected death started filling in when we hit Streator. She had been on the phone earlier that morning with my Aunt Marge, Mom's sister-in-law. Of all the relatives back home, Marge was the one who Mom and Dad hung around with the most. Marge helped them with things and often called or stopped by just to say hello. Her husband—my uncle—died many years ago when I was small, but Uncle Lee was always one of my favorites, and I remember spending lots of happy hours over at their place playing with my cousins. Mike and Pat hung around a lot at our house too, and they always liked Mom. And, it's funny, they never called her Aunt Jean. They just called her Jean.

Anyway, Mom was on the phone with Marge last Thursday morning, chatting about this and that. Dad was on the love seat in the little kitchen, just off the dining room where the phone is. Mom finished her conversation with Marge, hung up the phone, took a step or two, and dropped to the floor. Maybe Dad heard her go down, or maybe he just got to wondering where she was. He started calling out "Jean . . . Jean. . . ." He said he went to her and found her on the floor by the phone.

It saddens me to think about it—Dad finding his true love collapsed in the dining room. I remember them balancing the books together there after the auction sales I told you about. They had set up a couple of desks by the window near the phone. I watched them work sometimes. Mom called out the auction numbers and Dad confirmed the prices of each item sold while punching them into the green mechanical adding machine. And now he was alone with her there—in their little office, I guess—and she was dying, if not already dead.

Dad called 911, the ambulance came, and Mom was pronounced dead shortly thereafter. There was nothing Dad could have done. There was nothing any of us could have done. Mary and John and Chris and Jeff got home first, after receiving the call from Uncle Russ. They found Dad at home with Russ—Dad's brother—who lives next door. Mary said she talked with Russ for a while, then he left to go home. Gail and Sarah and Paul and I arrived a little later, in the early afternoon, as did my brother Jim and his friend Carol. I don't know about anyone else, but I cried nearly all the way home.

Jim and Carol stayed home with Dad and Gail and the kids the next morning while Mary and I went to Elias Funeral Home per our conversation with the funeral people the night prior. A woman came in the back door while we were waiting to be seen. She seemed to know what she was doing, but nonetheless I asked her if I could try to find someone for her. She said that she was okay, and added that she was the hairdresser. *The hairdresser?* I thought, before realizing that she was here to make somebody look good in the casket. Probably my mother.

Mary and I nailed down the details with Don Elias. Dad always told me that Don was a good guy, and it proved to be the case. We decided to have the wake service that evening and the funeral Mass the next morning at St. Anthony's church. We knew that if the burial wasn't on Saturday, we couldn't have it until Monday, and Mary and I thought the sooner, the better. Don said that this would be all right, because he could get the obituary notice into the *Times-Press* and Mom's death could be announced on WIZZ, the local radio station. The word was already out anyway, and I sensed that it was traveling fast.

I called a few people, but mostly I turned to Pat, a close friend who lives fifteen miles away in Ottawa. I asked him to get the news out to my old high-school and grade-school buddies. Like most of the guys I knew he would call, Pat had hung out at my folks' place a lot when we were all younger, and I could hear the surprise in his voice when I told him that Mom had died. "Your. . . your *Mom?*" Like me, and like a lot of people in town, I suspect, Pat thought Dad would go first. Surprise.

Another thing we had to decide at the funeral home was what to put on the front and back of those little memorial cards that often show up near the guest register at the wake. We didn't have a clue. We settled on some religious pictures for the front—the Virgin Mary praying, Christ hanging on the cross, that sort of thing—but we had a harder time picking out the words on the back. Don showed us some of the passages commonly used. The Serenity Prayer seemed like a popular choice, or some long verse about God calling his children home when the time was right.

We were about ready to pick something—anything—just to get the task behind us, when I remembered the words Mom used to say whenever adversity hit the Reynolds' household. It was simple, and appropriate, I thought, for the card detailing her death. Mom used to write me little notes and words of wisdom all the time, and she could put down her thoughts with the best of them. In truth, I've always fancied that my own writing skills, though meager, came from Mom. Whatever I wrote, no matter how bad it was, she thought it was great. And whatever I got published, she thought was Pulitzer material. Anyway, "Life goes on," she often told me, "and it is good." Thus a great writer is published posthumously on the back of her own funeral card. In my book, it's Pulitzer material, too.

The worst thing about our trip to the funeral home was having to pick out the casket. I never once thought about this, even after showing up at Elias's that morning—then Don led us into the casket viewing room. There must have been fifteen of them on display there, a model for every taste and pocketbook. They all looked good to me, and I figured they'd all serve their purpose. Still, they ranged thousands of dollars in price. Just like at the auction sales, Mom looked for a bargain in everything she bought, so Mary and I figured that this should be no exception. We shied away from both the top of the line and the bottom of the line models and ended up with something less than something more. We would find out later that evening—at the wake service—if our choice flattered her. It did, I suppose. And Mom's hair looked good.

I was surprised to see all of the flowers that had been sent, and the outpouring of support from family members and town folk touched me. Clearly, Mom was well liked, as is the man she married so long, long ago. Howard from Topco was there. It sure wasn't necessary for him to go all that way, but it was great to see him. He offered his condolences and told me to come back to work whenever I was ready. Thanks, Howard. And tell Topco thanks for the flowers. A lot of grade-school and high-school buddies were there, too. Pat must have made a lot of calls.

Dad sat in the front row of seats for most of the night. Mary and Jim and I tended to hang out by the coffin as people came by to extend their condolences. I sensed that even as Mom lay cold and white and quiet, people still had a hard time believing it was her and not Dad. Mom was the strong one, after all. She was the healthy one. She was the caregiver. How could she and not Dad be the one stretched out with good-looking hair in the moderately priced coffin that was something less than something more?

I did the best I could throughout the evening, and after all the tears I cried on the way home, maybe there weren't too many left. Still, Sarah saw that I was hurting and came to my rescue. Or at least she tried to. On a sheet of notepaper, which she had found in one of the desk drawers of the funeral home, she wrote me a note. "Dear Daddy, I know you are sad. I know how you feel. I love you and I'll always be with you. Love, Sarah." She's only eight years old. She doesn't understand that she can't possibly know how I feel. Her note meant the world to me nonetheless, because it gave me something tangible to hang on to, something that I could touch and hold and pull out of my pocket to linger over. It's only been a week, and I bet I've read that note fifty times.

We met again at Elias's the next morning before heading to St. Anthony's for the funeral Mass. A few people showed up there to offer their condolences. Pat was there, and some Topco folk. When it was time to go, the funeral people said they would be closing the coffin if we wanted to say our final good-byes. I hung back a bit behind Dad as he approached his bride. He'd been doing pretty good with all of this, and he'd shed only a few tears that I could see, but I choked back my own that morning right in front of the coffin when he bent down and kissed Mom good-bye on the forehead. It was a heart-breakingly gentle kiss, the saddest thing I have ever seen. "Good bye, Jean," perhaps he spoke to himself. "I'll miss you, Jean" perhaps he whispered. I know only that Mom and Dad loved each other, and that Dad's final kiss has forever sealed their love in my memory.

Father Ham at St. Anthony's said some nice words about Mom. He said how she and Dad used to walk to church every morning before Dad got sick. He said that everyone knew Mom to be a caring person. He said that she did a great job in taking care of Dad and how he would certainly miss her. And he said that she was a person of faith. Before the service, I asked Jimmy and Mary if they wanted to say anything about Mom after Communion. They both said no. Then I asked if they minded if I said anything. They both said no again, so I did. I did the best I could.

I began with a few words about Mom in general, having in mind to celebrate her life in eloquent fashion. She was many good things to many good people back in Streator over the course of her nearly eighty years there. But while she was generous, caring, and God-fearing, it is something far less lofty and far more down-to-earth that remains for me one of her greatest legacies. The woman could make a pie. Mostly, I talked about this—about how she was probably rolling out crusts even as we gathered in her memory; about how there would be a great feast in Paradise someday with her pies all around; about how if anybody had ever tasted one of her still-warm pies with a scoop of Sealtest on top, the person would have thought that it was he or she who had just died and gone to heaven. And in bittersweet fashion, I sensed that several people in St. Anthony's Church on that sad, sad Saturday morning understood.

Most of the people in the pews went home after the funeral. Only the family and a handful of others went on to St. Anthony's cemetery. It was cold for the first of April. Father Ham said a few more gentle words there—religious stuff about ashes to ashes and dust to dust. Then the cemetery people lowered Mom's body into the ground. Kevin and Barbara from Topco were there, and maybe some others. Kevin told me later that the sun shone through the clouds as the casket disappeared out of sight. I can't say that I noticed it, too, but I'm glad Kevin did. And I'm glad he told me about it.

Later on, everyone was invited to the Town and Country in Streator for the postburial luncheon. This is an odd ritual, I've always thought, but as the food was passed around that Saturday afternoon, I changed my mind. It was a nice thing—people sharing good food and quiet conversation after so much emotional trauma. "What are you going to do now, Jim?" I heard people ask Dad. He didn't know. Or if he did, he couldn't articulate it. But I knew, without even saying the words. And I think my sister knew, too. Dad couldn't stay by himself. As much as he liked his Streator home—he was born and raised in that house—he couldn't stay there alone. Too much general maintenance to do. Too many medicines to take. Too many meals to prepare. Too much of everything.

Jim thinks that Dad should go into a nursing home or an assisted-living arrangement there in Streator. Mary and I don't like the nursing home idea and think that Dad should be up by us in the Chicago area so we can see him more frequently. Jim isn't married and doesn't have any kids, but he has a mortgage. And he's an electrical engineer besides—a professional. He can't stay home from work to take care of Dad. And you know my story. I have two kids, a wife, a mortgage of my own, and I've been working for Topco for over seventeen years.

Mary, by comparison, taught school years ago but doesn't anymore; her husband pulls in a nice income between his long-time teaching job and his freelance work making educational videos. And they live in a spacious house in the suburbs. Of course, Dad would go to live with Mary. Where else would he go?

We spent one more night in Streator and headed back to Chicago the next day after taking from the house anything Mary might need in the short term. Medicines? Check. Portable commode? Check. Clothes? Check. None of us said much as we went about the final packing and walk-through. I helped Dad into Mary's car; then Gail and I climbed into our own and pulled out right behind them. I've probably backed out of my folks' driveway a thousand times since Dad and Coach Stevens taught me how to drive back in high school. But backing out this time knowing that we had Dad packed up, that Mary was taking him to live with her, and that Mom was buried in the ground was just too weird. It all seemed like a bad dream. Unfortunately, everybody was awake except Mom.

Dad is settled into Mary's place now, but what did Dickens say about the great art o' letter writing . . . leave 'em wanting for more? There is indeed much more to tell.

Part Two

What to Do Now?

"The great decisions of human life have as a rule far more to do with the instincts and other mysterious unconscious factors than with conscious will and well-meaning reasonableness."

SO WROTE THE Swiss psychiatrist and founder of analytical psychology Carl Jung in his 1933 work, *Modern Man in Search of a Soul* (Harvest Books, 1955). I don't know much about psychiatry and psychology, and I certainly didn't know Mr. Jung personally, but nearly fifty years after his death, I couldn't agreed with him more. Indeed, when any of us are faced with difficult decisions, we are often directed by our friends and loved ones—and perhaps even by our psychiatrists and our psychologists—to follow our hearts, not our heads. I've given this counsel myself, in fact. And many times.

All of which makes me wonder now why it is so difficult for me to decide what to do next in the Dad story. My father can't live by himself, this is clear. But should we put him in a nursing home? Or an assisted-living facility? And if so, where? Should we hire a caregiver? And if so, full-time or part-time? And again, where? Dad's house? My house? The major problem in nailing down any of these options is, I think, the knowledge that the decision is not mine and mine alone. And certainly, the effects of the decision are far-ranging.

Here, my own family would be the ones feeling these effects the most—Gail, Sarah, and Paul. Despite negative feedback from both my sister and brother, I eventually come to entertain the option of quitting my job of nearly eighteen years to become my father's paid caregiver here in my home. It seems like a crazy idea to nearly everyone I mention it to, but something seems right about it, too. Something that I am having a hard time shaking.

"Life's full of little choices, isn't it?" asked Ursula of the *Little Mermaid* in Disney's animated classic as Ariel tried to decide whether or not to sign over her voice in hopes of gaining legs and her true love. The ever-crabby Sebastian thought it was a stupid idea, and maybe it was, but sometimes, after all of the discussion, all of the reason, and all of the logic have been put on the table, we just have to go with what feels right, just as Mr. Jung suggests. And even then, we never know how things will go, for as the insightful baseball legend Yogi Berra suggests, it's hard to make predictions—especially about the future.

[6]

Mary says it's hard, but manageable. Like my father, she's a gamer, and is able to deal with stress more than her petite frame indicates.

S HE'S BEEN TAKING CARE OF POP for a couple of months now, and it's going okay, apparently. Not great, I get the feeling. But okay. And okay is not a bad thing, perhaps, especially when the terrain is all new.

Before Mom took Pop back home to Streator following Dad's drug holiday and his extended nursing home stay—but knowing that their return was imminent—Gail and I went and spent a day in my folks' house trying to ready it for the homecoming. Mostly, we got rid of the throw rugs. Mom and Dad had lots of them, but we knew instinctively—and we heard one of the therapists say— that Dad needed to be in an environment that would minimize the opportunities for his tripping and falling over things. Mom and Dad's place would never be clutter-free, but we did a pretty good job of getting rid of the trouble areas. Much to my mother's dismay when she got the news.

In somewhat similar fashion, Mary had to physically adapt her house to receive Pop. Not that there's much clutter in Mary's place. It doesn't have a throw rug in sight, come to think of it. They have a beautiful home. It's so beautiful, in fact, that shortly after they bought the place, Mary told me that it was the house she could die in. I thought it was a strange way to put it, but I caught her drift. And I've never forgotten her words. I wonder if Mom spoke similar ones upon marrying Dad and moving into his little place there on Van Buren Street back in Streator. Probably not, but she died there nonetheless. And way before her time.

Mary has a spare bedroom at her place, but—like the rest of the bedrooms—it's upstairs, and as much as Dad would be willing to climb the curving staircase up to the second floor, he wouldn't be able to do it regularly. Falling would occur sooner or later. Or maybe just sooner, period. Accordingly, Mary had to move her dining room table out into the middle of the living room to make room for Pop's bed where the table used to be. Pop is refusing to wear diapers at her place and she isn't pushing the issue with him, so she's also had to put a plastic tarp on the wall-to-wall carpeting under the bed to prevent any staining that might occur because of Pop's accidents. The portable commode—also with tarp—is in the corner of the dining room on the kitchen wall. Mary's house could be featured in *Better Homes and Gardens*. Or *Better (Nursing) Homes and Gardens*.

Dad goes to bed early. Real early. Mary says he wants to settle down at 6:00 P.M. or so, basically right after dinner. What's worse, he takes his shirt off when he thinks it's time, and he doesn't care if anybody is around. Including Mary's sons' friends. Chris is a sophomore in high school and Jeff is in eighth grade, prime time for having friends over. Mary says they've cut back on the visits a bit, though. And it's not even because of Dad's undressing. Mostly it's because they are trying to keep the house quiet for Pop. Mary tells me that she bangs pots and pans together to keep Dad awake after dinner, but once he settles into bed, she tries to keep the household quiet to give him a couple good hours of sleep. Of course, this also gives Mary a couple good hours of respite from Pop care.

I went over there once to give Mary a break so that she could go with John and her boys to a school sports banquet. Dad was pretty much settled in when I got there, and I left as soon as they got home with no Pop incidents to speak of. I'll have to do this more often—give Mary a break. I know she'd do it for me if the tables were reversed and Pop was at our place and under my care. Beyond the hard day-to-day work, one of the hardest things about taking care of Dad—or anybody like Dad—has got to be that unless you're away from home and someone else is in charge, you're always on the job. Mary says she sleeps with one ear open, listening for movement down on the main floor. When sleep isn't even your own, it doesn't give you much to look forward to at the end of a long day.

Mary says that Chris and Jeff get along pretty well with Pop, but that their interaction is limited. She says that her husband, though, is great with Dad. A lot of guys, I suspect, wouldn't be quite so agreeable to opening up their house to an invalid parent and throwing tarps all over the dining room floor—not to mention a bed and a portable commode. John isn't home much during the day because of his teaching job, but in the evenings and on weekends he's always there for Mary. He even takes Pop to the hardware store for no reason sometimes just to give Mary a break from it all. I don't know. Maybe because Mary helped John care for his mom for a while in their home, he shares Mary's value of watching after one's own.

"Bitterly she weeps at night, tears upon her cheeks. . . ." The words are from the Bible—the Book of Lamentations—and describe Jerusalem after the destruction it endured at the hands of the Chaldeans. Two millennia later, they could describe my sister. Mary says the tears come often these days because of Dad. She says she's frustrated, sometimes angry, and always tired. I feel bad, because we're leaving on a trip soon to Disney World. Gail and I have had this thing planned for a long time, now. Since before Mom died, anyway. Should I stay or should I go? I say the words rhetorically. I'm going with my family. Mary will be in my thoughts, but I won't cancel the trip to stay here just in case she needs me.

I'd ask you to tell me that it's the right thing to do, but I feel that it is. Other than being here for moral support, I can't do much on the short term to relieve Mary's situation. She says she's taking it day-by-day, but right now, the work is in her hands. Just as it was in Mom's hands for all those years. Dad is falling more, Mary says, but she's managing for the time being. She's capable, and we'll only be gone for a week or so. Time to start packing. I think I hear Mickey calling my name.

[7]

Dad's back in the nursing home again with aspiration pneumonia. Damned Parkinson's. His swallowing hasn't gotten any better since the last time he had the problem.

IN FACT—like everything else Parkinson's-related—it just keeps getting worse. He flunked the cookie swallow test again, too. Mary and I told the medical types that Dad would flunk it before he even took it, and now they're talking about the peg tube again. The speech therapist in particular says that Dad shouldn't be taking anything by mouth. She says he's always aspirating a little bit, and that by allowing him to eat even pureed foods we're putting him in danger. The way I see it, there's the textbook response, and there's the quality-of-life response. Ms. Speech Therapist may be well versed in the former, but she needs work in the latter.

This latest medical adventure began when Mary hauled Dad into the hospital last month. He was getting weaker and weaker and falling all the time. More tears from Mary, I'm sure. The chest x-ray confirmed the pneumonia, and the emergency room people put Dad on some intravenous antibiotics. I sense that some of the doctors who saw Dad after he came in thought that this might be the end for him. Dad's a fighter, though, and every night when Mary and I left the hospital, Dad gave us that firm handshake and a thumbs up. Poor guy. He got a bad deal, but he's playing his cards as well as anybody could.

He was still in the hospital when Mary said that she just couldn't take care of Pop anymore in her home. Actually, Mary would take care of him until she dropped, but her husband said no. He said that Mary would have a heart attack, too. Nobody's really said the words, but in the back of our heads, we all know that taking care of Dad these past several years may have been what did Mom in. We all know that lifting Dad every time he fell may have been behind her acute myocardial infarction on that Thursday morning.

It's not that John was kicking Dad out into the street. John's a good man and really cares for Dad. Like I said before, he helped Mary with Pop plenty whenever he was around. He gave Mary some options that made sense. He told her that they could hire someone to come in and live with them to take care of Dad full-time. It's not that Mary—or anybody—has to be with Dad every second, but when he needs somebody, he needs somebody. As Mary says, and Mom before she died, it's a twenty-four-hour job.

Part of the problem at Mary's place is that the house isn't well suited to taking care of someone with Dad's needs. I told you about the dining-room set-up. Also, they didn't have a hospital bed, so they had to prop Dad up at night to help his swallowing, but once the pillows fell away, Dad was flat again. Mary's place has wall-to-wall carpeting and Dad is incontinent. None of this made for a good arrangement. Finally, Mary just isn't strong enough. She's plenty strong, but even with Dad's difficulty in swallowing, he still weighs over 150 pounds. Mary's tiny by comparison, and when he falls, she can't get him up.

Mary wasn't keen on the live-in caregiver option, which John gave her, and I can't say that I blame her. I'm sure it was enough of a lifestyle change to have Dad in the house, let alone another person besides. Neither Mary nor I like the idea of putting Dad in a nursing home, especially knowing that Mom said she would never do such a thing. Jim sees it differently, though. He's still in favor of a nursing home or an assisted-living arrangement back in Streator.

Jim says Dad should be in Streator because that's where he grew up. If Dad was in good shape and could take care of himself, of course! But now? With advanced Parkinson's disease and with only a handful of aging brothers, sisters and in-laws to check up on him? Still, the decision to look for *any* nursing home for Dad was made easier by the fact that he was going there straight out of the hospital for rehabilitation from the pneumonia. He wasn't necessarily going as a long-term resident, but after things didn't work at Mary's place, we all knew what was coming.

Mary and I spent several days shopping around for a nursing home for Dad. The hospital had recommended one facility, but it was rather far from Mary's place, rather far from mine, and way far from Jim's. Accordingly, we began our search with facilities nearer to Mary's home, knowing that she'd be the one visiting Dad the most since she's not teaching anymore. Having never cased out nursing homes before, we weren't sure at the beginning what we were looking for. But before long, we got the hang of it.

Did the place smell of urine? Did the aides seem friendly? Were the rooms well maintained? What was the nurse-to-patient ratio? One thing for sure—none of the places were cheap, especially with extra charges like incontinent care added on. At the rates we were seeing, Dad's savings wouldn't last forever. We weren't too concerned about the price just yet—and still aren't—because Dad is there for rehabilitation, and right now, Medicare is paying for everything. But Medicare doesn't last forever, either.

Something else I want to tell you. As we were going along from nursing home to nursing home, I made a point to ask at least one resident of each facility we visited if he or she actually wanted to be there. "No!" I heard again and again. These gentle people elaborated that the food was good or the staff was friendly or the movies on Friday night were great. But did any of them actually *want* to be there? I mentioned this to one of the nursing home people walking Mary and me around one day, and she said she wasn't surprised. She said that nursing homes serve an important need, but that for most patients, being home or with family is always the best. Hmmm. . . .

We finally settled on a place in Arlington Heights called MedBridge. It's about fifteen minutes away for Mary, a little further for me, and a little further still for Jim. When we were scoping out the place, I bumped into a lady from work who was visiting someone she knew staying there for rehabilitation of some sort. She said it was a good place. The nurses and aides seemed friendly. So did the administrative type who walked us around. Dad seemed okay with the place, too, I guess. And no urine smell.

For a while there after Pop arrived, they rigged him up with one of those gastrointestinal tubes that went up through his nose and into his stomach. We said okay to this treatment because Dad wasn't swallowing much and the theory was that he needed the tube to get the meds into him. The meds, in turn, would get him moving a little, and then he'd be able to swallow more on his own. Neither Mary nor I could bear to watch when they put the tube in. That's gotta hurt!

Dad pulled it out a few times, prompting the nursing home people to tape the tube to his forehead so that he couldn't see it or get to it with his hands. I went home from the nursing home one night and climbed exhausted into bed after barely saying hello to my wife. All I could think of was Dad, there by himself in a strange place surrounded by strangers—albeit friendly strangers—with a tube up his nose. It didn't seem right. I prayed for him, but I can't even remember the specifics.

Dad's off the gastrointestinal tube now. The speech therapist at MedBridge said essentially the same thing as the one at the hospital—that Dad shouldn't be swallowing by mouth. He's getting a little stronger each day, though, and small progress is still progress. Mary has been terrific through all of this. She's stayed true to her word about visiting Dad. She goes every day. Sometimes twice a day. And she really can bring a smile to his face. Often she goes at dinnertime and feeds him his pureed spinach, pureed meatloaf, and pureed cottage cheese. When Dad is doing well, he can feed himself, and he can actually put a lot of that stuff away. Have you ever seen pureed spinach, meatloaf, and cottage cheese? Mary and I sometimes play the *guess-the-food* game. But Dad can gobble it up.

When Mom was still taking care of Dad she sent me a note. I kept it, I think, because she said some nice things about me in it. I kept it, too, though, because she said some nice things about Mary, and I thought of it not too long ago after seeing Mary at the nursing home with Dad. It's easy to see why Dad likes her so much. Everybody likes her. She talks with the other patients and the staff. She smiles. She cares. Mom must have seen all of this in Mary even when we were small, because this is what she wrote:

Nice chatting with you last night via the phone. The aide is here taking care of Pop so I'll get this off while I can. I'm glad you enjoyed your ice skating with the kids. Do you remember, John, when you were just a toddler and we'd go roller-skating? Jim and Mary managed by themselves and Dad and I had to hold you up. But you had determination and by the time we gave it up, you were rolling along on your own. Give Mary credit for taking you on the ice pond. She was so good to you, John. Just like a little mother. And you were never a problem, just a good kid always.

Love, Me and Pop.

Yep, Mary is a good one. I try to be nice to Dad's roommates, too, but by the time I get to the nursing home each night, I guess I'm too irritable to be friendly. I hate to say this—and maybe I'm embarrassed to say it—but I don't look forward to going to see Dad each night after work. I do it, though. Because of guilt? Sure. But mostly because it just seems like the right thing to do. Mother Teresa once said that it's not what we do, but how much love we put in the doing that counts. I don't think I'm doing too well in the love category. What I really want to do is just go home and veg out for a while. I don't even particularly want to play with the kids. Sarah is eight and Paul is six now. They're great, but work wears me down and sometimes I'm not in the greatest of spirits, even for them or for Gail.

Here's the usual routine. I get up around six or so, shower, have breakfast by myself, and go to the office. I spend the day putting out fires, shuffling papers, and going to meetings. Some days are rough, but some days are good, like when I give my class about quality assurance to new employees. A lady at work named Margaret coordinates the training sessions, and she tells people that my class is one of the best. I take a lot of pride in it. And on really good days, I get to evaluate product on the bench out in the lab. That's the best part of the whole gig—looking at product. Touching it, smelling it, tasting it, seeing what makes it good or bad, in specification or out.

But even the best of days can leave me unfulfilled sometimes. It's like I wrote before. I often don't feel that working at Topco is my great calling in life. At the same time, I don't doubt for a minute that it's part of my growth curve. Everyone treats me very well there. Howard can be explosive sometimes, but he's a great boss. And I really enjoy traveling with him. We have fun on the road. Not long ago, we took our mitts on the airplane with us and played catch for half an hour after the set-up work was done at our destination. I feel intimidated at work sometimes, especially with the computer stuff, but my conflict isn't with the job. My conflict is that I don't sense it's what I'm supposed to be doing.

Howard gives me a lot of good-natured grief about this, but there's a grain of truth in the grief. Heck. I sometimes wonder myself if I should be focusing all of my energies toward advancing myself in the foods field instead of writing poetry—or letters—at 5:00 A.M. Howard once asked me years ago, "When did you first notice that you were different from the rest of the little boys in Streator?" He has more insight than he knows.

When I'm not traveling, I leave right from work to go see Dad at MedBridge. I tried heading home first a few times to have dinner with Gail and the kids, but Dad goes to sleep early and if I don't get there by 7:30 or 8:00 P.M, I miss him. This isn't a good time for my family and me, and I'm the guy causing all of the friction. I give Gail a paycheck—and a nice one—every two weeks, but beyond that, I don't give her much at all. I barely see my family these days, and when I do, I'm not the best of company.

But little Sarah doesn't seem to care. When I came home from the nursing home last night the kids were in bed again. I went in and checked on them and gave them soft goodnight kisses, but they were both sound asleep. It doesn't make sense. I've become a lousy father for trying to be a caring son. And Gail cut me deeply when she told me about Sarah's prayer after the family said grace around the table without me once more. "Dear God, please let Daddy have dinner with us again sometime." Ouch.

And now it's time to start it all over again. My wife tipped me off to Steve Goodman—a folksinger, of sorts—years ago. One of his songs has a great line, and it defines how I've felt these past several weeks with Dad in the nursing home and me going out there all the time. "I'm weary, but weary is only a case / Of being unwound at the wrong time and place. . . ." I'm weary.

[8]

Mary and I keep going out to see Dad almost every day. We meet together at MedBridge on the weekends, and on weekdays.

SHE USUALLY GOES DURING the day or at dinner time—or both—and I still make it out there after I leave work. Jim and Carol make it out there on the weekends.

Dad got a little stronger, but then he stopped showing improvement and essentially planed out. And I don't know now how this works exactly, but Medicare only lasts so long. Also, the medical types at the nursing home review Dad's status every week and make assessments on his progress. Maybe the two issues are connected in Dad's case, or maybe not. All I know is that I got a call a few nights ago from the nursing home people telling me that it was time to either release Dad—to take him home somewhere— or to check him in as a permanent resident. His rehab days were through, his free ride was over, and it was crunch time. This was the phone call we all knew was coming but that we weren't yet ready to receive.

The call came to me because Mary was vacationing in Florida with her husband. The administrative type on the MedBridge end of the line was pleasant enough, but she kept asking what I wanted to do with Dad. How the hell should I know? Mom's gone, Dad can't even speak sometimes, and now she's asking me what to do?

This is the caliber of question I'd always take to Mom and Dad before making a decision. Mom, should I take the Topco job? Dad, should we buy the house? I even asked Dad if I was old enough to get married before popping the question to Gail—and I was twenty-seven at the time! Dad smiled and said yes, by the way.

So there it was—the dreaded nursing home question, and I had to field it. I executed the play flawlessly because I knew what the answer had to be. We had gone over all the options already, after all. Mary could no longer take care of Dad. Mary didn't want to hire someone to come and live with them to take care of Dad. Gail and I didn't want to hire someone to live with us to take care of Dad, either. And we definitely wanted to keep Dad up here so that we could see him more often.

At least this is how Mary and I see things, and I can't say that Jim's input even crossed my mind on this one. Dad was already in a nice facility. Between the two of us, Mary and I were seeing him everyday. Accordingly, I told the nursing home people to ready a room for him and slammed down the phone in anger. Mom said that she would never put Dad in a nursing home, and I just gave the order to do exactly that. What was that about being such a good kid always, Mom? Sorry to let you down.

I had taken the call on the wall phone in the kitchen. Gail, who was preparing dinner, heard the whole conversation. I quickly reiterated it to her anyway, and in a rush of anger and confusion and false bravado I added, "I wish I could just quit my job and take care of him myself!" My outburst was rhetorical, not seeking a response. Gail offered one anyway, and I'm both excited and nervous about where it will lead. "So why don't you?" she said.

Huh? This wasn't a game of double-dare-you in the school parking lot when we were kids. This was real grown-up stuff. I can't even recall what I said in return, but it was probably along the lines of "Yea, right!" But then we sat down and talked about it, and on paper, anyway, the plan had a chance. I couldn't just quit work without income, but Gail explained that if we hired a caregiver, his or her services would be paid through Dad's account. The money is there for his care, she explained, adding that I could be his caregiver if I really wanted to be. The nursing home staff had been nothing but kind to Dad, and he was happy there. Still, he had told me on occasion that he would rather be with family, and each time he did, I remembered the nursing home tour guide telling me the same thing during our shopping days.

I'm no Charles Atlas, but I'm stronger than Mary and can probably deal physically with Dad better than she could. Also, I have Gail around the house more than she has John around her place, so I'd have more help if I need it. The intangible element is important, too. I'd feel better about saying goodnight every night to Dad if he was just down the hall from me rather than ten miles away in a nursing home. And surely Dad would rather be tucked in each night by one of his own rather than by a man or woman dressed in white nursing-home garb. This is what I would want for myself, anyway.

And what about Sarah and Paul? Would they benefit from having their grandfather living at home with us? I've taken them both a few times on weekends to see Pop in the nursing home. Dad likes having them around. At least until they start acting squirrelly. But that's what kids do, and right now, Dad is surrounded by old people in wheelchairs who either call out for help for hours on end or who sit quietly with their heads on their chests. I have no problem with nursing homes. Really. And there may come a time when Dad truly needs to be in one. On his good days, though, he doesn't need to be in one. On his good days, he absolutely *shouldn't* be in one. But where should he be? With me?

Gail also added that I would be able to write a little more having Dad here at home with us. Mom always liked my writing. She was always my biggest fan, regardless of the actual literary merit of my work. She dies suddenly and Dad needs somewhere to go. Call it coincidence, but I'm beginning to see it as part of a plan. And I like the way it's looking.

Financially, the notion of quitting work to take care of Dad isn't a good one, but Gail reiterated again that Dad would have to pay the nursing home out of his savings. She reiterated again that his savings were for his care, and that if I quit, the money Dad paid MedBridge to care for him could come to me instead. I don't like the idea of taking money from Dad. But I also don't like the idea of putting him in a nursing home. Gail works only part-time, however, and there's no way that I could leave work without having some money coming in. We have to figure things out, but already I have an inkling that what I thought about upon hearing that Mom had died is on the verge of becoming a reality—that my life is indeed going to change in some profound and dramatic way that goes much deeper than just time away from home visiting my father.

I phoned Mary in Florida that night to tell her about the call from the nursing home and about how I had told them to check Dad in as a permanent resident. She said it wasn't the best thing but we pretty much had to do it. Then I bounced the idea off of her about quitting Topco to take care of Dad here at home. She didn't sound too positive about it. In fact, she thought it wasn't a very good idea at all. She told me all the things I already knew—that I had a house, a wife, two kids in Catholic grade school, and that this wasn't the time for me to quit a well-paying job of nearly eighteen years to take care of Dad. Besides, she said, it was hard work. Very hard.

Mary has never said it, but I think a part of her doesn't want me to take care of Dad because of guilt. I think Mary is thinking that if she had been able to take care of Dad in her home, that I wouldn't be faced with the decision to quit work and take care of him here. She may even be factoring my salary and my 401-K plan and the prestige of my position into her thinking. There is no question about it—I'm in good stead right now financially. If I quit to take care of Dad, I'll be giving up a lot. In part, at least, this may be what's in Mary's head, and she doesn't want anything to do with it.

I think it may also be a feeling of failure on Mary's part—that she couldn't do it and that maybe I can. Whether I can or not remains to be seen, should we decide to pursue this thing. You know that hokey, old Doris Day song, "Que sera, sera. . . ." Well, my mother never sang it to me when I was just a little boy. But she said the words to me often and I'm clinging to them now. And whatever happens, Mary has nothing to be guilty or down about. I've seen Mary in action on the parental care front, and she's great. She was terrific with Dad while he was at her place, and it's my hunch that she'll do terrific with him for the long haul, regardless of where he ends up.

I talked with Jim next. He doesn't want me to do it either. He thinks it's a bad idea, too, but I sense that his objections come from a whole different place than Mary's. Jim implied that it was quite a coincidence that I'm thinking of quitting a job which I struggle with at times to care for Dad in our home, write, and take Dad's money in the process. And he said that maybe I couldn't even do it. Physically. I think I can. Like I said, I'm at the nursing home almost every day. I see how the therapists have Dad up and walking with the walker when he's doing well. I see the way the kitchen purees his food. I see the way the aides change Dad's bedding, and how they change him and clean him when he needs changing and cleaning. I see how they transfer him from bed to chair and from chair to bed. I see how the nurses crush Dad's medicines and give them to him in little applesauce cups. I also see how they can miss his scheduled medication times.

Mary and I have both seen this, in fact. We chase down the nurses whenever we're there to make sure the meds are administered on time. I don't blame the nurses or the nursing home. The patient load is heavy and the staff is small. One time, a nurse told me this exactly, and that they do the best they can. She'd probably get in trouble if any of her bosses ever heard her say such things, but I know that she speaks the truth. Still, Dr. Rezak told us that it's important Dad get his meds on time. The way I see it, each nurse has to be attentive to the needs of several patients on their portion of the floor or wing. If we took care of Dad in our home, I would have to be attentive to the needs of only one patient, who happens to be my father.

Gail and I have discussed the notion further. We discuss it every day, it seems. For hours! What should we do with Dad? In the meantime, I keep going out there to see him. I keep missing meals with my family. I know that it's important for me to be here with Gail and Sarah and Paul. But I feel strongly that I should be spending time with Dad, too. If he was healthy and living by himself down in Streator, I wouldn't be compelled to visit all of the time. But he's not healthy. He has advanced Parkinson's disease. He floats mentally sometimes, and I think it's important to keep my face in front of him, to let him know that I'm in his corner.

Which brings me back to my brother and sister. Although Jim and Mary seem to have different reasons why they don't want me to take care of Dad, I still need to do what seems right to me. Howard at Topco kids me about this all the time, too. Whenever I take a course of action at work that he doesn't agree with, I tell him, "It seemed like the right thing to do." Howard's retort: "How could anybody ever argue with that?"

Again the dawn stretches into morning, and speaking of Howard, he'll be expecting me soon. Things are happening.

[9]

*When my brother suggested that I might
not be able to physically care for Dad and that
I shouldn't quit work to bring Dad into our
home only to find that I couldn't do the job,
it made sense to me.*

I THINK MY BROTHER IS WRONG about a lot of things pertaining to our father and his needs, but his comment prompted another battery of conversations between Gail and me. Fortunately, my wife is a remarkable woman, and she has vision, which often escapes me. And she's supportive. That means an awful lot at a time like this. Anyway, Gail thought that Jim had a good idea, too. We need to test the waters to see what it would be like for us having Dad here. We need to see how Sarah and Paul would react to it as well. And, of course, we need to see if Dad actually wants to be here.

We had a group meeting with the kids. We told them that Pop needed someone to take care of him and that I was considering being that someone. We also told them that I planned to take a week's vacation—the one I had been saving to take over the Christmas holiday—to bring Dad here and to see how it would go. They were both okay with the idea. I told Mary the plan. She was okay with it, too. I told Jim about it as well, and thanked him for the suggestion.

The nursing home people liked it when I asked for a lesson in transferring Dad in and out of the wheelchair. Dad doesn't need the chair all the time. When he is doing well, he can walk on his own with the walker, but his walking is shaky. In truth, he needs someone with him to make sure he doesn't fall. One of the therapists even gave me an old gait belt. These are belts that wrap around the patient's waist, and the therapist then holds onto it from the back. This allows the patient to walk unaided while also allowing the therapist the opportunity to prevent an imminent fall. The therapist's name was Marguerite. I sensed that she was pulling for me, and I told her thanks.

Then the nurses went over Dad's medicine regime. In truth, I already knew it like the back of my hand. More than one person at the nursing home asked me why I was doing this. I couched the whole thing in the context of a vacation for Dad—that it would give him a little change of scenery—not that they weren't doing a great job. This was true enough, but I also wanted to see how caring for Dad in my home would go. The bottom line—and I've told several people this—is that on his good days, Dad needs a little more life in his life. I wanted to see if I could offer it to him.

First we had to shift the kids' bedroom upstairs because we needed to put Dad next to Gail and me. Our house has two bedrooms on the main floor, one big (which Gail and I claimed when we bought the joint) and one small. When we showed Mom and Dad the house for the first time, Mom walked into the small bedroom on the main floor and said that it would make a nice nursery. Then she walked into the small bedroom upstairs and said exactly the same thing. Well, the small bedroom on the main floor did indeed become the nursery. For Sarah first, then for Paul. Eventually, we put bunk beds in there for the kids when they got a little older. Now, fifteen years after Mom thought we had a couple of nice rooms for children, the upper room takes on that very role, and the lower one becomes the bedroom for her widowed husband. It's funny how things go.

I picked up Dad two weeks back and told him I was taking him home with us for a while. "For a little vacation," I told him, as I had told him several days in a row before the big day came. I'm not sure if he understood. Like I said—he floats mentally sometimes. Mary met me at the nursing home that day and came home with me to help Dad get settled in for the week. Sarah and Paul were at school when I pulled up with Pop, and Gail was at work. They'd all be home soon enough, but I think it was good they weren't there when Dad arrived. It made everything a little quieter, a little less hectic for him. And for me!

Dad did pretty well with it all. One of my concerns was the stairs. We helped Dad out of the car and supported him across the walk. Dad gravitated toward the right side railing and I supported him from the left. Then with both hands on the rail, he worked his way up the steps. He tried to take the steps normally—one foot at a time—but I suggested that he pause on each step with both feet before tackling the next one. Back in Streator, we never used the front door—always the back. Here in Chicago, we never use the back door—always the front. I'm up and down these stairs all the time. I fly up and down them, in fact, taking two steps at a time when I'm in a hurry. But I can't say I ever counted the steps until Dad came. I counted the steps that day. We have seven.

Mary stayed with me until Dad got settled in. First we showed him his bedroom where he would be staying for the week. Remembering its earlier days, it's still dressed in nursery colors from the quarter round to the crown molding. The closet door trim and the window trim are neon pink. And I do mean neon. And the border nestled between the chair rails is complete with pictures of bunnies and clowns and little toy jack-in-the-boxes. Dad saw it and smiled. From the get-go, he was as pleasant as could be. As my wife has told me more than once, he's a nice old man. May I get such praise when I've put a few more years behind me. And may I be gracious and happy with pink!

Like I said, Dad's mobile, but he's shaky. Fortunately, he took to the wheelchair I rented for him from Kluza's Pharmacy down by the KFC. Dad used it to move from point to point throughout the house when he wasn't doing well. When he was doing okay, we went with the walker or sometimes with Marguerite's gait belt. The wheelchair rental cost was nominal, and I think it was money well spent for our little trial period.

Mary stayed with Pop while I picked up the kids from school. They both gave him a nice homecoming, although I sensed Sarah was more comfortable with him than Paul. Later that first day—after Mary left—Gail came home from her work at the dental office and Pop was happy to see her. He's always liked her, and it gave me joy to see the two of them interact. In truth, one of my favorite pictures from our wedding album isn't any of the pictures of Gail and me at the altar or cutting the cake at the wedding reception or dancing together on the Catering by Heck's dance floor. It's a close-up picture of Dad about to kiss Gail at the wedding Mass during the Sign of Peace. His eyes are closed. Her eyes are closed. Their lips are about an inch apart, and my mom is visible in the background through the space between them. If tenderness was ever photographed and put in a book, we have the book.

Anyway, Gail and Pop shared their hellos and our week as an extended family officially began. I made chicken burritos that first night. I have to tell you that Pop is a meat and potatoes kind of guy, and my mom was a meat and potatoes kind of cook. I can say with authority that when I told Dad what we were having for dinner, he didn't have a clue. And besides the dish being foreign to Dad in the first place, I had to chop it up for him, too. I didn't puree it quite as much as the people at the nursing home did. The dish still had some definition to it, at least. But Dad did okay with it, and he actually asked for more. Like I said earlier, when he's doing well, he can put it away.

After dinner, Dad wanted to go to bed. It was 6:30 P.M. I should have known this from Mary's experience, but I had forgotten.

Before Dad's Parkinson's took hold, my parents walked to church every morning, and to accommodate their early rising, they went to bed early, too. Easily by 8:00 P.M. Often earlier. And apparently it's gotten worse. We held him off from bed for a little while, but not much. I figured he'd crash before too long, and it was probably easier to ready him for bed when he was awake and stronger than when he was groggy and weaker.

Pop is wearing diapers all the time now, and generally without protest. I changed him just before I got him into bed. I had Dad stand up and hold onto his walker while I lowered his pants from behind, removed the old diaper, and put on a new one. It was wet, but not overly. Occasionally, Dad asked to use the bathroom. Sometimes we made it in time, and sometimes not. Oddly, I couldn't say the word "diaper" to Dad. To him, I'd say that I had to change his pads or even his shorts. Awkward for me. Awkward for him. This is the guy who taught me how to drive a car. This is the guy I turned to for approval when I was thinking of asking Gail to marry me. And now he's the guy who needs help cleaning his own behind.

Bed was something of an adventure, too. We used Sarah's old bed, which we had stashed away in the basement. Nothing fancy, but it did the trick. Marginally. I put two incontinent pads beneath Dad to keep the bed dry during the night. Dad settled in right away, just like Mary said he would. But a couple of hours later, he was awake. Not *I-want-to-get-up* awake, but *up-and-restless-in-bed* awake. I heard him stirring—or maybe Gail did—and I went in to see him. I calmed him down, but a couple of hours later, it happened again. A girl at work tells me that it's called "sun-downing" when a person goes to bed early then gets up several times a night. I have no idea if she's right about this, but I like the sound of it. What I don't like is dealing with it.

Morning came too late or too early, depending on how you want to look at it. Too late in that I was up twice more with Dad and felt awake throughout the entire night. Too early in that when

I finally did fall asleep, it was time to get Dad his 6:00 A.M. medicine. He was wide-awake and raring to go. I could have gone back to bed, and would have, but when Dad got up, I knew that my day had begun. Like Mom and Dad, I tend to be an early-morning person, too. In fact, a line from an old Lovin' Spoonful song speaks my sentiment well: "There's something special 'bout six o'clock / in the morning when it's still too early to knock. . . ." Of course, that's only when I'm not getting up every couple of hours. The whole thing reminded me of when Sarah and Paul were newborns. Infants and aging parents can really mess up a good night's sleep.

Dad wasn't totally dry in the morning, but he wasn't drenched either. I helped him out of bed and into the wheelchair. Then I brought him into the kitchen, had him stand against the counter, and cleaned his bottom and legs with warm, soapy water. It didn't seem like such a bad way to start a day. I helped him get dressed next, asking him if he was okay with the clothes I had picked out for him. He said they were fine. Dad couldn't really get his own pants on, so I helped him with this 100 percent. I also helped him with the shirt, but less so, and once it was on, he could deal with the buttons. Finally, I helped him transfer himself from the wheelchair to the pink chair in the living room, turned on the morning news shows on TV, and asked him if he wanted a cup of coffee. He responded with a yes, and a big smile. I got him the coffee, made him some pancakes for breakfast, and threw his sheets and pajamas into the laundry. It wasn't yet 7:00 A.M. Great to go on a vacation from work, you know?

The nights were the worst. Dad settled into a rough evening routine as the days slipped away, but he still got up frequently. Fortunately, he never fell, but I often found him unable to walk and clutching the dining room hutch or the living room end table. He would walk so far then freeze up. Damned Parkinson's. Sometimes I would hear him calling Mom's name in the darkness. "Jean! Jean!" The first time I heard it, I thought of how he called for her while she was laying dead by the phone back in their dining room.

Then there were the accidents. While Dad could occasionally let me know when he needed to use the bathroom during the day, he was completely incontinent during the night. Sometimes he would tear the diapers off or manage to slip out of them. Sometimes he climbed out of bed, too, and more than once I walked into his room only to step bare-footed into a puddle of urine on the floor. Yecch! Dad always insisted on going to bed with his socks on, so I would also find him with soggy socks and dragging a trail of urine behind him on the floor. I tried to be gentle with Dad during these moments. I didn't always succeed. Seldom, I must admit.

Despite the long nights, the week passed quickly. I crushed Dad's medicines between two spoons and gave them to him right on time: 6:00 A.M., 8:30 A.M., 11:00 A.M., 1:30 P.M., 4:00 P.M., and 6:30 P.M. In between, I had Dad walk around the house several times with his walker and me alongside. I pureed all of his meals except the things that fell apart quickly in his mouth—like pancakes or soft cookies—and he ate everything I put in front of him.

I also got him out of the house at least once a day, thinking the fresh air and sunshine were good for him. The seven steps down and seven steps up were good for him, too, and I quickly confirmed that he was much better coming up the stairs than he was going down. Dad always greeted Sarah and Paul and Gail as they entered the room, and they generally returned the favor. And we finished off the week by taking Dad—in his wheelchair—with us to church on Sunday. He said he had a great time and that he really enjoyed his stay. Then I took him back to the nursing home.

So. The week that was supposed to clear things up for us in deciding what to do about Dad just made it more difficult. Why? Because I discovered that I could do it—take care of Dad—and that he enjoyed our caregiving. I say "our" because Sarah and Paul and Gail were intimate players in this experiment. I did all of the crushing and pureeing and washing and cleaning and lifting and transferring when it came to Pop, but my family was always close by to lend a hand when I needed it, or to give Pop a kind word. Mary called every day to see how things were going. I put Dad on the line with her once or twice if he was up to talking at the moment, and he always smiled when he heard her voice.

A part of me, I think, was hoping that Dad and I wouldn't fare well during this handful of days. That would have made it easier for me to take him back to the nursing home for keeps. But he did okay. Actually, he did terrific! The nursing home people greeted him with smiles and kindness, so I knew that he was going back to a good place. Actually, I knew he was in a good place before I took the week's vacation. But I had sensed before taking the vacation that his home shouldn't be with these people, as kind as they are. I had sensed that his home should be with his own. The trial week did nothing to refute this feeling. In fact, the trial week reinforced it, leaving me with the same decision I had before.

Gail and I talk about it every day. Mary calls me every day about it, too, and she tells me that the relatives back home are talking. What should we do about Dad? I seem to eat, drink, and sleep the question. Even with all of the work I put in last week in caring for him, it was nice to have dinner with my family instead of driving out to MedBridge after work. And it was especially nice to see him sitting in his chair having cookies and a cup of tea at three in the afternoon.

10

"The journey of a thousand miles must begin with a single step." So holds the ancient wisdom of Lao Tzu, anyway.

IF THIS IS TRUE—and certainly it must be—then the first step on the journey I am now traveling was the week off with Dad at our place. When I left you last, I had just taken Dad back to the nursing home after he did well here for a week. Gail and I and my sister have been talking about what we should do next. Well, I've decided on that next step, the second step of the journey. I wish I could tell you I had full support from family and friends, but Mary is uneasy with the idea and Jim is against it.

As I pen this note, it is again early in the day—5:30 A.M., or so. I will be briefer than usual this morning, though, because I go to work at 6:00 A.M. these days. Yes, Topco still starts at 8:00, and yes, I'm still employed there, but I'm on week two of a three-month nonpaid leave of absence from work to take care of Dad full-time in our home. Dad said he really liked being here for the week back in August, so after he had settled back into the nursing home, I asked him if he would like to live at our place for a few months so that we could all figure things out a little better. He said he'd like that, and it was all I really needed to hear.

I heard plenty more before finally deciding to take the Family and Medical Leave, though. Mary said she thought it would be okay, as long as I'd have my Topco job waiting for me come the New Year when I wanted to go back to work. She told some of the relatives back home about the idea, and while I didn't talk to any of them directly, I knew that nobody there was in my corner. Their biggest concern, if I could read between Mary's lines, was the same as her own—that my job wouldn't be there when I was ready to go back.

Gail and Sarah and Paul, however, were with me, and with their support, I knew that I could take the next step. It was an additional bonus when Howard gave me his support to the proposed three-month leave of absence as well. I sensed that Howard really cared about me when Mom died so suddenly in March. And it was beyond an employer/employee kind of care. Howard's own dad passed away several years ago, but his mom has been having some of her own health concerns lately, and Howard is always there for her. He knows what having a sick parent is like.

Howard's been with Topco for over twenty years, but that doesn't mean he's a corporate guy. I was fired years ago in part for not having a corporate personality, and I've come to discover that Howard doesn't really have one either. And when I bounced the leave of absence idea off him before going ahead with the formal paperwork, he said I would have his blessing on it. Howard comes across as pretty gruff on the outside, but he has a softer side, too. I think he keeps it hidden from most people, but he showed it to me when he cried with the news of Mom's death. He showed it to me when he told me to take as much time as I needed in coming back to work after the funeral. And he showed it to me when he said he understood and respected what I was trying to do for Dad.

Basically, the Family and Medical Leave Act of 1993 requires employers covered by the Act to provide up to three months of leave to qualified employees. The employee's job—or at least, relative position—is also protected over the course of the leave. In other words, should Pop do poorly here and I try to go back to work in January, Topco would have to give me my same job, or an "equivalent" position in regards to pay and benefits. It's not too good to be true, however, because I don't get paid for three months, and I have to give Topco a check for $95.58 every couple of weeks to cover my portion on the group insurance premium.

All of this was spelled out in the upfront paperwork, which Howard directed me to obtain from the personnel department. For my part, I had to get a note from Dad's neurologist, Dr. Rezak, describing Dad's health status. Dr. Rezak wrote that Dad suffered from Parkinson's disease. Under "Probable duration of condition," Dr. Rezak wrote, "Indefinite." I know that we all start dying the very second we are born, but it's sad to know that even Dad's best days aren't real good ones, and that he is only going to get worse.

Dr. Rezak's most telling words, however, came under his description of Dad's current day-to-day existence. I've got the form right in front of me. "This patient manifests severe Parkinson's disease and cognitive impairment. He requires constant supervision and care. He requires assistance with all activities of daily living. He cannot walk without considerable assistance. He is taking an extensive amount of medicine." Damned Parkinson's.

In check-mark fashion, Dr. Rezak went on to say that Dad did not need hospitalization, that he did need assistance for basic medical, hygiene, nutritional needs, safety, and transportation, and that my time off with Dad would be necessary or beneficial for the care of the patient. I found it odd that the form includes parenthetically "this may include psychological comfort." Maybe the people at the Department of Labor responsible for form WH-380 should have listed psychological comfort as something more than just an afterthought.

Anyway, Dr. Rezak checked "yes" to Dad benefiting from my presence after reading my signed statement on the form to Item 17, which states: *When Family Leave is needed to care for a seriously ill family member, the employee shall state the care he or she will provide and an estimate of the time period during which this care will be provided. . . .* To this, I responded: "My father needs custodial care, pureed foods, assistance w/wheelchair and in walking and use of the bathroom. He is also on an extensive medication schedule for his Parkinson's disease. Emotionally, he seemed more responsive during a recent stay at my home (one week) and he has indicated he would like to return. I need to see how this option works out over a few months' time frame." Shortly thereafter, I got the paperwork back from personnel telling me that I qualified for the three-month leave. It began last week, on the second of October.

I think I was upfront with Howard. I've been telling him for years that even though Topco is a good gig, I didn't think it was my calling in life. So when I told him about the leave of absence— when I told him that I needed to see how Jim's one-week experiment would play out over the course of several weeks—every word was true. And what if Dad does well here over the three months? Then we'll have another decision on our hands. I told him all of this. But I also told him that I wanted to use the time I had at home to write more, and to see if the writing life had any interest or possibility for me.

Howard's secretary Fran coordinated a great party for my three-month hiatus, however long it ends up to be. Cake, ice cream, the whole nine yards. I was honored by the theme she chose for the gathering: "A man for all seasons." Just like Thomas More in the movie. I don't know if I qualify for the title, but it was nice to claim it, if only for the afternoon. I shared my thoughts on taking care of Dad with whoever wanted to hear them, and I kept singing the same song. Namely, that on Dad's good days, he needs more life in his life. As do we all at times.

Kevin wrote me a poem. Nice. And I got some cards from some of my friends throughout the building as well. The one that touched me most came from Mary Nell, a computer person of Irish descent who I don't work with day-to-day but who brings a smile to my face whenever I see her and who holds a special place in her heart for Guinness beer. She wrote,

> I'm so sorry to hear about your mother's passing. I will be thinking of you and sending you good thoughts and prayers during this time. I will miss your smiling face around Topco. You are always a breath of fresh air. I hope that everything goes smoothly as possible—it will be quite a challenge. Let me know if there is anything I can do—or just call to talk. I'll bring the Guinness. . . .

Thanks, Mary. I'll keep that in mind.

I got another nice note from a guy named Jim Bolton. Jim doesn't know this, but he's actually a personal hero of mine. As a product manager at work, he purchases some of the product that we do the quality assurance work on back in the lab, so he's over at our end of the building quite a bit. He was in the lab a few years ago in early March, shortly after Lent had begun. I knew that he was Catholic, as I'd seen him at noon Mass at St. Peter's near work on Ash Wednesday. So, making conversation more than anything else, I asked him what he was giving up for Lent.

I was surprised—and impressed—to hear that he was going to Mass every day. This is a busy guy with a fairly high-profile job at work. Still, he cared enough about his faith to take in weekday Mass as part of his Lenten observance. It's not a major time commitment, but it's still a commitment. And one that had never even occurred to me. "Cool," I thought. So cool, in fact, that just this past Lent, I started doing it, too, going to 6:30 A.M. Mass at St. Constance before work. And I only missed a few days, as things turned out—the days in late March and early April around my mother's death.

Anyway, in keeping with his commitment to God and religion, Jim wrote,

We will surely miss you over the next several weeks or months, but you will continue to be in my prayers as always. May God give you the strength to endure with any and all adversities. He never gives us more than we can bear.

Such platitudes—while certainly pleasant sounding on paper—may not have meant much to me if delivered from someone else. But I know that Jim Bolton is a man of faith, and coming from him, they meant a lot. I'm not sure what lies ahead for Pop, or for my family and me, but I am confident that we'll all do just fine with it. We come from good stock, after all. And besides, like John Belushi and Dan Akyroyd from the *Blues Brothers*, I sense we're on a mission from God.

Dad seems to be settling in just fine. In truth, he's doing better than I expected. The nights are still the worst, but even the midnight hours have gotten better thanks to Nurse Ratchet. That's not her real name. I don't even know her real name—I'll call her Rebecca. I used to call her Nurse Ratchet after the surly nurse in the Jack Nicholson movie, *One Flew Over the Cuckoo's Nest*. She was mean, that lady, and Nurse Rebecca reminded me of her. The MedBridge Nurse Ratchet seemed gruff with the patients, and often I saw her harshness—or what I perceived to be harshness—in the dining room when she was helping the people eat who needed assistance. Jokingly, I told my sister that the woman scared me. Jokingly, Mary agreed.

But my perception of Nurse Ratchet—of Rebecca—changed when she heard that I would be taking Dad out of the nursing home and bringing him to our place to live. She was friendly and caring after all, and I realized that she wanted only the best for Dad. Perhaps, she felt that my family and I could give it to him. Anyway, she told me that wherever Dad ended up, he really needed a hospital bed. I agreed. Then she asked me if I had one lined up for him. I told her no, but added that I was in the market for one. Then she told me about some old electric hospital beds that the nursing home was junking.

Seems they recently got some brand new beds and they were scrapping the old ones. She said that some had already been picked up, but that a few were out on the service drive behind the nursing home. I went there at once and found one bed remaining. It was a little beat up, but it looked fine to me. I got some paper and a marking pen as Rebecca suggested and put a couple of "Hold for John Reynolds" tags on the thing. Then I arranged for some helpers and the next day, we loaded it into the back of our van.

Man, it was heavy! Even with the rails off. It must be all the electrical works down beneath the springs. All I know is that it was almost as heavy as the upright grand piano I moved from my old grade school down in Streator to our home in Chicago several years ago. The pastor at St. Anthony's told me that if I wanted the piano, which had been damaged somewhat in a flood, I could have it. Provided I hauled it away.

A friend—one of several who helped me to get the thing onto Dad's old F150 pickup—gave me some advice I've never forgotten. He told me that if the piano should somehow fall off the back of the truck as I was cruising along the Dan Ryan or the Kennedy Expressway, or anywhere else for that matter, I should act like nothing happened and just keep on going. I laughed when David said the words to me, and I smiled to myself as I recalled them trying to get the hospital bed into the van. Fortunately, neither the piano nor the bed slipped away in transit, and now both of them grace our home. For wildly different purposes, of course.

I've gotta run. I hear Dad banging his wedding ring on the rails of the hospital bed again, and it's time to go to work. Not that getting up three times last night with Dad wasn't work! That's one thing I noticed right away about being home with Dad. I'm always on the job. At least at Topco, when I went home, I pretty much left the office behind me. Now the work follows me around. Remember that commercial for Dunkin' Donuts when the alarm goes off early in the morning and the guy in bed slaps at it and groans, "Time to make the donuts." Well, it's time to crush the meds.

11

Dad has been here for three weeks now, and I'm starting to get a feel for things. Probably, Dad is too.

IT'S EARLY MORNING AGAIN, my best time, it seems. I talked to Howard the other day. He called to see how things were going. I spoke with Father Tom the other day, too. He's our pastor. He asked me how things were going with Dad also, but he got a little more definitive than most people. He asked what a typical day was like. I told him as best as I could, considering that no two days have played out exactly the same with Dad since he's been here. Still, it was a good question. Father Tom's questions usually are, I have found. Here's how I answered it, with some additions thrown in.

I'm up early with Dad each day, usually by 6:00 A.M. Often sooner. Today, I'm up earlier still to write this. Otherwise, I'd probably still be in bed. But not asleep. I'll explain later. Dad was up only twice last night. The first time I heard him, he was once again banging his wedding ring on the hospital bed rail. It's an annoying sound, like a woodpecker pounding away on an aluminum Christmas tree, or a tinny machine gun going off. When Pop lived at Mary's place right after Mom died, she had given him a bell to ring whenever Dad needed her. Dad is soft-spoken to begin with, and his voice has lost a lot of its power as the Parkinson's takes control more and more. Mary was quick to respond to the bell, thinking that she might get to Dad before he got out of bed and fell. It didn't always work for her.

With the hospital bed, this is less of a concern here. Accordingly, when Mary suggested—right in front of Dad—that I give him a bell at our place, I looked at Mary with daggers and pulled a finger across my throat to say, "No!" without Dad hearing the word. I explained to Mary later that I didn't want Dad to think I would always be there for him in the middle of the night whenever he rang the bell. I would be, of course, but I didn't want to make it easy for him. He figured out the ring thing within a few days, though, so he didn't need a bell after all. Hello woodpecker and machine gun; good-bye quiet nights.

Dad was fine when I went in to see him the first time. He said he just wanted to see if I was still awake. "No, Dad," I told him, adding that it was two o'clock in the morning, and that nobody was awake. I told him that Sarah, Paul, and Gail were asleep. I told him that Belle (the cat) was asleep. I told him that the neighbors were asleep. I told him, in fact, that the only people in the whole house—and probably on the whole block—who were awake were him and me. And do you know what he said? With the trace of a smile, he said he thought he'd go to bed now, too. I could have screamed. I could have laughed. I kissed him on the forehead and said good night. I must admit that I could have been a little gentler with Dad though all of this. That's probably why I smiled myself and thought of Nurse Ratchet as I trudged back to bed.

A couple of hours later, I was up with him a second time when I heard a commotion in his room. He was trying—unsuccessfully— to get out of bed. When I found him, he had his legs wrapped up in the hospital rail on the wall side of the bed. I uncurled him as best as I could and asked what he was trying to do. He said he had to use the bathroom. I would have lifted him onto the wheelchair to the portable commode that Mary had given me, but I could tell by the odor in the room that it was already too late. I had seen the nurses in the hospital and in the nursing home change Dad by rolling him back and forth on the bed as they got the old diaper off, cleaned him, and put a new diaper on. It seemed like a lot of work to me, and I felt more comfortable with changing and cleaning Dad when he was standing up.

I got him out of bed and had him stand up with the walker positioned against the wall so it wouldn't go anywhere. As he stood there on fairly strong legs, I took the old diaper off from behind, ran a wet wipe across his cheeks and down between his legs, and slipped a new diaper into place. Then I had him settle back into the chair, and I transferred him from there back into the bed after I had put some new pads in place. If it all sounds like a lot of commotion at 4:00 A.M., you're right. Last night, Dad settled right back to sleep. I didn't.

When Sarah and Paul were newborns in that very same bedroom years ago, I would go to them when I heard them crying in the night. I brought them to Gail, who breast-fed them and took them back to the crib. Meanwhile, I fell right back asleep in a heartbeat. I barely woke up throughout this almost nightly task. I was so used to doing it that I practically got Sarah and Paul in my sleep. Pseudo-sleepwalking, I suppose. But the work with Dad last night—and many nights so far—tends to wake me up to the point that I can't get back to sleep. That's why I'm up now and writing this.

Getting back to the "normal" day. . . . By 6:00 A.M., or so, Dad is usually stirring. I get him out of bed, change him, clean him lightly (the shower is later), and get him dressed. Then I crush and administer his early morning Sinemet. I used to crush Dad's pills between two spoons, but Gail bought me a mortar and pestle the other day at a local science supply store. Much better than spoons. Then I usually mix the crushed meds with a little applesauce before giving them to Dad. There is no way he can swallow the pill whole with water. Heck, if he could do that, he'd probably be back in Streator and on his own. But Dad's swallowing has long been suspect, and aspiration pneumonia has already landed him in the hospital a couple of times now.

Occasionally when I give him his meds, he can't swallow them at all. I wonder what Dad thinks about during these times. Does he say to himself, "Why can't I swallow this?" Or maybe, "I don't *want* to swallow this!"? Or does anything cross his mind at all? In the selfish and insignificant scope of things, it's frustrating for me. I put the small spoonful of Sinemet and applesauce in his mouth and tell him to swallow. He sits there with the stuff in his mouth. On occasion, it comes pouring right back out onto his clothes or onto the floor. He doesn't mean to do it, but I get short with him nonetheless. "Dad, Dad, Dad," I often say in anger as I rush a towel up to his mouth as if to force the meds back in. I can be such a jerk sometimes. And if you don't believe me, ask Gail.

I heard one of the physical therapists at the nursing home say once that walking is the best exercise Dad can do. After I get Dad dressed each morning, I have him walk with the walker to the pink chair on the dining room side of the living room. On his bad days, it's a slow go, if he makes it at all. Sometimes I have to whip the rented wheelchair in behind him and let him sit down right there on the spot. On his good days, though, he can walk all the way to the bay window, turn around, go to the kitchen, turn around again, and return to the living room before he says he's tired and wants to sit down. These are the times when I sing his praises.

I'm harsh with Dad sometimes, true, but I'm also his biggest fan and cheerleader. "Excellent, Dad. Excellent! Who's the man. . . . you the man. Oh, yea! Oh yea!!" He may tire of hearing it, but for now, at least, he seems to enjoy the limelight. And remarkably, he shares it with me. Not that I deserve it, but he offers it anyway. "Great job, Dad!" I'll say when he sits down. In ever humble fashion, he often counters with something like, "No, you did great." As Gail always says, he's a nice old man.

And I do love him, but it's funny. I can feel my love for Dad forming more over the days and weeks of his care here, but when

I was small, I don't know if love is a term I would have used to describe my feelings for my father. Respect, yes. I had tremendous respect for him. Even when I was in grade school, I could see and appreciate how hard he worked to put food on our table and clothes on our back.

He was often gone by the time I got up in the morning, and he usually didn't get home until six o'clock or so. He would eat with us—something that Mom always prepared—then often he would head back to the bank to work for a few more hours. Until past my bedtime, usually. Mom taught me how to throw a baseball. Mom helped me with my homework more times than not. Mom showed me how to balance the paper route books. I sense that she enjoyed spending time with me on these things, but primarily, I think she did them because Dad was never around. I loved Mom, and I miss her every day. I'm learning to love Dad. And as the author of Ecclesiastes—and the Byrds—say, there is a time to every purpose under heaven.

I respected Dad also because I saw how well regarded he was in the community. Everybody in Streator loved Dad. He was always quick to share a smile, a handshake, and a word hello. In high school, my buddies always wanted to use my dad as a reference when they went looking for part-time jobs. Who could blame them for wanting James Reynolds, Vice-President, Streator National Bank, for a reference? I heard Mom and Dad talking about kids in town who made the WIZZ news for violating curfew, or worse, for underage drinking. I didn't want to get caught up with that crowd for a lot of reasons, not the least of which was that I didn't want to disappoint my father.

As usual, I digress. Next, I throw Dad's clothes in the wash. Being home from Topco for a while, I've taken over the laundry. It just makes sense, because most of it is Dad's anyway. I do easily one load a day, often more. Dad's sheets are almost always wet in the morning—sometimes drenched—despite my efforts to keep them dry. The hospital bed from the nursing home came with a big, plastic covered mattress pad, so I can just wipe that down. On the fitted sheet each night I put two of those large incontinent bed pads, one on top of the other.

In his tossing and turning, though, Dad often displaces these over the course of the night, so I've taken to pinning them down with safety pins. The sheet is already starting to show it's wear with pin marks and tears where dad has pulled and stretched the pads. I watched him in his sleep one night for several minutes, and was amazed at how agitated he can become while still remaining asleep. And one morning I found him with the safety pin pinned to his diaper— I don't even want to know, okay?

After laundry comes breakfast duty, one of my favorite times of the day. First, Pop has to have his morning cup of coffee. I forgot it once or twice when he first came here, and he quickly asked me about it. I know that he and Mom enjoyed the stuff, for whenever I'd spent the night back in Streator, I could always smell it in the morning. I also remember Mom and Dad taking us out to breakfast at the Town & Country restaurant in Streator after the Sunday papers had been delivered and how they would sit around afterward with cups of coffee in their hands. "Can I heat that up for you?" the waitress would ask, and Mom and Dad would always say, "Please, just half a cup." Or something like that. I've never been much of a coffee drinker myself, but I have a cup sometimes with Pop in the morning, and I'm beginning to see the appeal.

By this time it's usually pushing 7:00 A.M.—time to tune in "Good Morning America" on the television for Dad and get Sarah and Paul moving for school. Sarah is in third grade now and Paul is in first. They're cute. Gail would normally get them up, but since I'm home now with Dad, she takes advantage of a few more minutes under the blankets, and I'm happy to give them to her. In truth, it's kind of a treat for me to hang with Sarah and Paul in the morning. Usually I'm gone for work right about now and they're either still in bed or just starting to stir. Now I get to be a part of their early morning routine, and hopefully, I can be as cheery and as bright for them as sunshine. Or orange juice, at least.

Now I'm the breakfast guy, and I relish the role. I've always been big on the morning meal, but I seldom took the time to make it for myself when Gail and the kids were still in bed. I've eaten a lot of cold cereal and frozen waffles over the recent years, but not many real breakfasts, not the kind of breakfasts Mom often made for us when we were small. But all of that changed when Dad came. Waffles, pancakes, French toast, scrambled eggs, oatmeal with apples and raisins. Not all on the same day, of course.

Dad seems to like my cooking, and he often greets whatever I put in front of him with a big smile and an "Oh, boy." God bless him. He doesn't have many passions left anymore. He can't drive. He can't work around the house. He can't crunch numbers at the bank or at the auction sales. But he loves to eat, and when he's doing well, he can handle a fork and a spoon in fine fashion. I feel most at ease with serving him pancakes, because the syrup pretty much dissolves everything and this makes it easier for him to swallow. A therapist told me that this is always a good choice.

I actually put French toast into the food processor, because the crusts sometimes can be chewy, and I try to give him as few raisins as possible, just enough to be able to tell him that I'm serving oatmeal with raisins. Mary said she served him lettuce once by mistake when Dad was at her place and thought he was going to die for the coughing. I've learned from her mistake, and if anything, I've taken my caution to the extreme. With few exceptions—breakfast entrees, mostly, or cookies—whatever I give Pop goes into the chopper first. Against his wishes, I might add. Sorry, Pop, but it seems to be working.

After breakfast, I clean the dishes and take the kids to school, while Gail catches her final few Z's. Again, this is a treat for me. I don't know what's going to happen down the road with Dad and his longer-term care, but right now I'm digging being home. More than one person I've mentioned this arrangement to has responded with words akin to, "Mr. Mom, huh?" Well, yes, and no. Yes, in that by virtue of my being home I've assumed some of Gail's roles and I'm able to spend a lot more time with my children. No, in that my primary focus right at this moment is not Sarah and Paul or giving Gail a little extra sleep. My primary focus right at this moment is Dad's day-to-day care as Gail and I discuss alternative options that don't include sending him to a nursing home. Mr. Mom? Maybe. Mr. Son? Definitely.

Of course, none of this conversation would be possible if Mary, as the executor of Dad's estate with power of attorney status, wasn't floating us some "Pop care" money from Dad's savings. I'm a practical man, as Howard told me once or twice while discussing the financial element of my leave of absence. It would have been a heavy financial burden on my family—not so much now, but in lost savings down the road—to give up a paycheck for three months while I took care of Dad. Mary conceded that the leave of absence would be a good thing provided I'd get my job back in January if things didn't work out well here with Pop. After I assured her in this regard, she felt better about the leave and agreed that I should have some money coming in.

I read somewhere that the time off work allowed for by the Family and Medical Leave Act of 1993 hasn't been utilized by many who would otherwise have loved to take time off for a medical or family reason because they just couldn't afford the loss of income for three months. Fortunately, Dad (with Mom) has some money saved up—more than I would have guessed based on their lifestyle. Their earnings and savings came to light shortly after Mom died since Mom and Dad didn't have a will and we had to meet with a lawyer to settle some financial affairs. The meeting was in Mary's home because Dad was living there then, and that's when Mary got her executor and power of attorney labels.

I remember the meeting very well. We were all sitting around Mary's kitchen table when the lawyer—Mary and her husband

John's lawyer—said that we needed to assign these titles to someone. He said that traditionally, they befall the oldest son. That would be Jim. Silence took over as we all decided what we wanted to do. That's when I stood up and interjected, I think, a little humor into the air by saying that I wanted no part of either assignment.

I next shared the story about how I once had to borrow forty bucks from a business contact in Columbus, Ohio, so I could pay for my parking at O'Hare International when I got back home. I told everyone assembled that I have many gifts, but that keeping track of money isn't one of them, and I closed my argument by saying that the whole executor and power of attorney thing sounded like a lot of paperwork. And I hate paperwork.

It was the lawyer, I think, who suggested that it might make sense to give the jobs to Mary only because Dad would be living with her and all of his medical bills would be coming to her house anyway. It sounded like a fine suggestion to me. Mary was reluctant at first. Maybe she was thinking about all the work it would entail, too. But she said okay in the end. Not with authority, but okay nonetheless. I applauded her commitment. Jim never objected, and so it was settled.

Dad was going through his cash pretty quickly at the nursing home. It would have been nice if he could have used it to travel with Mom to exotic spots around the globe. Maybe to Hawaii. Maybe to Europe. Or even just to Weaver's for chicken every night if they wanted to. But Mom's dead and Dad's sick and now the money is intended for his care. Mary is paying me significantly less than my Topco salary, and a fair amount less than what Dad was paying the nursing home. This is a good thing, I think, provided we can give Pop the care he needs. And so far, so good, it would appear.

I have to go away for a while. It's pushing six bells, and I just heard Pop banging his ring on the bed rail again. I'll be back.

12

Okay, Pop is square for the moment, the kids are at school, and I have a little more time left before I'm back on duty.

GETTING BACK TO FATHER TOM'S "routine day" question, I am reminded of something a quality assurance person told me at one of the food plants I was visiting probably fifteen years ago. I asked him something about the planting and harvesting schedules of the various products his company canned. Peas, beans, and corn, primarily. He gave me rule-of-thumb answers, but he added that he had been in the business over twenty years, and he wasn't yet quite sure what a "typical" year looked like. I've only been caring for Dad for a few weeks now, and I'm still looking for the typical day.

Whatever it is, it's pretty mundane. After coming back from dropping Sarah and Paul off at school, I transfer the laundry from the washer to the dryer and add the second load, if there is one. Usually next, I take care of the breakfast dishes and grab a quick bite myself, if I haven't already eaten (I sample liberally from the meal as I prepare it, just like Mom used to do). I give Pop his second medicine of the day at 8:30, and then it's time for one of Dad's most dreaded experiences here so far—the shower.

I don't know why Dad hates showers so much. But I'm pretty confident that he's taken more showers here already than he's taken in the past several years back in Streator. In truth, I'm not particularly fond of giving them to him either, but I think they're good for him. One of the nurses at MedBridge told me that sponge baths are nice, but to really clean someone well—especially someone who is incontinent with occasional bowel movement accidents—showers are best. I don't have an official shower chair, but I use a plastic-coated metal lawn chair that fits right into the tub. Whatever works, works.

I've taken to giving Dad showers three times a week—on Monday, Wednesday, and Friday—but typically I get one of these days off when the home health aide comes. Her visits were set up when I first brought Dad here. They were suggested by the social worker at MedBridge as I was winding down all the paperwork regarding Dad's upcoming three months at our place, and I must say, I look forward to the time off. Dad takes to the company, too, even though he typically complains when I tell him someone is on the way.

A nurse showed up within the first several days of Dad being here. I went over the day-to-day gig with her—like I'm doing right now—and answered all of her questions. She said that it looked like Dad was in good hands. Then she listened to Dad's breathing for the rattling sounds of pneumonia. She said he sounded good. His blood pressure was also on the mark, as was his temperature. She even clipped Dad's toenails for him. I was so happy, I could have kissed her. I know Jesus washed his disciples' feet, but it's going to take me awhile to grow into some of these things, okay?

A physical therapist comes two times a week. She works with Dad on his walking primarily, but she also does some exercises with him. She has him raise his arms above his head and out to the side. She has him stand straight-legged and straight-backed against the wall while holding on the walker. Dad hates this one. Finally, she does some bed exercises with him. Dad lies in bed while she flexes his legs and rolls him back and forth. She says this is "passive" exercise in that she is the one physically moving Dad's legs, but it's exercise nevertheless because the muscles are being worked.

I like the notion. It goes back to the old *you'll-do-it-whether-you-like-it-or-not* concept. Dad, of course, often can't control his muscle movements like you and I can, and when he can't, it's nice to know that the movement itself is more important than who is doing the moving. I try exercising with Dad in similar fashion on the days the therapist doesn't come, but I don't always pull it off. What I always pull off, however—much to Dad's displeasure—is walking.

Finally, the home health aide comes once per week. If Dad is due for it, she'll give him his shower instead of me. I've only been at this a handful of weeks now, and already I can appreciate the importance of caregiver rejuvenation time. I get a lot of support from Gail, and to a certain extent from the kids, but day-in and day-out, I'm the guy here with Dad, and it is a little bit wearing. Mary continues to call every day to see how we're doing. She even came over a few times to chat with Pop and to give me a little respite from the one-on-one thing with Dad. So far, it all seems to be working just fine.

Shower-wise, Gail and I installed one of those hand-held shower sprays at the suggestion of the aide, and it seems to help the process by controlling—and containing—the water a little better. Howard called the other day, in fact, to see how things were going. I told him I had just gotten Dad out of the shower and that my father was sitting in the bathroom dripping wet with no clothes on. Howard paused for a second or two, perhaps picturing the scene in his mind's eye, and then said, "I'll get back to you." I smile every time I think about it.

I spend the next half an hour or so drying Pop off and getting new clothes on him. It takes longer than you might think. Three times a week, I also give him a shave with one of those disposable razors. This works pretty well, but I'm so afraid of nicking him. I have, in fact, already. And more than once. One of these days I'll probably have to buy him one of those electric shavers. I know that Dad doesn't like the things because they just don't give as close a shave as a blade. Still, if an electric shaver will keep Dad's face intact a little better, I'll probably go that route sometime soon.

Next, it's exercise time if Dad is doing well. Up and back the length of the house with the walker. Everyone in the house—and probably the neighbors—know when Pop is on the move. Gail has compared the sound to a sick cow. Those poor sick cows get compared to a lot of things, don't they? Anyway, the sound is caused by the rubber tips on the legs of the walker. We have hardwood floors throughout the place, and when Dad puts downward pressure on the walker and moves forward at the same time, the rubber must rub the wood the wrong way. It's not as bad as fingernails across a chalkboard, but it's close.

After exercise, I usually change him again just like I do when I get him out of bed first thing in the morning—by having him stand behind the walker while I stand behind him. Once or twice now, Pop's legs have given out on him as I go about unfastening his pants, lowering them, removing the old diaper, putting the new one in place, and pulling up and fastening his pants again. Then I find myself supporting nearly his entire weight on my thighs while either yelling at him to stand (on my bad days) or encouraging him to stand a little straighter (on my better days). If you ever find yourself in a position like this—taking care of your dad or your mom or anybody who needs help and who may be incontinent—I have one word for you when choosing their clothing: elastic!

Mid- to late-morning, I usually get Dad a snack. Cookies, maybe. Pound cake. Carrot cake. Or donuts, if we have them. Pop loves donuts. As I mentioned earlier, all these foods dissolve pretty well in Pop's mouth, so I don't have to mince or dice them. Often he asks for seconds. And sometimes thirds. That's okay, Pop, ask away. And we buy one treat—chocolate, chocolate-chip pudding cakes—through a school fund-raiser program, and along with the donuts, I'd have to put them at the top of Pop's list. I prefer giving him donuts, however, because of the mess factor. Picture a little kid polishing off a serving of mostaciolli. That's how Dad is with a chocolate, chocolate chip pudding cake in front of him. He always comes up smiling, but washcloths and towels to the ready!

I may have a little quiet time just before the noon entree, but if I haven't finished the dishes and the laundry by then, it goes away quickly. Lunch is usually a chopped meal—macaroni and cheese, canned soup, ravioli. I categorize Pop's meals by how many times I have to put them through the food processor. If it's a single dish, like ravioli, it's a "one-chop" meal because I only have to use the food processor once. Easy. If it's a salad and a plate of stew, it's a "two-chop" meal. Harder. If it's a salad, a chicken breast, green beans, and rice pilaf, it's a "four-chop" meal. You get the idea.

After lunch, I take care of the dishes again, then prepare Pop's 1:30 medicine. Also, I try to get him out of the house at least once a day. I do this whenever the weather and timing seem right. When both are on the mark, I help Dad down the seven stairs to the sidewalk, walk with him (or wheel him) to the car, load him, and hit the trail. Sometimes we go down to the local drug store. Sometimes to get gas. Sometimes just around the block. Dad likes being in the car. I remember that he used to take Mom and my brother and sister and me out for drives when I was smaller. Now I'm taking him. What goes around, comes around.

I pick up Sarah and Paul from school at 2:30. I actually wheeled Pop down there a couple of days ago. I'm pretty good with the wheelchair and I know how to take a curb with it. That day, though, I nearly lost him. I saw a small bump in the sidewalk where one slab of concrete had risen against another. I thought the wheelchair would just ride right over it so I didn't even slow down. Instead, the wheels hit the lip and stopped cold, causing the entire chair to tilt forward. I hadn't strapped Dad in as I should have so he began sliding out of the chair. Holding on the handle of the chair with one hand, I swung my arm down hard across Pop's chest to keep him secure. It worked, and within seconds I was back in control. I apologized to Dad about the rocky road. And even now I wonder about the rocky road that is stretching out before the both of us.

Sometimes in late afternoon, Pop takes a nap, but seldom. Mostly he watches the television news starting at 4:00, which is also his next medicine time. It's easy to forget these appointments, so I set three timers to help remind me. I've got an alarm on my watch, one on the refrigerator door, and a third on the stove. With all of these buzzers and bells going off, along with my wife to help me pick up the slack when I miss one, we've got Pop covered pretty well. Sometimes, when he's in a bad mood about something, he'll say as I approach with the meds, "Again? I just had one of those!" Well, no, Dad, it was actually over two hours ago.

Dinnertime is probably my worst time of the day, especially on Gail's workdays. Then I've got Pop, Sarah and Paul with their homework, and dinner to worry about. It can get pretty hectic around here between 4:00 and 6:00. Pop's last med time is technically at 6:30, but I've been cheating toward 6:00 P.M. with it. Dad fades pretty early, and the medicine perks him up a little bit before dinner, which usually ends up going on the table around 6:15 or so. I asked Dr. Rezak about this, and he said it wouldn't be a problem. Basically, he said that in Dad's case, the pills could be given at times that best suited him to a certain extent, provided that they were given consistently at the same times from day to day. We're consistent, okay, and I've got the timers to prove it.

After dinner, I walk with Pop some more if he's up to it, change him again, lead him to the pink chair in front of the TV, and put a dessert or snack in front of him. Then I get his bed ready. If Pop had his way, we'd have dinner at 5:00 and he'd be in bed by 6:00. Gail and I are trying to push him back to a more reasonable schedule. At least at our place, he has a separate bedroom, which helps. Like I said, at Mary's he was going to bed at 6:00 in the living room. In truth, I'm beginning to know how Dad feels, because by early evening, I'm about ready to cash in my chips and go to bed, too.

One thing I've learned very quickly is how much time it takes—and how exhausting it can be—to take care of someone. To really take care of someone, I mean, the way Gail took care of Sarah and Paul when they were very young and I was traveling a lot for Topco. Once, I went to Europe for two weeks when Paul was only a month old. I've come to appreciate what I didn't appreciate then—that the time isn't sucked up in actually being with the person in need of care. It's sucked up in tending to all of the associated things that need tending to: the laundry, the medicine, the food preparation, the constant cleanup.

A friend told me that shortly after their daughter was born, he asked his wife if she could mail a letter for him during the day while he was at work. He returned to find the letter unmailed. Dismayed by his wife's inability to carry out a simple task, he told me that the next day he asked his wife if she could just *stamp* the letter while he was at work. Gutsy, I must admit, but even before my taking care of Dad, I knew that this was the wrong thing to say. Anyway, now I'm the housewife in many ways, Dad is the infant, and I spend my days trying to find time to stamp the letter. Note to self: Thank Gail later, and tell her that you love her.

I usually get Pop a bedtime snack around seven or so, then start getting him ready for bed at 7:30 or 7:45. When he's doing well, it's not much of a problem. I again change and clean him, then put him into one of those open-in-the-back hospital gowns that someone at the nursing home was kind enough to give me. Pop has pajamas too, but he doesn't seem to mind the gown, and it's a lot easier for me when he's wearing it, especially when the urine soaks through the diaper at night. I've always been pretty utilitarian, and I've become more so over the past several weeks. Whatever works best is best; style notwithstanding.

And did I tell you about my father's bowel movements? Mary tipped me off to this when Pop was at her place and one of his BM's plugged up her sewer line. Dad is less regular than more, with bowel movements occurring only once every several days. He seems fine with the arrangement, so I guess I am, too. The trouble is that when the BM's finally come, they're big and—even with the stool softener I give him once a day—they're firm. Sort of like footballs. I've taken to keeping a little piece of wood trim in the bathroom. Now, after Dad goes, I get him out of there and lock everybody else out of there as well, then I go about breaking Pop's BM into smaller units that the toilet can handle. I'm sure I've told you way more than you wanted to hear.

Getting Pop into bed can be tricky, especially when he locks his grip onto the arm of the wheelchair. Once when I was transferring him into the bed from the chair, I didn't know that he was holding on. I ended up picking both him and the wheelchair up off the floor. *"Let go!"* I yelled, even though I knew that he wasn't doing it on purpose. I had to pry his fingers off the chair that night, then I gave him a towel to hang on to as I quickly completed the transfer. I've been a runner for the past twenty-five years, but I've never been much of a weightlifter. Now all that has changed, and I don't even go to the gym.

Pop doesn't always settle down right away, but he's getting better. I think shifting him to a later bedtime instead of his original schedule has helped. Even now, though, he often takes a long time to get comfortable. Sometimes, he just sits up in bed. This worries me, for I fear he'll topple over and hit his head on the bed railing. It hasn't happened yet, but that doesn't mean it won't happen tonight or tomorrow night. I don't settle into my own evening until Pop settles into his.

And I do a few special things with Pop each night before leaving his room. First, I bless him by tracing the sign of the cross on his forehead with my right thumb. "May Almighty God continue to bless you and heal you," I say. And, "I ask this in the name of

Jesus Christ, his Son, our Lord. In the name of the Father, Son, and the Holy Spirit, Amen." I say a prayer of thanks silently next, followed by a prayer of petition that I may do better with Pop tomorrow. Then I extend my hand to Dad and say, "Let's check the grip." When Dad gives me his firm handshake in return, I know that everything is going to be okay, at least for the night. Finally, I kiss him on the forehead and tell him that I love him, dim the lights, and close the door behind me. He should be good for a few hours after that. From 10:00 P.M. to the following morning, it's a toss-up.

Don't hold me to this "typical day," okay? The recap of my response to Father Tom's question has turned into the ramblings of a sleep-depraved madman. I didn't want to interrupt your train of thought anymore than I have already, so I didn't tell you that I was setting my pen down over the course of these past several hours to walk with Dad two times, run with him to the drugstore, give him his meds, change and clean him twice, give him lunch, mop up the resultant spill, fold his laundry, and clean his dentures.

You probably didn't even know that I was gone all of those times. Gone or not, I'm back, but now it's time to get Pop his three o'clock snack. How does that old saying go? "Man may work from sun to sun, but woman's work is never done." I'll never, ever again—as I did in my ignorant youth—ask a mother of young children if she works. My question from this day forward will be, "Do you work outside the home?" The difference, I know now, is significant.

Anyway, what began as a predawn note because I couldn't fall back asleep has turned into another long letter, with these last few pen strokes being completed about fourteen hours after I began. Not a bad effort. Especially for someone who doesn't work outside the home.

13

Just a quick note to give you the Pop update. Bottom line: he's doing fine. At least that's what the nurse said on her follow-up visit.

At THE TIME, Dad's vital signs were good, and he actually appears to be putting on a few pounds. He doesn't like the way I chop his food, but he's been pneumonia-free since he got here. Maybe there's a connection. Two of his favorite meals are pizza and burritos. I'm sure he had a pizza or two at Mary's place, but like I said, the burritos were all Greek to him.

Dad continues to do well with the stairs (still better on the way up than on the way down), so we've been getting out almost every day. He enjoys going to church with us on Sundays, and the parishioners at St. Constance have really taken to him, even in this short amount of time. In truth, some people even fawn over him. It's nice to see. I still don't know how Dad is feeling following Mom's death. We talk about her sometimes. I bring up conversation of Mom in the past tense hoping to remind him that she is gone now. Still, I often hear him calling for her in the night—"Jean, Jean"—and referring to her in ways that make me think that he thinks she is still alive. Touching. Sad. And a little freaky at three o'clock in the morning.

Which brings me to Dad's mental condition. He continues to float mentally at times. Dr. Rezak used the term "dementia" during Dad's last visit there several weeks ago. He's probably right, especially when Dad says things to me and I have no idea about the thought behind the words. Like, "There's someone standing there," when no one is there. Or, "The house is on fire," when it clearly is not. Dementia. When I hear the word, I always think of that crazy disk jockey, Dr. Demento. Dementia. I can't bring myself to use the word with people in conversation. "Floating mentally" is easier for me to deal with, so that's how I plan to keep referring to Dad's cognitive difficulties.

Dad's doing well physically, though. So well, in fact, that on his really good days—the days when he absolutely should not be in a nursing home—he sometimes even ventures forth on his own by using table tops and chair backs for balance along the way. Only when I'm not looking, of course. I actually found him in the basement the other day. Huh? I take a three-month leave of absence from work to take care of my father, and when my back is turned putting laundry away or something, he shuffles down the stairs with a makeshift handrail and into the basement. I get sweaty thinking about what might have happened. When I saw that he wasn't in his usual spot, I ran upstairs, outside, and all through the house before I found him down below. "Dad," I hollered, "what are you doing?!" "Just walking," he said. Great!

Last week, the drain in the bathtub backed up. Remember, I was telling you how I helped Dad when I was a kid and he was working on the drain? Decades later, the roles are reversed. This time, I was in the tub and wearing the grimy work clothes while Dad—in his wheelchair—was alongside of me giving me moral support. Dad handed me the screwdriver as I did some repair work on the faucet, then he handed me the rodder and watched as I snaked it into the drain while squatting in three inches of murky water. We chatted about this and that. Mostly, I recounted the story I already told you about the problem in Streator, and how he told me there was no sweeter sound in the world than the sound of water rushing through a cleaned out drain.

I worked the rodder back and forth several times, each time coming back with a clump of hair, or worse, something I couldn't identify. I was making progress, though. We were making progress. Finally, the head of the rodder gave a little and the water started to go down, making the same sucking sound I had heard years ago. Dad was all smiles and patted me on the back. I thanked him for showing me how to do it years ago. And then I said something that broadened Dad's smile even more: "I bet they wouldn't let you do this in the nursing home." He agreed, and despite the chilly dampness swirling about my ankles, I felt plenty warm inside.

Meanwhile, the longer-term discussion of what to do with Dad goes on. Mary and I talk every day. Gail and I talk every day. I've met with Howard a few times for lunch. "What are you going to do?" they all keep asking. I don't know anymore than Dad did when people asked him the same question at the Town & Country luncheon following Mom's burial. I had better decide pretty quickly, though, because I'm due back to work come January. I can't say that I really miss the actual work, but I miss the camaraderie of the office, and I do miss the paychecks.

Mary tells me that the relatives back home are glad to hear that Dad is doing well, but at the same time they're saying that I should wake up and go back to work. Uh, try showering and dressing a hundred-fifty-pound man who doesn't move so well on his own. Or lifting him into and out of an automobile a couple of times a day. Or crushing twelve pills a day and administering them on time. I've long held that those who work the hardest get paid the least. And often, it seems, the reverse is true. Go back to work? As if what I'm doing here with Dad isn't work.

Mary, by comparison, knows what goes on here day after day because it went on at her place when Dad was staying with her right after Mom's death. Mary knows the work involved because it was the work she did herself. Anyway, she thinks I'm doing great with Dad, and she tells me this often. We share thoughts and ideas because I know she understands. There was a song several years ago with the lyrics, "Before you abuse, criticize, and accuse, walk a mile in my shoes." Well, Mary has walked a mile in my shoes. So has Mom. Several miles, in fact. More than ever now, I admire them for it.

I just got a letter in the mail the other day from Dad's neurologist, Dr. Rezak. It's addressed *To Whom It May Concern*, and it opens with the words: "Mr. James Reynolds is under my care for severe Parkinson's disease." The letter goes on to say that Dad requires a wheelchair for transportation. Actually, I asked Dr. Rezak for the letter because the pharmacist at Kluza's Pharmacy—where I've been renting Dad's wheelchair since he came to stay with us—asked it of me. It all has to do with Medicare. Apparently, I get a discount on the monthly wheelchair fee if the chair is requested by a doctor for a legitimate medical reason. We still have money coming in from Dad's estate through Mary, but it's way less than what I was making. Saving a few bucks on the wheelchair each month is money in the family's pocket, and the family can use it!

Gail and I have discussed the option of me going back to work and then hiring someone to be a full-time, live-in caregiver for Dad. We talked about this before I took the leave of absence, too, but the conversation didn't really go anywhere. Recently, we've been talking more specifics. There seems to be an underground network of middle-European caregivers in this area. I know people who know people who have used one, and it sounds like a hit-or-miss proposition. Some—probably most—are great. Some are horror stories of theft and neglect. And even with the greatest non-American caregiver, the language is always a problem. And besides, where would we put a live-in aide?

We've also discussed the option of hiring someone part-time during the day while I'm at work. This doesn't seem like such a good idea either, because I travel for my job, and who would help Gail get Pop in bed at night when he is doing poorly and I'm gone?

I'm sure Howard would be understanding on the travel element and let me get away with traveling less, but that's not the job for one thing, and for two things, I'd be gone sooner or later, leaving Gail on her own to take care of my father.

In addition to these logistic problems, I've also talked to a few nursing agencies and the hourly rate for professional nursing care-givers is pricey—much more on a part-time basis than my sister is paying me on a full-time basis. I know that money isn't the issue here, Dad's care is. Fortunately, we've been able—so far, anyway—to give Dad what appears to be good care, while saving him money over the nursing home at the same time. And I am convinced that being with family is an added benefit for Dad here, one that cannot be measured in dollars and cents.

I don't want to brag, but I'm kind of a big shot back at work. I've been there nearly eighteen years for one thing, and I'm the manager of Quality Assurance Audits. This puts me over twelve professional food and nonfood technologists, a wonderful bunch of people that I feel privileged to work with everyday. I work well with them because I did their job for over twelve years, and I know what they have on their plates. Anyway, I used to judge my days by seeing what we had going on together—meetings, product evaluations, travel. Now I wake up and see if Dad's sheets are dry. Dry sheets. They don't occur often, but I've found that when they do, Pop usually has a decent day. Dry sheets, I think, are an indication that he slept well the night before. As I've told more than one person since early October, when Pop has a good day, I have a good day.

It's pushing 6:00 A.M., and I'm on Dad duty. More later. Much more later.

14

It's nearly crunch time on the Pop decision. Howard has been great about this whole thing as I've tried to decide what to do.

LIKE I TOLD YOU a while back, Howard seems to have a better understanding of what I'm going through than most people do. Since I've worked for him for all these years and since I've kind of left him in the lurch, you might think he'd be the least supportive of what I'm doing. Oddly though—other than Gail and Mary and a few people at church—he's been more supportive than anybody else. Every time we talk he tells me not to feel pressured, but that he needs to know if I'm coming back or not.

In a goofy sort of way, the decision would be a lot easier if Dad were doing poorly here. Just like it would have been easier after taking my week's vacation here with Dad if he had done poorly then. But he did well then and he's doing well now, so where does that leave me? "Well, Dad, I hope you enjoyed yourself for these past several weeks. You're looking great, You've been pneumonia-free ever since you got here, and the people at church love you, not to mention your grandchildren. I'm taking you back to the nursing home now, because I have to go back to work."

The funny thing is, Dad would handle the news just fine. In taking him from the hospital after his latest bout with pneumonia to the nursing home to my place for that week, then back to the nursing home, then back here in October when the leave of absence began, I've found Pop to be pretty good at settling into a place. So what does it matter if he's in a nursing home or here with me, especially if on certain days he doesn't seem to know where he is? What's wrong with it, I guess, is how it makes me feel. The bigger questions, I think, are these: Why should a physical therapist walk with Dad each day when I can walk with him? Why should a nurse crush his meds for him six times a day when I can crush them? And why should an aide tuck him in each night when I can tuck him in? And give him a blessing and a goodnight kiss besides.

And speaking of blessings, did I tell you that I'm Dad's Godfather. And that Gail is his Godmother. We were there with him in church when the priest poured the water over Dad's head. We were there with him in church when we said that we would help him grow in his faith. And we were there with him in church when his baptismal candle—the candle that is now upstairs on my bookshelf—was lighted to symbolize his new life in Christ. I held that candle during the ceremony. It's a white taper, about ten inches long, and it has a picture of a dove coming down from the sky with a golden sun in the background. Below are waves of the sea, and directly above the waves are green and blue tongues of fire, or what I take to be fire. These are images of Catholicism from my youth. Now they are images from my adulthood, while Dad slips more and more into the role of the child. Life gets stranger every day.

I told you about how Mom and Dad walked to church every morning. Years before that, Dad went with us to Sunday morning Mass before driving us around in the car to deliver the papers. I can't remember, but it seems to me that I knew even then that Dad wasn't Catholic. I seem to remember Mom telling me that he wasn't anything—that he had no religious affiliation—and that she hoped he would convert someday. When I asked about why he went to Mass with us, she said that he just thought it was nice. This impressed me—this going to Mass without having to go to Mass—and Dad taught me more about going to church by his actions than he ever would have guessed.

But what I remember most about Dad's faith—or lack of it—from long ago is snooping through Mom and Dad's big desk in the front room one day. I wasn't looking for anything in particular when I came across a black book about the Catholic faith. I figured that Dad was studying up on Catholicism. And in that book was a picture of hell. At least some artist's vision of hell. And it was awful. It was pretty tame, I'm sure, by today's standards of high-tech, special effects movie wizardry. The hell in Dad's book was a simple black and white drawing showing all these people in agony surrounded by liquid flames. I knew they were liquid because one guy was holding up his hand—in supplication, perhaps—and the flames were dripping down his hand into the rest of the flames all around him. Yow!

I never talked with Mom about Dad and about what we could do to keep him out of that horrible place. But they must have kept on talking about it. Several years later, I came to learn that Dad was taking some classes from the priest at St. Anthony's Church. "Great," I thought, even though I didn't have the initial zeal I felt when I was small to have Dad baptized. I guess he had since proven himself in my eyes. With or without the baptismal font, I knew what kind of man my father was. And whether he was officially churched or not, I wanted to be like him.

Still, I was surprised and honored when my folks asked Gail and me to be Dad's Godparents. He was baptized nearly ten years ago now by Father Joe there at St. Anthony's, the same church where my brother and sister and I were baptized, again proving that what goes around, comes around. When I was small—probably about the same time I found the black book in the desk drawer—I remember reading somewhere that if a person caused the direct conversion of another to the faith, then the person behind the conversion was assured a place in heaven. Well, I'm not sure if I believed it then, and I'm not sure if I believe it now. But true or no, I'm sure of Mom's place in paradise, and it's nice having someone there to talk to.

As I was saying before I took you on a religious tangent, I'm still trying to decide what to do about Dad. Money keeps playing a role in the decision. As does fear. I've worked at Topco for nearly eighteen years. Beyond my Oscar Mayer fiasco, it's been my only job since college. They pay me well, but I'm actually considering not returning so I can take care of Dad on a permanent basis. I had talked with Gail before about spending more time writing with Dad here. In truth, it hasn't happened. Taking care of my father consumes more energy than I ever thought it would. Do I really want to quit doing all that I know how to do in order to take care of Dad and maybe put some words down on paper?

My brother is still shaking his head over all of this. He's angry. I've already told you how he feels, but I bring it up again because it keeps playing on me, just like everything else, as my leave of absence from work winds down. I have different responsibilities now, but one of my jobs at Topco was traveling around the country—and the world—accepting or rejecting production facilities that wanted to pack product for my company. I made these decisions on my own, with potentially millions of dollars of business hanging in the balance. Now I can't decide what to do about Dad. About my work. About my life. What's happened to me?

It's nearly 6:00 A.M., and Dad is stirring. I have to go, and I have to make my decision over the course of the next several days because Howard needs his answer. I wrote a poem a while back entitled "Evening Prayer." Here it is:

Thank you, Lord, for one more sunset.
Let the magic of this moment linger always in my heart,
    and may my soul forever behold your face
       in the blush of the evening sky,
          in the rush of sunlight upon the sea,

in the mystery of shadows
that the afternoon misunderstood.
Any good I've done this day
is just my way of saying I love you,
and for all the times I've fallen short
I ask you for a kind report.
Remember—
it was the sinners you came for, not the saints.
I do not pray for wealth or fame
yet I seek two blessings always the same—
grant me wisdom, Lord, to see your light
and strength to do whatever's right.
And Godspeed, sweet Jesus.
Open my eyes so that I may better discern the kingdom
as you envisioned it;
renew my spirit so that I may better live the life
provisioned by your cross.
If the path is revealed in the treading,
then walk with me, Lord, and I will surely find the way;
for while I don't understand the entire plan,
I put myself in your holy hands.
and you give me Peace.

I need wisdom and strength now more than ever. And Peace.
Go once more with God, and pray that I do the same.

[15]

Dad continues to do well. The decision about what to do with him and the decision about what to do with my life—as if they're two separate decisions—still weigh heavily upon me.

BUT IT'S THE HOLIDAY SEASON, one of my favorite times of year, and maybe I can forget about all of the problems for a minute or two. If you're in the mood, maybe I can share a little Christmas magic with you this morning before my day begins.

A few years ago, Gail and I made our own Christmas cards, and the tradition continues. I write the text of the message, hand-letter it onto our page design, and make copies of the finished card. Gail usually does some artwork by hand on each individual card, then off they go to family and friends. It's a lot of work, but it has become one of my favorite ways of keeping the Holy Day. And I tell you this because we went out with Dad last night to pick out our tree. We purchased it from a Christmas tree lot, leaving Dad in the car as Gail, Sarah, Paul, and I made our selection. Dad liked our choice, and the experience reminded me of one of our very first Christmas card messages:

Isn't it nice to see the Christmas trees?
They come from all around, these joyous pines.
And they take their time, I'm told—
 up to eight years from seedling to needing a home.
Then they show up come December
 on empty lots and root beer stands
  in stands that nature could never imagine:
   urban forests, imploring us to take them home
    one tree at a time.

I remember a Christmas long, long ago
 when my father and I embraced the cold
  in search of evergreen gold.
I was only three and smaller than every tree
 but I was not without an opinion.
Even in that towering dominion
 I foolishly voiced my displeasure
  for the lack of perfect treasures to be found.
All around were trees too skinny or too fat
 or too tall or too short
  or too full or not full enough. . . .

Enough!

My father took me by the hand
 and helped me understand.
He told me that every tree was special
 in its own imperfect way,
  much like little boys.
And big boys, I now suppose. . . .

No son, I'm not blind—
 that skinny tree will do just fine.

How ironic that thirty years later, I'm taking Dad out to get a Christmas tree after he took me out for years when I was small. And after we got the tree set up at home and trimmed with the lights and the ornaments and the garlands, Dad just looked at it with wonder. Just like my children. Just like me, I'm sure, when I was small. And when I was small, I had another Christmas tree adventure that I hope is worth the telling. It was the night the fully decorated tree came crashing down in our living room.

I can't tell you if I pulled the tree down by a string of lights, by a branch, or by the cord that plugged into the wall. I can only tell you that I pulled it down, and it came down hard. I was unscathed, but it caused one hell of a commotion. There were pine needles everywhere. And bubble lights that were no longer bubbling. And sparkling strands of tinsel. And long, plastic icicles. And broken glass ornaments and light bulbs. Mary, Jim, and Mom all came running. And yes, Dad came running, too. Now, he sits in the soft glow of a tree that comes from a much different time in his life. And mine. To my eyes, at least, the glow becomes us.

I heard from someone not long ago—maybe Dr. Rezak, or one of the health care nurses—about the stages of Parkinson's disease. There are five of them, apparently. The initial diagnosis is Stage I, when the patient is exhibiting minor Parkinson Disease symptoms, and it progresses to stage V, which, as it was described to me, is when the patient is essentially bedridden. Whoever I was talking with put Dad at Stage IV to Stage V—in other words, not good. When Dad can't walk, or when he can barely stand for that matter, I see him at Stage V. When he can't speak or can't swallow for hours at a time, I see him at Stage V. These, too, are the times I see him in a nursing home.

But he's not like this all of the time. When he's up and about with his walker and me beside him, I know that he doesn't belong in a nursing home. At least not yet. When he's saying hello to folks at St. Constance following Sunday morning Mass, I know that he doesn't belong in a nursing home. At least not yet. He just won a wreath in a church raffle. You should have seen his face when I told him about the phone call telling me to come and pick it up. You should have seen his face when I walked in the door with the thing and Sarah and Paul and Gail gathered around to see what Pop had won. I don't know anything of the diagnostic intricacies of the stages of Parkinson's disease, but I know how I feel when I see Dad enjoying himself under our roof.

What are we going to do about Dad? The answer, as ill-defined as it is, seems to change everyday. It's nearly time to decide.

16

Every year at Christmas, Topco hands out a holiday box to all of its employees. The box is filled with various Topco-labeled items, and it's a pretty good haul.

THE FROZEN TURKEYS are handed out separately, and there is usually a lot of commotion because the birds are stored in the parking lot in a trailer unit, and employees are given little slips of paper telling them when they should go to claim their Christmas meal. People are walking out of the building all of the time throughout the day, it seems, carrying frozen turkeys from the trailer to their cars.

The boxes are distributed the same day, and it' always fun to plow through the goodies to see what's going home with us for the holidays. Working in the lab, the technologists and I often joke that it's the stuff nobody else wants, like maraschino cherries and orange marmalade. I must have ten bottles of cherries stashed in the back of my cupboard, and Howard said to me years ago, "Show me a food technologist who likes orange marmalade, and I'll show you a bad food technologist."

But there's good stuff in the box, too. Over the years, I can remember getting wild blueberry preserves and cans of cashews and upscale olives stuffed with real pimiento, not the pureed pimiento paste that passes itself off as real pimiento. I can remember getting boxes of club crackers and rounds of Gouda cheese, and more times than not, I've come away with some imported Jarlsberg cheese as well. I can't say that it's one of my all-time favorite cheeses from a taste and texture point of view, but I've always liked the name.

I am reminded of the Christmas boxes and turkeys in such detail because earlier today, I came home with my eighteenth and final holiday gift from Topco. I told Howard about six hours ago that I wouldn't be coming back to work for him after the first of the year.

I swear, I didn't know what I was going to tell him even as I drove to the office. The family discussion of what to do about Dad has gone on and on and on, and Howard did us all a favor by forcing a decision. I'm embarrassed to tell you that I weighed myself this morning, and I've lost nearly twenty pounds in trying to decide what to do. I know that I haven't been eating the way I should. I haven't gone running in months. I've been sick with worry and indecision. Should I quit, or should I go back to work and send Dad to a nursing home?

In many ways, sending Dad to the nursing home would have been the easiest thing to do. Then life would return to normal, relatively speaking. But not really. Because I would still be going out to see Dad on a regular basis, disrupting my evenings and weekends. Perhaps down the road, this would have gotten the better of me, and I would say to myself, "I'll go see Dad tomorrow." Or, "I'll go see him when I get back from Pittsburgh." I saw a lot of lonely people in the nursing home while I was visiting Dad there. Some of them complained to me that their children were too busy to come in for a chat. Was I one of those children? "No!" I told myself. Maybe. . . .

I thought I had my answer early last evening, but by the time I hit the pillow that night, I was already waffling again and dreading the next day. We have snow here, and early last evening, I was taking out the trash. On the way back from the alley, I scooped up a handful of snow and packed it into a ball. My thoughts and actions were unplanned, but like a little kid, I was looking for direction, and my eyes went to the deck in our back yard, the deck which my wife and I built when Sarah was small and Paul was still a glint in Gail's eye. "Dear Lord," I prayed, "if I'm supposed to quit work and take care of Dad, let me hit the cornerpost of the deck."

I was on the sidewalk, fifteen to twenty feet from the front of the deck and a little bit to the right of it. I let the snowball fly, and it did, indeed, hit the front cornerpost, but not squarely. Incredibly, the snowball then broke apart, and what was left of it continued on and hit the back post which is supporting the lattice work we put up years ago. So there it was. My sign. I don't know if it came from God or Mom or the Snow Queen, but somebody was telling me that I not only should quit to take care of Dad, it was a very good thing besides. I just stared at the two snow marks for several seconds, then I went into the house, too embarrassed to tell Gail what I had done.

The positive connection, like I said, didn't last long. My sign from above, I later told myself, wasn't some cosmic revelation. It was instead the result of coincidence and, possibly, years of playing organized baseball when I was small. Fate cannot be decided by the flight of a snowball. I tossed and turned last night, despite Gail's support, and too soon, it was time for me to face Howard. Gail asked me what I was going to do as I left the house yesterday. I told her I didn't know. And truly, I didn't.

Many years ago, I was coming up Stink Creek Hill back home with my buddy Gary. It was our senior year in Streator High, just days before graduation. I cannot recall where we were coming from that day or where we were going, but I remember Gary saying that it would be the last time we'd come up Stink Creek Hill as high-schoolers. His comment has stuck with me ever since, and I have often recalled it as I pass from one phase to another in my life. I recalled it as I traveled the familiar four-mile route from my home to the office, thinking that if I tell Howard I'm quitting, it would be the last time I take Foster to Central to Lehigh to Howard to Gross Point Road as a Topco employee. Pulling into the Topco lot, I had not yet nailed down my answer.

I took care of getting my turkey and my holiday box first as it was give-away day. I tried to avoid people I knew, preferring to talk to no one until I talked with Howard. I had gotten everything into the car and was walking from the north parking lot door through the warehouse toward Howard's office when a remarkable thing happened, even more remarkable than the snowball the night before. I bumped into Barbara.

I've known Barbara for the entire length of my Topco stay as she started about three months before I did. I've also had the pleasure of having her work directly beside me for several years, and, as I told Howard often, she is the hardest working woman in the building. I've relied heavily on her over the years for assistance in all sorts of projects, and she has always come through for me. Always. Ironically, I often joke with Barbara the same way that Howard has joked with me: "Don't quit before I do." I would be lost without her, and now, I'm the one who's thinking of leaving.

Beyond her work ethic, something else impressed me early on about Barbara and it has made me one of her biggest fans. She is a caring person, a family person. She talks often about her husband and her children, and while I've never gotten to know any of them, I sense in conversation with Barbara that they mean the world to her. When she and her husband celebrated their twenty-fifth wedding anniversary several years ago, I presented her with a poem I had written for them in calligraphy and which Gail had framed. Barbara must have liked it, for she sent a note a few days later on a beautiful card that carried the image of a flower painted by hand in watercolor and Barbara's name scripted in dark pink. More beautiful still were the words inside the card:

Dear John and Gail,

Your gift is priceless. It is obvious that it is a gift of love that took many long hours of care and thoughtfulness. Both Leon and I were moved beyond words needed to express our appreciation.

We will cherish this gift forever, but most of all your friendship shines through as the real present. I hope we can live up to these beautiful words and wish you both the same pleasure of growing old together in love, health, and happiness. . . .

Barbara and Leon.

Nice, huh? Well, that's Barbara. Nice. Sometimes Gail would stop by the office to say hello and bring Sarah and Paul with her. Barbara loves seeing my kids, and she is always quick to get them candy treats from the sample cage back in the warehouse. Sarah and Paul are still learning to remember names, but Barbara, I suspect, will be held in their memory for years and years to come as the "candy lady." It is a term of description, of course. But it is also a term of affection. And I will always cherish the colorful, hand-knitted afghans she gave us when Sarah and Paul were born, along with the white one she gave to Gail and me as a wedding gift over fourteen years ago.

I bounce ideas off of her constantly—both work-related and non-work related—and she's never led me astray. I've asked her about gift ideas for Gail over the years. I've asked her about children's name's before Sarah and Paul were born. I've asked her how she dealt with newborns in the house when she was a new mother. She's easy to talk with, Barbara, and I've come to know that she is wise.

I give you all of this Barbara info because you need to know how much I value her opinion and counsel. I hadn't spoken with her much beyond hello on the phone since I began my leave of absence three months ago. And suddenly, there we were in the warehouse yesterday—she enjoying the festive mood of the day;

me still trying to decide what to tell Howard as I trudged toward his office. When we met, she asked me what I was going to do. I told her the truth. I told her that I didn't know.

Then she said something, which made everything clear. She said that I didn't really have a choice. I never asked her what she meant by the words. Did she mean that I didn't have a choice in that I needed to get back to work? Or did she mean that I didn't have a choice in that Dad needed someone right now, and that I was the someone? I told her that she was right and continued on, but in that instant, I knew what I was going to do. I walked into Howard's office and told him that Dad was doing well. Then I told him that even though what I was doing may seem foolish to some, I was quitting to take care of Dad full-time. Howard didn't try to talk me out of it. Better yet, he told me that he understood. Later as the news spread, people often told me, "You have to do what you have to do."

I heard the words ten times if I heard them once, and almost every time, I heard them with some degree of misunderstanding and disbelief. At least that's what I perceived. People generally seemed to be saying that this is a really stupid idea. I wasn't looking for praise from my co-workers. I was looking for a little support, however. The kind of support I sensed was coming from Howard and Bob, another guy who works for Howard and with whom I share an office wall.

Like Barbara, Bob is good person, too. I actually worked for him for a few years when my responsibilities shifted somewhat. Eventually, though, both Bob and I ended up working for Howard. As a hobby, Bob does woodworking away from the office, and he's very good at it. He once gave me an intricately carved "R" in honor of my last name, and he also gave me a carved version of my creative-writing side business, "Train of Thought." Like Barbara's afghans, I will long hold both pieces dear.

One of my favorite work memories of Bob is computer related. Bob is the lab's computer genius. He just took to the computer a few years ago when we got our first one, and he's been reading manuals and banging on keyboards ever since. Me? I'm not much on computers now, and years ago, I was borderline illiterate. But I had a big project due for Howard one day. Bob knew it was due because he heard it assigned to me during the same staff meeting. I got to work early—about 6:30 on the day it was due—and Bob was already there. We shared hello's and I told him why I was there, even though I think he knew. I was working on something that Bob had set up on the lab's computer network, so Bob could access the work, too.

And he did. Without saying a word, he sat down on the computer behind me and started banging away at one portion of the assignment as I worked slowly at another. I knew at once what he was doing, and I smiled to myself—and breathed a little easier—because I knew that I would make my deadline. It was like two people shoveling the driveway after the snowstorm instead of one. The work fell away from both screens—much faster from Bob's, of course, because he actually knew what he was doing— and not long after the official workday began at 8:00 A.M., the report was finished. I would have been at it for hours. I told Bob thanks and he said "No prob," and in that instant, I realized what a kind and decent man this was. Whenever I did something wrong when I was working for Bob, he would gently chide me, then add, "It doesn't make you a bad guy." Maybe yes or maybe no, but Bob is a good guy, no questions asked.

Anyway, I sensed compassion from Bob in the wake of my decision. I sensed compassion from the likes of Jim Bolton and Mary Nell, who had written such nice notes when I began the leave of absence three months ago. I sensed compassion from Barbara, too, even though I never did ask her what she really meant by her "no choice" comment in the warehouse. Other people's "You have to do what you have to do" is a far cry from something like, "I'm sure your Dad will like staying with you. Let me know if you need anything." I can understand the former type of response, but I embrace the latter—now, and in the weeks, months, and possibly years to come.

Howard told me that what I was doing was the right thing. He also told me that he would need a letter of resignation. I'll work on it and get it back to him. My three-month leave of absence extends until the end of the year, so until then, I guess I'm technically employed. Come January 2, however, I'll be unemployed. And by my own choosing. Am I nervous? Yes. But I'm excited, too. For Dad. For me. For my family. I think it was Helen Keller who once said that life is nothing if not an adventure. Here's to the adventure.

Part Three

A Day in the Life

I've always felt that my wife and I make a good team—not in spite of our differences, but because of them.

CASES IN POINT? I'm a morning person; she's a night owl, so I make breakfast and the kids' school lunches and she deals with homework at the eleventh hour. I like winter; she likes summer (but she's winning me over), so I go sledding with Sarah and Paul in the snow and she takes them to theme parks in the heat.

Additionally, I'm a doer; she's a thinker; and we've talked about this one at length. I tend to jump into things and then figure out what to do when I get there. Gail tends to figure things out first, then jump in. Nine times out of ten, her way works out better. But there is something to be said for my way, too, and day-to-day now, we're living it. I quit my job. Dad's settled in, and every day is a day in the life of my father and his care-giving family.

I get most of the care-giving recognition because I'm the one here with Pop nine times out of ten, but Gail and my children and my sister and brother are key players in this saga, too. Still, when one of the first social workers came to see how Dad was doing here shortly after he moved in, she was very surprised to learn toward the end of her visit that I was Dad's primary caregiver. She said she just assumed it was my wife. She said that it was not so unusual these days for a spouse to quit work in order to stay home and care for an aging parent. She said it was very unusual, though, when the person quitting work was the man. In care-giving circles, females rule.

In true leap-before-you-look fashion, I am learning everything as I go along. Perhaps there is no other way, really, in circumstances such as these. And besides, Parkinson's disease is a funny thing, at least in my father's case. I've learned to pick up on certain trends that Dad exhibits, but mostly, each new day is a new day.

Some days are pretty good for Dad. These are the days when he can walk, exercise a little, and swallow his medicines, so I spend my hours doing laundry, cleaning, tending to his needs— and even writing a little—in good spirits.

By comparison, some days are pretty bad. These are the days when he can't walk, exercise, or swallow his meds, and my days are darkened accordingly. And some days are just terrible. I've never cared much for the term, "emotional roller coaster." I've always found it trite and overused. Perhaps this is because I have never really been on one before. I'm riding one now, though, and the term is not trite at all. It just tells it like it is. My wife—my opposite in many ways—is alongside me for the ride, and I thank God she's with me in the car.

17

We hung a stocking up for Pop over the handle of his wheelchair. He was thrilled on Christmas morning when I showed him that Santa had brought him chocolates and cookies. Pop enjoyed going to Mass with us, and later opening gifts.

EVEN MORE, I ENJOYED having him there, in our home, and not celebrating Christmas in the rec room of the nursing home. Again, I'm sure that would be nice, too, but for now . . . for now, I think Dad is better off here.

I continue to walk with him frequently, and exercise with him, and get him out of the house when the weather is good. Sometimes the children seem to rattle him a little, especially lately with their being home from school and running back and forth throughout the house. Paul gets on Pop's nerves the most, but I am convinced that the commotion isn't a bad thing. It gets back to the premise of Dad needing more life in his life. With Sarah and Paul sparring, Gail coming and going to work, the paper carrier ringing the bell to make her collections, and the phone ringing off the hook, there is plenty going on here that Dad can focus on, and somehow, I think it's all helping.

Dad is even sleeping better these days. Or nights, I guess. Like I said earlier, Gail and I have shifted him back to a more respectable schedule. He's sleeping basically through the night now, with only an occasional 2:00 A.M. "ringing" of the hospital bed, whereas when he first came here in October, getting up with him several times a night was not uncommon. Besides the shift in sleep schedule, much of the credit goes again to the hospital bed, compliments of Nurse Rebecca. Only a few times has Dad managed to scale the walls, and I usually get to him before he can cause any damage to himself. No falls so far.

Gail has been great through this whole thing, even though it's really just beginning. She has a wonderful rapport with Dad, and vice versa, it seems. I'm sure a lot of women wouldn't deal well with a husband who takes a massive pay cut to care for his ailing father and to try his hand at writing. Nor would a lot of women deal well with the father himself, who occasionally pees on the floor and whose wheelchair has managed to ding almost every door jam and piece of furniture in the house.

Well, Gail not only deals with Dad and me, she seems to actually embrace the situation, and the other night, she had me laughing so hard that I was actually crying. It was the middle of the night—1:00 A.M. to 3:00 A.M. territory—when we both heard something that stirred us from our sleep. Instinctively, I asked out loud, to myself as much as to Gail, "Dad?" Just then, Belle, our cat, went cheetah-like from one end of the house to another as she is sometimes inclined to do. The sound was one of racing paws and the rush of wind. It was the sound of speed in the darkness. Immediately afterward, Gail responded to my question: "Nope," she said, "too fast!"

We took Dad to see Dr. Rezak just before the end of the year. Mary met me there. She was against me quitting work to take care of Dad full-time because she didn't like the idea of me leaving a good job, but now that the decision has been made, she has swung completely into my corner. I have no idea what the future will bring, but I sense that Mary will be in my corner through it all. I've tried to tell her how much this means to me, but I've probably fallen woefully short of expressing my true feelings. We tend to kid a lot. I tell her, "You take care of Dad's paperwork, and I'll take care of his laundry." We talk often. We laugh. It's good to have her. Jim remains as distant as before.

Dr. Rezak had Dad do some exercises for him. Dad most enjoys "turning the knobs." Here, he extends both arms out in front of him, then rotates his wrists both left and right as if he were turning two doorknobs or shower controls. Dad does the turning well, and seems pleased with himself at the effort. But he turns his hands back and forth way faster than Dr. Rezak wants him to go. I've noticed the same things in my exercises with Dad at home. Slow, controlled movements are hard for him. Fast twitch movements appear to be easy for him. And he can't seem to understand the direction that will take him from one to the other.

Dr. Rezak had Dad stand up, too, then walk for a little bit. Dad got up out of the wheelchair with minimal assistance, and he walked—again with help—maybe twenty feet down the hallway outside of Dr. Rezak's examination room. Dr. Rezak seemed impressed. I told him of the routine I was doing with Dad at home and he told me to stay the course. He also gave me a sample of something called Ambien after I told him of Dad's earlier sleeping problems. It's a sleeping pill, I guess. I told Dr. Rezak I'd see how it went over the next few weeks and consider it, but you know what? I've already considered it. This poor man is already on twelve pills a day to help him get moving. I'm not about to add another medication to his repertoire to help him calm down.

January 2 came and went, but with highlights. I needed to pick up some calligraphic artwork which I had on display at Chicago's Newberry Library. Maybe I'll just share with you the journal entry which I jotted down that night after I got Pop tucked in and shortly before I tucked myself in, too. "I was officially due back at Topco today. God, I hope this decision is the right one. It still feels right, and I take hope in that. I took Sarah and Paul downtown today to pick up the Newberry pieces. Paul chased a flock of pigeons away in the park. They flew low. He laughed and laughed and ran low to the ground with birds all about. Such joy! If I was at work, I would have missed it." Every day, whether I write it down or not, the journal of my life is filling up. I pray now more than ever that I fill it up with good things.

[18]

*I've settled into my day-to-day life as a
caregiver, a writer, and a stay-at-home father.
Gail and I have placed a few ads in North
Shore magazine, an upscale publication
focusing on lifestyle issues for Chicago's north
suburban well-to-do crowd.*

I'VE ACTUALLY RECEIVED a few phone calls from this and some assignments—enough to keep me busy but not nearly enough to bring in any serious money. I enjoy the work, but I don't know how much I can even take on, as I spend so much time caught up in some element of Pop's care.

Gail takes care of our financial books, such as they are. I got a phone call the other day from some investment firm out in San Francisco, of all places. It sounded like a young woman on the other end of the line—an attractive one, no less—and maybe that's why I listened to her entire spiel. She said that as I was a mover and shaker in my field, she was calling me with some hot investment tips, which she thought I might be interested in.

I asked her how she got my name and number. She gave me an evasive answer—something about how she heard that I was someone who may have some investment money available and who might be interested in doing something with it. I listened to the choice of options, and when she was through, I told her that I had recently quit my job and had taken a substantial salary hit to take care of my father and to write. "Oh," she said. And added, after several seconds of dead air, "Do you know anybody else you could refer me to?" Click.

Dollar-wise, I've come to learn that we can get by with much less than I thought we needed. Gail and I were never too extravagant in our spending patterns, but we went out to movies every once in a while. We went out to eat. Things have changed. Now I make pizza on three Friday nights out of four instead of ordering out from Joe's. Fast food meals with the kids are practically nonexistent. We haven't been to a first-run movie in months. I've taken to changing the oil in my car and Gail's van, and I haven't bought any new clothes in a year. We're not saving anything, but day to day, we have food on our table and a roof over our heads. Day to day, it's working.

My official occupation these days—the one that puts the food on the table and keeps the roof over our heads—is "caregiver," and unless my writing career really takes off, it will be what I put on the "Occupation" line of next year's tax return. Actually, I'm pretty good at it, and I've already added a few new things to Dad's calendar, which he isn't crazy about but which I think might do him some good. First of all, I've started taking him to a Parkinson's support group. Pop was against it, if he even understood it as I explained it to him. I had read about it in the paper, and Father Tom tipped me off to it as well. We went to our first meeting a few months ago, although in truth, I didn't want to go either. One more time commitment, you know?

I'm glad we went, though. And Dad seemed to enjoy himself once we got there. Pop remains very soft-spoken when he can speak at all. Even when questions from the group were directed toward Dad, I did most of the responding because Dad just wasn't up to it. It was attended by many Parkinsonians whose disease had progressed much less than Pop's. Some were there on their own, some were there with their caregivers. We talked about medication schedules, doctors, and exercises. Dad seemed to have the most advanced case (stage IV–V?), and was on the heaviest medication schedule. Poor Dad. He's not alone in this world, although at times it must certainly seem so to him.

A couple of months ago, I added a Monday-Wednesday-Friday seniors' exercise class to Dad's schedule. The class meets at the Leaning Tower YMCA, not far from here. I knew about it because I had seen the signs while going to the same Y to swim during my lunch break at Topco. Gail and I have been members for years, in fact. But when I was swimming there just over a year ago, I never dreamed I'd be unemployed from Topco and bringing my own father to the seniors' class three times a week. Of course, that was before Mom passed away. One woman dies, and everything changes.

Pop really enjoyed his first session there. We met Elmer, Evelyn, and Stanley, and we said hello to several others. Dad sat in his chair for the entire forty-five minutes while the others stood up or sat down depending on the instructor's direction. He actually did pretty well, even with the dumbbell weights, though I had to help him through several of the exercises. Passive exercise, I now understand, is still exercise.

And I had to chuckle to myself that first time because as we were leaving two of the gray-haired women in the class passed us up in the hallway going the opposite direction. They smiled at Dad and asked if he was coming again. Dad smiled back and said yes. Later, in the car, Dad said to me, "Did you hear those two girls? They asked if we were coming back?" I responded, "Yea, Pop, I heard them. Pretty cool." But what I was really thinking was, "*Girls*? Those women were both over seventy years old!"

Mary has come over several times already to watch Pop and give me a breather. Like I said, it's great having her support.

Sometimes she comes and Gail and I sneak away either by ourselves or with Sarah and Paul for a couple of hours. Sometimes she comes over during the day when Gail is at work and the kids are at school just so I can write uninterrupted for a while instead of being up every several minutes to check on Pop. But beyond needing her to give me more writing time, I also need her to just give me time away from Dad. A friend of mine told me once that when her children were very small and she was home alone with them, she actually called her husband at work and told him to come home right away if he didn't want her to abuse them.

Her words were tongue-in-cheek, of course, but perhaps not totally so. I couldn't relate to them when Sarah and Paul were infants and toddlers because I was doing the fifty-hour a week thing at Topco when I was in town and traveling the rest of the time. Gail may have felt that way more than once, but me? No, I was the hero. I was the guy who showed up every once in a while and wrestled with the kids on our bed or took them to the park to make snow angels or walked them down to the 7-Eleven for Slurpies. Gail was the one who had to deal with them day-in and day-out. In a sense, I am Gail now, and my father is my child.

I hardly abuse Dad, but I've become mean-spirited toward him at times. I heard the phrase from Howard at work as he described the demeanor of certain Topco personnel, usually executive types who had power over their underlings. Now I find myself being mean-spirited toward Pop on occasion. I've shared this concern with my wife and with Father Tom. Both have told me the same thing—that I'm being too hard on myself. As Gail said once, "It's not like you yell at him and call him a stupid old man!"

No. But there are times—more than I like to admit—that I am less than kind to my father. The world only sees me when Pop is doing well and I'm taking him to church, or to the St. Charles pumpkin fest this past October, or out shopping and to lunch at the mall. The world doesn't see me when I am wiping up Pop's urine from the floor in the middle of the night, or picking up the entire plate of food that he has dropped on himself and the rug for the second time in fifteen minutes. These are the times when I am far less than the person I should be, as if Dad wants to do these things any more than I don't want him to do them.

When I took Pop to exercise class several sessions ago, the instructor told me that it makes her cry to see what a good and loving son I am. She doesn't know my darker side. I feel a lot of nonloving attitudes toward Dad at times, like when he's up several times a night. It happened again just last night, in fact. I swung Dad around in the chair quickly after transferring him out of bed to change his sheets, not saying a word but showing by my actions that I couldn't wait to be done with the task of cleaning him up.

I also made a point to sigh loudly—loudly enough to let Dad hear how angry I was to be in his room again, tending to his needs. Less than six months on the job, and I'm already turning into Nurse Ratchet. Nurse Rebecca at MedBridge showed her golden side. May I ultimately do the same. Dear God, help me to put more love into the doing. Mom, pray for me. And Mom, how did you do this by yourself for all those years?

Dad got a nice note from somebody back in Streator when he was in MedBridge and before he came here to live. The guy's name was Paul Ahearn. I don't think I know him, but the surname sounds familiar. Anyway, his card ended up coming home with us and I put it on one of the shelves in Pop's room. The Hallmark sentiments were nice, but it was the hand-written note inside that caught my attention: "Jim, you are very special to me. My prayers and friendship are always with you. You always brighten up the lives of all the people you come in contact with and that makes you special. God bless you and your family." Truer words were never spoken, and yet sometimes I treat Dad in ways that I wouldn't want to be treated. And he's paying me for the privilege.

When I catch myself acting mean to Dad, I at least try to snap myself out of it. And fortunately for me, Dad is pretty under-standing. I tell him that I am sorry for being short with him, and he tells me that I am doing a great job. He's easy. I also thank him often for letting me take care of him, which allows me to write a little at the same time. When Dad was in the hospital and nursing home a few years ago, I used to read to him from a storybook nearly every time I went to visit. Dad seemed to like it, so now I've taken to reading him my own work. It always brings a smile, but like I said—Dad's easy. At Father Tom's suggestion, I wrote bulletin columns for each of the four Sundays of Advent this past Christmas season. Father Tom knew I was home with Dad, and he knew I liked to write. I guess he put two and two together. I never would have volunteered my services—too shy, perhaps. But I wasn't about to tell my pastor no, especially when I was secretly happy to get the nod. Each of the four columns—one each about seeking light, hope, joy, and peace—were well received by our parishioners, and I got some very nice feedback. Here's one of the pieces:

THE FIRST SUNDAY OF ADVENT:
SEEK LIGHT

Admit it. The approach of winter is a dreary thing. It's cold outside. And often gray. And the days just keep getting shorter and shorter. In fact, the winter solstice is December 21—the shortest day on the calendar; the day when this part of the world is the furthest away from the sun. Studies have shown that some people suffer from chronic depression during the onset of winter because of this lack of sunlight, and medical types have come up with a name for the problem. They call it Seasonal Affective Disorder, SAD. Even the Advent Wreath has at its origin the idea that light must battle darkness until springtime comes again.

How ironic that we have come to celebrate Christmas in the midst of the darkest night of the year. Actually, how appropriate. "I am the light of the world," Jesus told us. Need we seek any other brilliance to chase away the shadows abundant upon the earth? Or in our hearts? But you know how when you're driving down the highway late at night and you need to turn on your interior car light for a moment, and suddenly you can't see the road nearly as well? It's that way with us around the holidays: sometimes we let other lights get in the way.

We have been commercializing and secularizing Christmas for centuries now. I'm certainly not immune to it all. You'll see me at the mall one of these nights, getting frustrated with the crowds and with the high prices and with the sheer madness that is "Toys-R-Us." And you'll see me on my porch with five strands of tiny blinking lights in my hand and calling to my wife for just one more extension cord. And you'll see me at the O'Hare Post Office—the one that never closes—hoping to get the cards into the hands of family and friends before Christmas. And none of these are bad things, really. In truth, I enjoy the hustle of the holiday season (except for that "Toys-R-Us" business . . .) and immerse myself in it as much—if not more—than anybody else.

The only trouble with any of it is if it causes us to lose our focus. Christmas isn't about finding the perfect tree or pulling off the perfect party or getting everything on our list. These are nice extras, to be sure, but that's all they are. Extras. Gravy. Icing on the cake of life. Because Christmas isn't about us. That's darkness. It's about the Child. That's Light. It's about the fulfillment of a promise made to humankind long, long ago. And that's the dazzling radiance that we cannot even begin to look upon or to understand.

It's hard for me to imagine this now—during the first week of Advent—but before I know it, I'll be packing the ornaments away, unplugging all of the extension cords, and hauling the tree away for mulching. All of the glitter will be gone. All of the tinsel. And all of the lights. All of the lights save one, that is. Because while this may be the winter solstice season, when we are furthest away from the sun, it's also the Christmas season, when, hopefully, we are closest to the Son. Let's help each other remember that. Together, may we always seek his True Light, and may He forever dispel the darkness in our lives.

When I read it to Dad, he just looked at me, smiled, and said, "I don't know how you do it, John." I've been writing occasional columns since, and our parishioners still seem to like them. I know that Dad does, or at least he puts on a pretty good act. Anyway, this has led into my first serious writing effort now that Dad is here with us—a small Christmas book with the rest of the Advent essays, two Christmas stories, and all of the Christmas card messages I've written for the past several years. I really dig working on it, and Dad has become of my first listeners. "I don't know how you do it, John." If he's said it once, he's said it ten times, and each time with a smile on his face. Dad has become my boss and my editor of sorts, and a finer one of each I couldn't ask for.

Once again, I run out of time before I run out of words. I have more tales to tell but now I'm needed in Pop's bedroom. I'm tired. I'm always tired these days, it seems. Many years ago, when I was very small, I remember my Mom telling me that she was always tired, too. You'd never know it to watch her. She was always doing something here or doing something there—baking pies, working the auction sales, delivering newspapers when Jim or I were sick. I understand her words more, now. Much more. I don't have three little kids to take care of. I have two growing children and one aging father. Maybe it's a wash in the end.

19

Dad has been here for over a year now, and he continues to do well. He had his latest appointment with Dr. Rezak just a couple of months ago, in fact, and per the good doctor, everything is clicking along just fine.

I TOLD DR. REZAK that I had cut back on Pop's milk, yogurt, and ice cream intake until late in the day—after his last medicine dosage—because I had read somewhere that milk proteins might slow the uptake of the Parkinson's meds in the bloodstream.

Dr. Rezak wasn't convinced that this had any positive effect on Dad, but told me that Dad is doing as well as he's doing partly because of the care he's getting at home. It made me feel good to hear the words, for I've expressed some of my doubts to you already, and if anything, they've grown stronger. It's always me and Dad, me and Dad, me and Dad. I'm happy for the time with him, but often, it's too much time. I know a guy in Arkansas who told me once that he wanted to make enough money to have his Dad move to Arkansas, too. I asked him if he wanted his Dad to move into a house right next to his own. He laughed and said he loved his Dad, but he didn't know if he loved him that much. It struck me as funny then. It strikes me as less funny now.

I'm on the parish pastoral council at St. Constance, and they had an overnight retreat a while back. It was meant to be a quiet time of reflection for all of the council members, and I'm glad I had an opportunity to attend. I didn't know if I'd be able to, because mostly I spend my days and nights here with Dad. He's been doing so well, lately, though, that Gail told me she thought she could handle Pop while I was gone, especially since I'd be only an hour away. It was really nice to remove myself from the home front— where something always needs tending, it seems—even though I was gone for less than twenty-four hours, all told.

I got the chance to run at dawn after spending a restful night in my retreat room—a room, I should add, that had no television or phone. Here is my journal entry for the day:

It is 7:00 A.M. now. I awoke at 6:00 and ran around the lake— about three miles. It was beautiful. Dawn came slowly to the water, filtering through the forest that surrounds it. I stopped a few times just to take in the view. Trying to pray, I kept getting distracted by the face of God in nature. We can be so foolish at times. Today will be spent in study and prayer—things that at some points in my life I probably would have balked at. But not today. Today I embrace the opportunity.

I think of Gail and Sarah and Paul often. While it's nice being away, I miss them, and I pray for their continued health and happiness. I pray also to do better with my father—to see also the face of God in a faltering old man who sometimes cannot walk, who sometimes cannot speak. May the good God smile upon him this day and all days.

Like Pop, I have good days and bad days in my care for him, and they are directly proportional to his very own good days and bad days. When he's doing well—when the showers are relatively easy and he helps with the transfers into and out of the car and he navigates the porch steps okay, I'm all smiles and good will. When the sheets aren't drenched in the morning and his dentures stay in his mouth instead of ending up on the floor and he swallows his medicine without spitting it up first, I'm gentleness personified. I'm Mr. Congeniality when everything is going the way I think it should.

But when I'm sitting up with him at 2:00 A.M. trying to convince him that the house is not on fire, or when his knees are buckling as I change his diaper, or when he's sitting on the toilet for over an hour straight trying to get something to come out, my patience wears pretty thin. When he calls, "Jean! Jean!" in the middle of the night, or bangs his ring on the bed rail just to see if I'm still awake, or refuses to walk—even when I know he can—at exercise time, I won't be winning any perfect host awards. Not by a long shot. And I am reminded at such times of a scriptural passage when Jesus says, essentially, that it's no big deal to love your friends, adding that anybody can do that. The hard part, he says, is to love and pray for your enemies. Or your own father, I suppose, when he's not doing well.

One of the benefits of being home with Pop, of course, is that I'm also home with my children. I like taking them to school. I like picking them up. I like hearing about their days while those days are still fresh in their minds. And by all accounts, they—and Gail— still seem to enjoy having me around. Sarah asked for waffles recently for breakfast, and as I was preparing them for her, I heard her call out, "And you know how I like them." I smiled. I do indeed. She likes them torn into bite-sized pieces, placed around the perimeter of the plate, with the syrup poured into the plate's center. Before Pop came to live with us and I was gone to work before they got up in the morning, I didn't even know she liked waffles.

Unrelated, but in a similar vein, Paul told me what he had learned the other day after I picked him up from school. Specifically, he had learned that liver was good for you. He followed this by saying that my running is good for me, too, and concluded, therefore, without any prompting, that liver must be like running. You can't fight logic, and I would never try. At least not now. Right now, I'm just happy to be here at home for a second-grade little boy with blonde hair and deep brown eyes, and to be on the receiving end of his great pearls of learned wisdom.

As for my writing, I've finished the Christmas book; I'm still writing bulletin columns for our parish; and I've sold a few more commissioned pieces under my new banner, "The Write Occasion." My income from the paying jobs hardly pays for groceries, let alone the rent. I find satisfaction in it, though, and feel that I'm utilizing the gifts God gave me whenever I sit down to the words. But if I didn't have the income coming in from Dad, none of this would be happening. The other day, Sarah asked me, quite out of the blue, if I would have to go back to work if Pop died. "Tough question," I told her. And I didn't have an answer.

And talk of Pop's death reminds me now of my mother's passing, and a church service I attended not long ago. For several years now, St. Constance has been inviting people to mourn their departed loved ones by attending a grieving liturgy associated with All Souls' Day. The mechanics of the service are simple enough. Up near the altar, a shrine is established which becomes the focal point of the remembrance. It consists of a pedestal carrying the parish's death registry, twelve unlit candles, and several vases of red carnations to symbolize the living.

As grieving family members enter the church, they are greeted by ministers of care who offer them one or more white carnations to symbolize their loved ones who have passed away in the preceding year (or earlier, as the mourners are so moved). After the homily, the names of the deceased are spoken out loud on a month-that-they-died basis, and during the moment of silence between each month, a candle is lit to remember all of the loved ones who passed away in that particular time period. Attendees are then invited to come forward with their white carnations and deposit them in the red carnation vases, thus symbolizing that the people we care about are still with us even after they are gone.

As a volunteer minister of care—a group of parishioners who visit the homebound and sick of our parish—I have had the opportunity to work at several of these celebrations. Over the years, I have greeted people at the door, ushered them to their seats, and handed them their white carnations. I've always had compassion for the mourners, of course. And yet, I didn't know their stories so I couldn't really know their hearts. But when Mom died suddenly early last year, everything changed. No longer was I on the outside looking in. I was now at the eye of the grieving storm looking out, and I discovered what a sad and lonely place it can be.

Even though Mom died in the preceding year, I got a call a month or so ago from Sister Marie Ellen—who directs the Ministry of Care program at our place as well as the Grieving Mass—asking if I would like Mom to be remembered at the upcoming liturgy. This surprised me because she wasn't buried from there, after all. She wasn't registered there and she didn't have envelopes—the two things Catholics often joke that their pastors are most concerned about. "Uh, yes, that would be nice," I think I said, and went about trying to tell Dad what to expect.

Dad and I never really talked much about Mom's death since the funeral, but the way he keeps calling "Jean! Jean!" makes me wonder if he thinks she is still alive sometimes. With this primarily in mind, I kept an eye on my father throughout the service to see how he was doing. He remained emotionless as I stepped forward with our carnation when the March names were called, but upon returning to his side, I could see—even by the way he sat in his wheelchair—that he had at least some handle on the solemn proceedings. After the last candle had been lit and all of the white and red carnations had been brought together, Dad looked at me with tears in his eyes and said simply, "I miss her." It was, in fact, the first time I had seen him cry since Mom's passing, and it prompted my own eyes to mist as I responded, "I miss her, too." And ours weren't the only tears in the house.

Do you remember the story of the disciples on the road to Emmaus? They were walking along talking about Jesus rising from the dead when Jesus came up and asked them what was going on. They didn't recognize him, but they were moved by his words and invited him to join them for supper. And when he broke bread at table with them that evening, they finally realized that he was the Lord. Well, I used to view mourning as a private passage, and to a certain extent, I still do. And yet the St. Constance parish family has given me a new compass for the journey, for they have taught me—just as the disciples learned on their way to Emmaus—that a little company along the road can be a good thing. Whether we recognize it at first or not.

Christmas lights are all around as we come to the end of our first full year of taking care of Pop. I've told Dad "thank you!" several times for the opportunity. He says I'm doing a great job. You already know what I think. But the tree is up, Pop is doing well, and life is indeed good. Actually, Dad helped us pick out the tree again this year from his seat in the car as my family and I ran about in the cold with our possible selections. I close with this year's Christmas card message, inspired by the year we've had:

I so love the things of Christmas,
    and as the familiar songs play now in my memory,
        I long to send you the perfect holiday greeting.
Perhaps peace should be my wish for you—
    the gentle and lasting Peace that only the Child can bring.
Or perhaps joy . . . yes, unceasing joy
    is surely my wish for you this night—
    the joy of a blazing Yule log;
    the joy of dogs barking "Jingle Bells" slightly off-key;
    the joy that lives in the deepest heart of friendship and family.
Or love. . .
Perhaps I should send simply my love.
But even while tending such thoughts I realize that a single prize
    encompasses all of these blessings and more.

Home . . .
I bid thee go home this Christmas season.
Go to that place where Peace and Love and Joy abound
    and surround you like golden sunshine on a warm autumn day.
Home—be it a mansion or a manger or a snowy forest glade;
    be it a father or a sister or a face smiling back from the crowd;
    be it the aromatic trace of gingerbread men
    or a silken-winged angel on top of the tree
    or a porcelain crèche figurine chipped and broken
        from too many years of being handled with love.
It has been written that we can never go home again.
Oh, but I say differently.
I say that we can go nowhere but during this holy time,
    because upon all of God's shining earth
        there is nothing more comforting, inviting, or welcoming
           than the places, persons, and things
              that we call home.
And I say also that if home really is where the heart is,
    then this Christmas, as always,
        you are heart and you are home to me.

[20]

I haven't written now in so long. Taking care of the kids. Taking care of dad. Time goes by quickly, but I put in some long days. I'm sitting this morning outside the blood bank office at Children's Memorial Hospital. I committed to give blood a month ago, but that's when Dad took ill, and I've been doing the hospital/nursing home visitation thing ever since.

POP HAD ANOTHER ROUTINE visit with Dr. Rezak shortly after the New Year, and he continued to do well at that time. Once again my sister Mary met us there. Dr. Rezak and his nurse Sue know that Dad has a sweet tooth. I think it came up back when Mom was alive and she told Dr. Rezak about her pies. Anyway, Mary and I usually take Pop out for Dunkin' Donuts and coffee after visiting the good doctor. We must have mentioned this once, for now it's become a running joke of sorts. Both Dr. Rezak and Sue kidded Dad about filling up on donuts and asked if we were going that way again after the appointment. With a big smile on his face, Dad said that we were. Moments like this—when Pop is out and about and grinning—nearly bring tears to my eyes. These are the moments when I am most convinced that we are doing right by him. I hope he feels the same way.

About a month after the visit, Dad got noticeably weaker. I knew from Pop's previous bouts with aspiration pneumonia that fever can sometimes be a sign of the problem. I began checking his temperature accordingly and found that it was running a bit on the high side. I called Mary. I always call Mary when Pop doesn't seem just right. She suggested that I give him some acetaminophen to bring the fever down and make him more comfortable. I did, and the stuff did the trick on the short term. The fever returned hours later, though, and Dad was still weak. I told Mary that Gail and I were going to take him to the hospital, just to play it safe. Mary met us there. As I've said, Mary calls every day to see how Pop is doing, and it's always great hearing from her. Once I told Pop that she had called to say hello, and Dad smiled and said (as much to himself as to me), "Good old Mary." Indeed.

The hospital people confirmed a mild case of aspiration pneumonia via a chest x-ray and hooked Dad up to an antibiotic IV. He perked up a little, but not much. Mary and I visited him there every day and were surprised when they decided to release him after only four days, but the fever had broken and they said we could take him home. Taking him home for the first time since he came here—nearly a year and a half ago—was a mixed blessing. It was great to get him home again, no question. But it was also great for those four days to sleep late, to forget about the medicine times and beepers, to not launder his sheets every morning, or change him, or exercise with him, or chop his food, or clean his dentures. Or break his bowl movements up with a piece of wood trim so they wouldn't clog up our sewer line.

He did okay the first day back, but I've got a pretty good read on Pop by now, and he wasn't back to where he was before the hospital visit. He got weaker the second night home, and really weak the third night. Plus, his swallowing seemed to shut down and I couldn't get any medicine into him. It's a catch 22—he needs the medicine to help him swallow better, but he's too weak to swallow the medicine. He coughed badly after trying the first spoonful of dinner on his worst night yet, and it was then that Gail and I decided to take him back to the hospital.

We wheeled him to the top of the front porch then tried to have him walk down the stairs, just like he had done hundreds of time before. But this time was different. This time, he locked his grip on the railing halfway down, and I'm telling you, it was like a vice on metal—immovable. All the while his knees were buckling, and Gail and I tried to loosen his hand from the rail so that we could get him back into the wheelchair waiting at the base of the stairs. "Let go, Dad! *Let go!*" Before the silence came, there was a lot of shouting, bells, and whistles that night.

Pop finally loosened his grip—or we loosened it for him; I cannot now remember—and we got him into the chair. I caught my breath and wheeled him toward the curb to begin the next struggle: getting him into the car. Sometimes Dad grabs the top of the car as I transfer him onto the front seat and when his grip is frozen there, it is nearly impossible to get him into the vehicle. It often becomes a two-person job then—I do the lifting and Gail holds on to his hand to prevent him from locking on to the car with it. These are the things we've learned as we go about taking care of Pop day to day.

Unfortunately, we had much more important things to worry about that night. Gail was standing near the open car door and I was pushing Dad near enough to it in the chair so that we could begin the transfer when Pop's head slumped forward onto his chest. Gail—a good man in the storm, as I often tell her—checked Dad and found that he had stopped breathing. She raced back into the house and said she was going to call 911, leaving me alone with my father, dying—or already dead—in the chair.

I didn't know what to do. I know CPR. Should I try to revive him, like I helped to revive that lady in Walgreen's parking lot years before when the woman she was with cried out in the darkness for help? Medically speaking, we've listed Pop as a DNR—Do Not Resuscitate—patient. Mary has even had to sign off on a few forms in this regard. But did that apply to a son in his own front yard and his father slouched over in a wheelchair? And for that matter, did I even want to revive him? Did I want to keep struggling with Dad here at home? These are the thoughts that ran through my head that night, and they're thoughts that I'm not particularly proud of. Later, I would recall the first thought I had after receiving the call at work that Mom had died: "Why couldn't it have been my dad?"

In truth, I hadn't reached a decision to do CPR or not do it when I got down to face my father in the chair. He wasn't moving. "So this is how he dies," I thought. "Dead in his wheelchair out on our front sidewalk." But even as I thought this, I sensed that it wasn't his time. Not yet. Not here like this out in the cold and the dark. I began shaking him and shouting his name, looking for some sign of life. I remember saying out loud, "Help me, Mom; help me!" Curiously, I didn't go to God directly in my moment of deepest need. Instead, I turned to somebody I knew well, somebody who used to play catch with me in the back yard when I was small. Instinctively, I turned to my mom, the only saint I knew. And she didn't let me down.

Within seconds, Dad sat up in his chair and started breathing in deeply. "That's right, Dad," I said. "Suck it in. Suck that fresh air in!" Moments later, Gail came out followed closely by Sarah and Paul. Focusing on my wife, I told them all what had happened. Focusing on my children, I tried to assure them all—or myself—that Pop would be okay. Then we heard the sirens. An ambulance and a fire truck pulled up, and what seemed like twenty people jumped out. Oddly, it reminded me of pulling into the Hi-Lo gas station years ago. . . .

Streator's Hi-Lo gas station. I've never seen another place exactly like it, and I probably never will. Located on the east end of Main Street back home, it shut down years ago—gone the way of the early-morning milk man, perhaps. High service and low price were its claims to fame, and to pull into the station when it was fully staffed was to see poetry in motion. The attendants flew around the car like trained moths around a light. One dispensed the gas, one cleaned the windows, one checked under the hood, and another checked the tires. And on top of it, they all seemed to be enjoying themselves as they were doing these things. Great service. With a smile.

Except for the smiling part, that's what I thought of when all of these emergency medical personnel converged on Dad and me. "They said it was a cardiac arrest!" one of them said in a less than pleasant tone when they saw Dad in his chair looking around wide-eyed at the goings-on. Gail said no, and reiterated what she had said on the 911 call—that Dad had stopped breathing but that we didn't know the cause.

I explained to them in person what had taken place over the past several minutes, in addition to giving them an abbreviated version of Dad's medical history. They all listened attentively. Then the fire truck and its contingent of paramedic types took off, and the ambulance people went about getting Dad into the back of their vehicle, giving him some oxygen, and hooking him up to some machinery—heart monitors, I think. I noticed a few of the neighbors had come out, standing in the fading light of the ambulance flashers and perhaps wondering whether or not they should approach me. I told them what was going on. I kissed Gail and told her that I'd call her when I had any news. She said she'd call Mary. Then I climbed into the front seat of the ambulance. They wouldn't let me go into the back.

I got word on the way to the hospital that Dad's oxygen level was good and that he seemed to be resting comfortably. Thanks, God. Thanks, Mom. It was my first time in an ambulance, and I saw the traffic ahead of me pretty much as the driver did. We were flying with lights on and sirens screaming, and I was amazed at the drivers who didn't even slow down, let alone stop. I asked the driver about this. He said it wasn't uncommon. I learned a lesson that night. These ambulance folks may have a life-or-death situation going on in the back, and the last thing they need are drivers who are too inconsiderate—or maybe just too stupid—to stop as the emergency vehicle speeds by. From now on, when I see an ambulance running hot, I stop. Somebody's dad could be inside.

The news at the hospital was good. The emergency room squad checked Dad over, and a doctor reported that he showed no signs of a stroke and no signs of a heart attack. He speculated that maybe Dad just passed out from the exertion on the stairs. "Maybe," I thought. But unlikely. I've seen Dad in a deep sleep before. This looked a whole lot more severe. I'm more inclined to believe Gail's later speculation—that a mucous plug blocked his airway for a few seconds. Perhaps because of Dad's swallowing problems, he occasionally gets a severe mucous build-up in his mouth. Sometimes, Pop coughs the stuff up. Yuck! Sometimes I sweep his mouth out with a towel. Double yuck! The rest of the time, he swallows it, I guess. It's pretty thick and, well, mucousy, and I could see it blocking his airway if it settled in just so.

Anyway, Dr. Rezak and Dr. Stone, Dad's internist, eventually got the news. They both work out of the same hospital—Glenbrook—but we took Dad to Resurrection Hospital that night because it was the closest one to home. Since Dad was stable, though, Rezak and Stone suggested that we transfer him directly to their location. Dad said he was up for it—if he understood what I was telling him. Mary had arrived by this time—good old Mary—and we agreed to send Dad on to Glenbrook. Not too much later, some transfer personnel loaded him into another ambulance and off he went. Mary drove me home and went on to Glenbrook to be with Dad. I told Gail the news, then got into my car and headed north, too.

Dad had a rough week and ended up with one of those tubes that runs though his nose directly into his stomach again because he wasn't swallowing his food or his medicine. Poor Pop. I called Jim and gave him the update. Meanwhile, Mary and I go to see Dad everyday. He's pretty nonresponsive, and his mental capacity is poor even when he does respond. Mary and I joke about whether or not he even knows who we are. But it's no joke. In truth, I often think that he doesn't have a clue.

Dad just lies there with his eyes half-open or half-shut, depending on how you care to look at it, with food—those liquid drinks—and medicine coming in via the tube. Mary and I try to get some sparks of recognition from him, but they seldom come. Still, I think it's important that we visit. I think it's very important, in fact. Maybe Dad knows we are with him but can't acknowledge us. Or maybe he doesn't really know we are with him at all, but can sense that support and love is about. At least this is what I like to think.

It's finally my time to give blood. I'm A+. Need any? A guy I used to work with said I was one of the most energetic persons he knew. He often talked about blood doping his system with my blood to give him some energy, too. I'd give way more than a pint today if it could go to Dad directly and maybe do him some good. Wish it were so easy. Anyway, it's time for me to tell them for about the twentieth time that I've never taken money or drugs for sex. Actually, I'm not big on giving blood. As I tell my children, I only do it for the cookies. And were Pop home, Gail would have to transfer him for the rest of the day. No heavy lifting, you know? The story continues.

[21]

*By the end of the hospital week, Dad
had improved enough to be sent to ManorCare,
the new name for MedBridge, the nursing
home where he has been in the past.*

POP STAYED ON THE NG TUBE (nasal gastrointestinal?) for a while; then they took it out. Actually, he pulled it out. More than once. One of the times when it was out, they gave him another cookie swallow at the hospital across the street. This was about a week or so after he arrived. We suspected that he would fail, and he did, but they said that they needed to test him anyway.

The speech therapist at the nursing home acted just like the rest of the speech therapists I've encountered along the way in caring for Pop. She was kind enough, but she felt that Dad should have the peg tube inserted back into his stomach. I guess the doctor at the nursing home is saying the same thing. All I know for sure is that when Dad has been alert enough to talk about it in the past, he has maintained that he didn't want the stomach tube put back in, and Mary and Jim and I are trying to abide by his wishes. Mary and I gave the okay to try feeding Dad by mouth, and he responded to some extent. Pureed carrots, here we come.

Mary and I kept a close tab on Pop's medication schedule both at the hospital and at the nursing home, and we found what we've found in the past: The nurses administering the meds to Pop aren't perfect when it comes to timing. My mother-in-law—a nurse—was right. At seventy-something, she isn't practicing, but her training and life-long interest in good health have given her significant insight into the state of well-being. According to Shirley-Mom—we call her Shirley-Mom because none of the daughters- and sons-in-law really wanted to call her Shirley and none of us really wanted to call her Mom. Anyway, according to Shirley-Mom, regardless of how professional and caring the staff at any given medical facility—be it a nursing home or a hospital or something in-between—the patient always benefits from having a friend or family member on the outside working as a personal advocate on the patient's behalf. Makes good sense to me.

I don't think I told you this, but when Dad was hospitalized with aspiration pneumonia a few years ago, then transferred to the nursing home for convalescence, he failed to respond as we thought he should and kept getting weaker. Some of the medical types thought it was just the progression of the Parkinson's disease, but given his rapid decline, we held the explanation suspect. Enter my wife, the advocate. "Check the medication dosages," she said. I had already confirmed that the medication schedule was properly forwarded to the new facility, but subsequent scrutiny showed that while Pop was being given the proper meds at the proper times, he was being given only two-thirds of the proper dosage. Pop rallied, and then as now, my wife and I are honored to be his advocates.

Pop came home in early April, about three weeks ago now. The ManorCare team did a great job with Dad and he regained a lot of his strength there. He eventually peaked out in his therapy, though, and we were told that we had to check him in as a full-time resident or put him somewhere else. He said he wanted to return here with us, and here he is. For a while though, while he was so emotionally detached at the nursing home, he said that he didn't want to come back here. When he said a few days later that he wanted to come back, I told him okay, but added that if he ever changed his mind and wanted to return to the nursing home, I'd take him back in a heartbeat. I explained again that I wanted what he wanted. I think he understood.

I know he understood what happened his first night back, however. Sarah and Paul were happy to see him, of course, and he lit up when he saw Gail, as he always does. He ate well that night, then later, when Gail helped me get him into bed, he sighed deeply upon settling into that old, creaky, salvaged hospital bed and said, "It's good to be home." I smiled, blessed him, and prayed over him as usual; then I turned out the lights, walked out, and closed the door behind me. I think he was already asleep. Sometimes, everything just seems right with the world.

At the same time, Pop's comforting words brought sadness, too. I had occasion to see Jim and Carol at the nursing home one afternoon. Jim and I exchanged a few words, and they weren't pleasant ones. He's still not happy with me for taking care of Dad, but he won't talk about it. When I bring it up he acts like I'm being pushy and unreasonable and shuts me down.

And at the center of it all—almost ironically—is Pop. Dad seems to like being at our place, he's with family, the medical professionals say he's doing well here, and I'm getting the chance to care for his needs and write a bit at the same time. It all seems like a win-win situation to me. Jim, by comparison, seems to think that what I'm doing is wrong. Maybe someday, we'll reconcile over this. It is my prayer, but right now, we're fairly estranged.

These digressions aside, Pop is doing well again. The visiting nurse, Alice, came only once. Mr. T is Dad's therapist for this round of home health care, which was set up by the nursing home before Dad was discharged. Mr. T is a soft-spoken Asian gentleman whom Pop seems to hold in bemusement. Nearly always when Mr. T is working with my father, Dad just looks at him with an open mouth and with a goofy look on his face. Still, Dad responds well to him and he is walking and standing as well as ever. Mr. T taught me how to cut tennis balls and put them on the front legs of Pop's walker. The house is a lot quieter now when Pop is up and about. And the other day, Mr. T said that Pop was lucky to have such a supportive family. It was nice to hear the words.

Not long after Dad was released, we took him to Dr. Stone, his internist, for a routine visit. Dr. Stone worked with Dad when he first ended up in the hospital following his drug holiday. Mom didn't care much for her because Dr. Stone was pushing for the peg tube and Mom didn't think Dad needed it. And Mom found Dr. Stone to be less than encouraging about Pop's prospects. My experiences with Dr. Stone have been pleasant enough. She's a realist, true, but I sense that she cares a lot for Pop and has only his best interests at heart.

Mary met Pop and me at Dr. Stone's office. I bopped out of the car and opened the trunk of my '85 Dodge 600—another in the long line of used cars I've bought from my Dad—only to see that I had forgotten Pop's wheelchair. I had walked Pop that morning down the stairs as I always do. He was doing really well so we walked together to the car, which was parked in front of the house. Normally, I help Pop into the 600, then run back up to the porch, get his wheelchair, and throw it into the trunk. This time, I just climbed into the driver's seat, started chatting with Pop about how nice it was to have him home again, and started heading north. I never thought once about the chair until I saw it wasn't there. "Duh!" as my children would say.

Fortunately, Dr. Stone's office had a chair at the ready. Pop did well that day, his vital signs were right on the mark, and Dr. Stone said that he looked to be in fine shape. She did some blood work on him, too. The numbers came in a few days later and over the phone, and Dr. Stone's office staffer told me that everything was "perfect." Guess you can't get much better than that. Since Pop was doing so well, I suggested that we take him out to Starbucks. Mary and I helped him walk to the table, and he looked like he owned the joint. I ordered three cappuccinos for the three of us. I liked mine. Mary was dubious. Pop—a Hills Brothers man— looked at the foamy thing and said, "What's that?"

Dad got some nice get-well cards from the seniors at the YMCA while he was rehabbing from his pneumonia. I was touched that the good folks there remembered him and took the time to track him down here. I think Dad was, too. "Dear Jim," they wrote. "We all miss you at exercise class. We are praying for your speedy recovery. We look forward to your return to our class when you are all better."

Actually, Dad liked the sentiment, but he didn't like the idea of returning to class. He'd been going for just about a year when he made the hospital run, and the nursing home stint tuckered him out even more. I think the "Y" has been good for him, but it was becoming more and more of a struggle to get him there. More often than not before he got sick, he said that he didn't want to go. "Exercise class today. Pop!" "Oh, geez. . ." he would say in return. I asked him if he wanted to return to class after he returned home here. He said not really. I didn't push it.

Several of the people in class would see Pop on a good day and say to me afterward that he was getting better. Not everyone knew he has Parkinson's disease. By their comments anyway, I think several of them thought that he was recovering from a stroke. It angered me sometimes to hear them talk, even though the words were words of encouragement. Without question, the exercises helped Dad. But barring a miracle, Dad will never "get better." That's just not the nature of what he's got. Maybe people get better from strokes. But Parkinson's just keeps taking them down. Day by day, week by week, month by month, and year by year. I'm seeing it happen, and it's not a good thing.

Pop's being in the hospital for a week or so and then the nursing home for three weeks put me in an interesting position as my father's paid caregiver. By the books, my job is to take care of Dad. I get paid for it. Even though I was spending several hours a day driving out to see Dad and spend time with him, I didn't think that I was fulfilling my assignment. At the hospital, someone else was cleaning him or changing him or crushing his medicines. At the nursing home someone else was pureeing his food or exercising with him. I was going to just say hello and to show him a little support, even on the days I didn't think he knew who I was.

Accordingly, I told Gail and Mary that I didn't think I should get paid for the time Dad was out of our home. They both disagreed, saying that I was, in fact, still caring for Dad by my presence with him each day. Besides, Mary said that the monthly check was already being reported to the IRS and that it would be difficult to explain the missing check at income tax time, or something like that. I could see the accounting dilemma so I took the check, but I've set up a payment schedule going out several months to pay the Pop care money back into Dad's account. It'll take a while, but I'll return the funds in full.

I faxed a poem to a radio station the other day based on the morning show schtick of the on-air personality. Getting my phone number from the fax paper, the personality called me later the same morning to thank me. She said she thought it was great. And I'm telling you this because of what she said next: "Are you a writer?" It was the first time anyone has ever asked me that question. I answered, "Yes, I am," marking the first time, also, that I had ever said that I was a writer. The word has always been intimidating to me in the past, but I'm beginning to feel a little more comfortable with it now. I told Dad about it and read him the poem. "I don't know how you do it, John." He was excited for me, and he showed his excitement by shaking my hand with his firm, firm grip and sharing with me his easy smile. Thanks, Dad. And in a bizarre way, thanks, Mom.

Gotta tell you one more thing before I get into my Pop routine for the day. My son Paul had his First Communion back in early

May. He wore a black double-breasted suit with dark shoes, and he looked so handsome with his fine blonde hair and his big brown eyes. We had a party at our place afterward. The whole family on both sides was invited. Most of them made it, and Pop did great all day. From the Mass to the feast to the camaraderie, he was never better. Then, when I was getting him ready for bed that night, he reached out, grabbed me with both hands, and held me at arms' length. He stared right at me, but didn't say anything for a few seconds. "Pop," I asked, "what is it?"

"I love you," was his response. He said it clearly and he said it slowly. I smiled and told him I loved him, too. Next, I patted him on the shoulders and told him thanks for sharing the words. It was the first time we had ever had such an exchange, but maybe he's been growing into love for me just as I've been growing into love for him. Pop is seventy-five years old. I'm forty-three. Some would say we waited too long to say it. I maintain, however, that we waited just long enough.

[22]

We're back from our vacation, and we had a great time. Last summer we drove to Colorado, camping along the way. This year we packed up the old, blue-smokin' Dodge Caravan and headed northeast.

WE SPENT SOME TIME in the Boston area with a college friend of mine and his family. We hit Quebec next, then Niagara Falls, and spent a night with my wife's grade-school friend and her family in Indiana. Again we camped along the way, but it was nice to have a bed and friendly faces on both ends of the trip.

My wife is big on family vacations, and I've learned the tradition from her. When Jim and Mary and I were small, Mom and Dad took us to Starved Rock State Park, not too far from Streator. We often hit Mother Goose Gardens along the way, a small amusement park for kids. I have fond memories of these outings, but they were all day trips, and we usually got home before dark. Mom and Dad didn't like driving at night. They never took us anywhere out of state, or anywhere that we had to spend the evening. Topco introduced me to overnight business travel when I started there almost twenty years ago now. My wife introduced me to vacation travel when she married me about three years later.

I put up a fight of sorts last year before we left for Colorado. The destination was fine with me. I love the mountains as much as the next guy. What troubled me wasn't even the idea of putting Dad into ManorCare for a couple of weeks. I knew they'd take good care of him there while we were gone. What troubled me was the financial element of the whole thing. I didn't think we could afford to take the trip. It's not that we didn't have money in the bank. We did. But with the income loss we experienced bringing Dad into the house and paying our own insurance, I didn't think it was money we should spend, especially when we would be losing two weeks of Pop care money in the process.

That's when Gail gave me one of those "Oh, brother" looks. "Didn't you get two weeks paid vacation at Topco?" she asked.

Actually, when I left there I was getting four weeks of paid vacation, but I knew immediately the point she was trying to make. "Well . . . yes . . ." I said. She had me and she knew it, going on to explain at length that the situation with Pop was no different than any employment setting, and that I was entitled to time-off benefits just as any salaried employee is entitled to them. Mary agreed.

Mary arranged the nursing home stay with the ManorCare people last year, and she did this year, too. I told Pop about it. He didn't seem too thrilled about it either time, but he grew into it more as time went on and as I explained to him that it was called "respite" care. It's a respite for us, true, but it's also a respite for him—a respite from my cooking; a respite from the kids and their friends running back and forth throughout the house; maybe even a respite from all the walking exercises I put him through. Besides, I told him that he knew the people at ManorCare from his previous stays there, and that they would certainly treat him well.

This "time off" notion is one I always hear about. The social experts say that it is important for us to step away from our daily routines and responsibilities to refresh and renew ourselves, whether we go away to do it or not. I've read that this is especially true for caregivers, and now I know why. I used to put in some long days at Topco. Some mornings I got there at 6:30 A.M. and didn't get home until dinnertime. Twelve-hour days were rare, but ten-hour days were not. Still, when I came home, the work was over.

Now, the work is never over. As long as I'm here and Pop is here, I'm on duty. It's a 24/7/365 gig. Again, it's not that I'm always dealing with him directly, but I'm dealing with him either physically or mentally all of the time. Having Dad in the nursing home for two weeks allows me to stop worrying about him, and I can't tell you how good it felt—both this year and last year—to drop Pop off at ManorCare and hit the bricks. Both times he was doing well when I left him, and both times I knew that for two weeks he was on somebody else's watch. Mary met me at ManorCare this year and last, and we went for a hot dog and fries at Portillo's after Pop was settled in and we had said our good-byes. Before leaving, Mary said she would visit Pop when we were gone. Pop smiled, and I did, too.

Mary and I are much different in our approaches to Pop care. I'm pretty utilitarian about it. I get the work done. The lifting, the transferring, the meds, the exercise, the laundry, the meals, the cleaning, the changing, the showers, the shaving, even the toe and fingernail clipping. I get it done. I don't do it with a lot of banter or cheer, but I do it. Mary, by comparison, like Gail and even my children, is a lot more giving. The notion of good cops and bad cops popped into my head a while back after one of Mary's visits, and it ended up as another column:

GOOD COP, BAD COP

Good cop, bad cop. I don't know if the stereotyped image is true, but I've seen it portrayed several times on television shows like NYPD Blues. In a typical scenario, somebody (often the alleged perpetrator) with knowledge of the crime under investigation is being interviewed by a pair of police officers. The person is noncooperative at best, belligerent at worst. One of the officers— the "bad" cop—starts getting upset with the suspect, perhaps raising his or her voice in anger, perhaps pounding his or her fist on the table and demanding cooperation. The other officer—the "good" cop—is more soft-spoken and understanding of the suspect's situation and generally takes a gentler approach in resolving things. Usually the teamwork works, and the suspect gives up his or her confession.

Good cop, bad cop. During my nearly eighteen years in the corporate world, I often played the former while my boss played the latter. We even joked about it on several occasions. In a typical scenario, a manufacturer supplying food or nonfood products to our company was not performing in a manner consistent with our specifications or overall expectations. Howard would get upset with the supplier accordingly, perhaps raising his voice, perhaps pounding his fist on the table and demanding cooperation. I was more soft-spoken and understanding of the supplier's situation and generally took a gentler approach in resolving things. Usually the teamwork worked, and the errant manufacturer got back on course.

Good cop, bad cop. I found myself thinking along these lines in the context of my father's care recently upon a visit from my sister. Mary makes Dad smile; I make him exercise when he doesn't want to. Mary brings him bites of candy, cake, and cookies; I bring him medicine, milk of magnesia, and pureed chicken, knowing that he hates all three. Mary gives him surprise gifts; I give him showers, even though he argues he doesn't need them. Mary lifts his spirits; I lift him into bed each night. And at times—more than I like to admit, actually—I'm not the most tolerant soul in any of these undertakings.

With my sister's gentleness and my chiding, it's clear to me that she's the good cop and I'm the bad. At least that's how Dad must view it. But when I get down on myself for this, I realize quickly that we're both playing important roles. In NYPD Blues, the good cop and the bad cop are a team. Back in my corporate days, Howard and I were a team. And in caring for Dad, Mary and I—along with my wife and children—are a team. They're the good cops. I'm the bad cop. All of which, I believe, is positive news for my father. It's always good to be good. Sometimes, perhaps, it's good to be bad.

I read it to Dad after I finished it. He grinned and said, "I don't know how you do it, John." The same words every time, and they always make me warm.

Anyway, we had a great time in Colorado and in the Northeast. I'm beginning to see not only the appeal, but the importance of these family vacations. And they are especially important now, with the unusual situation within our household. It's funny. I'm home all the time, but I'm missing more family functions than I ever did. Sarah plays basketball at her grade school but I've missed several of her games because I was here taking care of Pop. Mary has been real good about coming over to "Pop sit" so that we can get away at times as a family. She even calls us and tells us she'll do it without us having to ask. I know it's hard for her, because she lives half an hour away, and she has a family of her own.

I've become well known in certain church and school circles for leaving meetings early, particularly school board meetings and parish pastoral council meetings. It's not that I'm a slacker. Usually these things begin at 7:00 P.M. That's great, but Pop's bedtime is around 8:00 P.M. these days, and I start getting him ready about 7:50 or so. Accordingly, I quietly leave the meetings to go home and take care of Pop. Sometimes it's a hassle to do this, because a key agenda item may be coming up which I don't want to miss. Sometimes, though, it's a blessing. I'm not big on meetings, and it's nice to have a built in, no-questions-asked excuse for leaving them. If Pop is doing well, Gail can usually get him into bed on her own. But we can't really count on this, because when he's having a rough night, or when he's got the grip thing going on, it's serious work getting him from the chair to the bed.

All told, Pop continues to do well, but he wasn't in great shape when I picked him up from the nursing home after vacation. He apparently came down with some sort of respiratory infection while he was there. A cold, Mary thought, and he was pretty weak when I brought him home. Pop also suffered a wrist-drop on his left hand. Nobody could tell me the cause, but basically, Pop's left wrist can't seem to support the weight of his hand. Maybe a pinched nerve or something. Dad's neurologist, Dr. Rezak, called it "radial nerve palsy." The hand kind of just flops there. Dr. Rezak prescribed another home health therapist who's been coming over to see Pop on a regular basis, and the problem seems to be improving with specific wrist exercises and a temporary splint. Pop had a routine visit with Dr. Stone shortly after his visit to Dr. Rezak's office. Dad was a little off his mark during the Dr. Stone visit, but he did well enough, and both of the doctors said that overall, he was doing okay. Hang in there, Pop.

Got some sad news from Barbara at Topco shortly after vacation. Howard's mother passed away. Barbara said that Howard wanted it to be a very private service, but that she was going to the burial and asked if I wanted to join her. I'm glad she called. Howard was the first person I went to when Mom died, and I was glad to get the chance to attend his own mom's burial. Seemed fitting, to me. We're a strange pair, Howard and me—opposite in a lot of ways, but I feel a connection to the man at the same time.

The grave was in a huge Jewish cemetery. I said to Barbara as we approached the site that something looked different about this cemetery, but I couldn't quite place it. "No crosses," she said. Interesting. Barbara says that Jewish people don't recognize heaven or hell, but believe that one's spirit lives on in the memories of the offspring. A nice thought, and certainly true enough. Sorry to hear about your mom, Howard. She was lucky to have you. And vice versa, I'm sure.

Sorry to close this note with a story of death, but there is life to attend to. Time to get Pop out of bed and crush the medicines and do his laundry and make his breakfast. I'm glad to have the chance to do it all once again. I'm glad Pop's home and doing well, all things considered.

[23]

Holiday Greetings! Hard to believe we're at year's end again. Here's wishing you all the best this holy season has to offer.

Christmas . . .
Its magic is unmistakable—
sparkling in the lights that encircle the tree;
    dancing in the stars;
    romancing our senses
    and caressing the frosty air that we breathe.
Of course we can feel it on the wind now,
Of course we can hear it in the church bells now.
Of course we can see it in the glitter of the season now.
But what becomes of Christmas magic at the end of Christmas day?
What becomes of Christmas magic when the carols stop playing
    and when all of the ribbons are packed away?
May we ever remember that the Infant calls us
    not only at this moment
        but at every moment throughout the untold ages.
And certainly this engaging call
    goes far beyond the magic of Christmas,
Certainly this call is Christmas.

For Christmas happens whenever heart speaks to heart,
    whenever we put aside our differences
        and embrace our universal oneness.
Christmas happens whenever soul speaks to soul,
    whenever we put aside those things that keep us apart
        and embrace the love that connects us all.
And Christmas happens whenever the Child's joy is upon us,
    whenever we recognize His face in the face of our neighbor.
It is my sincerest hope this holy season
    that as I see Him in you, you may see Him also in me.
And may His Peace and Joy be thine,
now and always.

WHAT'S NEW? I ran the Chicago Marathon this past October. I did it in just over four hours. In my racing prime fifteen years ago, I ran it in sub-2:50 twice, getting me to Boston a couple of times. Clearly, I've lost a step or two in my old age. I hadn't planned on running this year particularly, but I sold some artwork, which had been on display at the Newberry Library, to a lady who just happened to work in the marathon office. Along with the check for the artwork, she gave me a free entry for the race. The entry fee was something like sixty-five dollars, so I figured hey—why not? Every morning after I put my training miles in, I gave Pop an update of my progress. Once after a long run, I told Pop that I had gotten up well before dawn and hit the streets for twelve miles that morning. Dad looked amazed. He said that he couldn't run a mile. In truth, Dad couldn't run to the kitchen and back, but his response made me smile.

The weather on race day was perfect—about forty-five degrees and sunny at the gun. After twenty-five miles, I knew I was going to take it home one more time. Running to my right and ahead ten feet or so was a woman about my age who must have made the same assessment of her own finishing status. I remember her words and the manner in which she spoke them. "I love you, Dad!"

she cried. Her sobs were audible, but her voice was strong and proud. It was clearly the voice of triumph in a quiet moment before reaching the tens of thousands of spectators and finishers waiting in Grant Park.

"I love you, Dad." Why these words? Why near the end of the marathon? My thought then is still my thought now—that she spoke them to a deceased father, someone who over the years had held her, walked her, sang to her. Someone who had laughed with her and cried with her. Someone who had gotten angry at her, who had been disappointed by her, who was often proud of her to the point of bursting. And someone who above all (and like nobody else ever could) had loved her rock-hard, yet silken-soft, and who had always, always, always encouraged her to do the very best she could do, and to be the very best person she could be.

This assessment could be wrong, of course. Her dad may have been on the side of the road cheering her on, and I may have just missed him. But I don't think so. Still, all I know for sure is that her words prompted me to whisper the same thing to my own father a few steps later. Dad didn't hear me, of course. He was back at home with my sister. Mary had come over earlier in the day so that Gail could take Sarah and Paul downtown to see me finish. I ran the race, but I didn't run it alone. And in a sense, my family runs a much longer race with me everyday. Hopefully, it's a long way from being over.

And the other big news as the year ends? We got a puppy. We had been talking about getting one for Sarah and Paul, but we couldn't pull it off when I was at work in the corporate world and traveling as much as I did. Being home with Pop, however, I'm able to walk the dog and be around during the day with him. We got him at the anticruelty shelter downtown for fifty bucks. And that included shots and a leash! About five months old now, he's a shepherd mix and we call him Phantom, since we got him just before Halloween. He's a handful, just like the kids. Just like Pop, for that matter. But what's one more family member to care for?

I sent a few recent columns to Catholic News Service, a wire service out of Washington, DC, and it looks like I'll be doing some freelance work for them in the upcoming year. And thanks to a friend's intervention, a large suburban parish will be carrying my columns next year, too. I continue to read them to Pop, and he's still smiling and saying the same thing.

Pop finishes the year strong and in good spirits. He had a follow-up visit with Dr. Stone the other day, and she said she was amazed at how well he was getting along. Way to go, Pop! Still, I can see that he's weaker now than when he first came here just over two years ago. Damned Parkinson's. Mary continues to be supportive, and once a month or so, we take Pop to the mall for lunch and to do a little shopping. Pop's closet is jammed with shirts, and every time we go out, he is looking for more. Mary and I have to laugh, because when Dad sees something he likes, he plants his feet on the floor and his wheel chair comes pretty much to a dead stop. The man knows what he wants. And what he wants is almost everything in almost every store we pass by, it would seem.

Gail continues to be supportive, too. And more than she knows. We celebrated our sixteenth anniversary in late November. After Mom and Dad had gotten to know her nearly twenty years ago now, I remember Dad telling me that she was a good woman. And so she remains. And she's so good with Pop. Maybe Dad somehow saw these days coming when he clicked with Gail so long ago. All I know for sure is that he is still clicking with her now, even as an old man. When we took a walk behind the falls on our vacation this past summer at Niagara, I wrote "John & Gail" inside of a heart with my finger in the moisture on the walls. The letters and the heart, I'm sure, didn't last very long. The love, I'm sure, will.

[24]

Pop is hanging in there. When people ask me how he's doing, my standard response has been unchanged since he came to stay with us. "He has good days and bad days."

DON'T WE ALL? I remember Mom often telling me when we spoke on the phone that Pop was doing either very well or very poorly. I understand her better now. I talk to Mom often when I run in the morning. I tell her how impressed I am with her to have taken care of Dad for so long. I tell her I'm sorry for not giving her more credit—or even the time of day—when she wanted to talk about it. And I ask her to pray for me that I might be able to care for Pop now a fraction as well as she did then.

I started charting Pop's temperature several months ago, in October of this past year. On October 20, to be exact. It's not that I hadn't taken it before. I've been taking it sporadically since he moved in. Right now, I'm recording all of the temperature readings—which I take just before bedtime—on the envelope of a birthday card Pop received from Mary, John, Chris, and Jeff. "Happy birthday," the card reads, "to someone really, really special." I couldn't have written it better myself.

Taking his temperature is nothing new, like I said. But when Pop had his pneumonia bout last spring, I remember one of the aides telling me that I should take it a little more frequently, stressing what I already knew—that a high fever can be indicative of an onset of aspiration pneumonia. Right after that, I started taking it every day, but it took me a few months to realize that I might as well record the information. The envelope is filling up fast now, but I've got a notebook at the ready.

A benefit of this daily temperature thing is that I have found that Pop doesn't do well when he gets warm. I don't know if it's a Parkinson's thing, or just a Dad thing. All I know is that he runs a rather low baseline temperature—more like 96.8 than 98.6. In truth, when Dad starts running above 98 or so, I can see his physical deterioration. His speech goes away even more than it's already gone away, he becomes much weaker in terms of standing and walking and exercise.

Often, I have to battle with him to take his sweater off on warmer days. Unless the day is really cold, I don't like giving him his sweater at all. I told all of this to a friend the other day when she asked about Dad, explaining that I'd rather take him out in 20-degree weather than on an 80-degree day. I've even been known to turn the air-conditioning on in the winter to cool him down. The temperature monitoring helps me in all of this. Sometimes, when Mary calls to ask how he's doing, I give her general information, then tell her that I'd have to check his chart for the specifics. I'm nurse material, no question.

I use one of those little under-the-tongue digital thermometers. I don't know how precisely accurate they are, but they give me a pretty good indication of what's going on. When Pop's doing poorly, it's hard to get a good reading with it because he cannot keep it under his tongue. Then I go under the armpit with it. One of these days, I'm going to buy an ear thermometer. I guess I've been holding off because I've heard stories that they're expensive and not really accurate at all. I'll keep my eye open for a good one.

When Pop is doing even reasonably well, though, the little one works just fine. Here are some recent entries: 97.5, 97.5, 96.0, 97.2, 96.5, 96.3, and 97.7. You get the idea. When Pop's temperature is on the rise—or if an elevated temperature is suspect because of the way he's acting—I might check it several times in a single day. The night before last, for example, he settled into bed with a 98.5 reading. That's high for Pop, so I watched him very closely yesterday. He did okay, but he was up to 99.4 at bedtime and very restless, so I crushed two 325-mg acetaminophen tablets and gave it to him in a little water slurry. He calmed down later and slept well through the night.

I checked on him a little while ago, and he looked to be resting comfortably. We'll see what the day brings, but I think he's out of the woods. I've been taking care of him so long, I've developed a sense about such things, you know? A maternal sense, perhaps. When Sarah was small, she was crying one night and I told Gail I'd go in and check on her. After calming her, I went back to bed and told my wife that she was fine. Several minutes later Sarah was crying again, and this time, Gail went and checked on her. "She's burning up!" I heard Gail call. Fifteen minutes later, we were waiting with Sarah at the emergency room.

The doctors and nurses took fine care of her there, and gave her something to get the dangerously high fever under quick control. Thank God! I felt like a real mope that night, and I've often wondered what would have happened to Sarah had Gail not been there to see that she was in serious trouble. Anyway, I'm getting a better feel for that kind of care now. And I think that it boils down to just paying attention to things—like I wasn't that night when Sarah ran the high fever.

I often call Mary when Gail's not around to bounce ideas off of her regarding my care for Pop. Should I put him down for a nap? Should I give him some milk of magnesia? Should I give him some acetaminophen? Should I take him to the hospital? Mostly, I know these answers before I call, but it's nice to corroborate with someone. My sister and my wife are the best corroborators going.

One thing about having Pop here, especially as the disease progresses, is that we're never quite sure what he's going to say. Some of these things aren't really funny, but they're funny, if you know what I mean. Shortly before the end of the year, Pop asked me if I was wearing new dungarees. "Dungarees?" I mused, wondering how long it had been since I last heard that term. Dad was referring to the faded Levi's 505 jeans I was wearing. They certainly weren't new—Mary had given them to me recently after her sons had outgrown them—but they were new to me. I explained this to Dad, and made a mental note about Dad's occasional tendency to live in the past.

Just two days later, I was getting Dad ready for the day per our usual routine. "How'd you sleep?" I asked. "Pretty good," he responded. "How's the weather?" he asked. "It's chilly, but it's supposed to warm up," I responded. "Is this shirt okay?" I asked, offering him a wardrobe selection from his closet. "Oh, I like that shirt!" he responded. But then he came out of left field as he is inclined to do on occasion,

"So, who lives here now?" Dad asked me very matter-of-factly. "Huh?" I said. He repeated himself word for word, so I said slowly, "You know. . . You, me, Gail, the kids." I could tell by the distant look on his face, however, that my answer meant nothing to him, so I repeated myself—still slower this time—with some degree of elaboration. "You . . . me . . . Gail . . . Sarah . . . Paul . . . the dog . . . the cat. . . ." Something must have clicked, for then Dad lit up and I finally saw a spark of recognition in his eyes. "Really?" he said. "I didn't know that!" Answering in the affirmative, I added, "Pretty nice place, no?" to which Pop enthusiastically responded, "Oh, yea!"

Albeit goofy, at least this conversation had some degree of sense. A few weeks ago, Pop was watching Phantom, who was asleep on the floor about five feet away from his chair. I walked into the room bringing a snack for Pop, and he said to me as he pointed to the dog, "We should buy some clothes for him. He just lies around naked all the time." Okaaaaay. . . .

Later that night, Pop had a hard time settling in. Gail was at a meeting, so I asked Sarah to come into Pop's room and calm him down. Sarah and Pop get along amazingly well, and I think that Dad's being here is as good for my daughter as it is for my father. After Sarah had gotten Pop over the rough spots, I explained to her that it's hard for me to deal with Pop when he's so weak and mentally confused because I grew up seeing him so strong and sharp. Maybe someday Sarah and Paul will be saying the same thing about me. Hang in there, Pop. Pray for us, Mom.

Mary has been helping me with Pop from day one. She still spells me so that Gail and I can get away and do something with the kids. She's so good about it. I've asked Jim a few times over the past two years, but he's always been busy with other plans. He's also turned down the invitations we've extended to him to join us for Father's Day, Easter, Thanksgiving, and Christmas. He has come over to see Dad, but it's usually a week or so before or after the actual family gathering. Dad always lights up when Jim's here.

Jim came over on our request the other night, though. Gail's niece was getting married, and I really wanted to attend with Gail, especially because Sarah and Paul were in the wedding party as junior bridesmaid and ring bearer. Jim said he could come in the afternoon but had to leave by early evening. Mary and John said they could come in the early evening to relieve Jim and Carol, giving me the whole night off. Excellent!

I called home from the wedding reception and heard that Pop had a rough night, and that Jim and Carol stayed a little longer than they had planned to help Mary and John settle him in. Mary said it was maybe good that Pop was off his mark that evening, because it showed Jim and Carol just how hard it can be to take care of Dad.

Developments with my writing: I've just started writing for a Catholic newspaper—*Senior Connection*—this should get a little income heading my way month to month. I've also sold an Easter essay to Catholic News Service. It had to do with Mom's passing and with Dad coming to live with us. You know the story as well as anyone, but maybe you'd enjoy the essay anyway. It says a few things I haven't shared with you yet, and I don't think the CNS people will mind:

ON DAFFODILS

"The flowers are blooming!" I used to say, in the springtimes of my youth. We had a batch of daffodils growing alongside our house—directly beneath the living room window—and every year without fail, they came magically to life. It was my mother, actually, who tipped me off to their enchantment. "The flowers are blooming!" she told me once over thirty years ago. And then the mantra became our own. Breathlessly I would race home when the paper route was finished and sound the call before hitting the driveway. And Mom kept it coming right back at me. Even as I went off to college and took a job in a distant city and got married and began a family of my own, she remained as dependable as the daffodils themselves. Sooner or later with every springtime came her call or her letter, "The flowers are blooming," and the words would always make me smile.

Ironically, it was in the spring of the year three years ago when I got the phone call at work telling me that she had died of a sudden and massive heart attack. I still shake my head when I think about it. I had been home with my wife and my children to see her and Dad just two weekends before. We talked. We laughed. Mom showed me in person that the flowers were blooming. And so they were. She was then—as she was always until that day the phone call came—the picture of health. Apparently, she was talking on the phone with my Aunt Marge one moment. She hung up, turned away, and literally in the next moment, she was gone.

Taking Care of Dad

Shortly thereafter, my father came to live with us. He has advanced Parkinson's disease and needs around-the-clock attention. The kind my mother used to give him. The kind my wife and I now try to provide. It's funny. In all those years of growing up and living at home, I never thought to ask him who actually put the bulbs down in the first place. Well, now I've finally gotten around to it, and just moments ago, Dad told me that it wasn't him and it wasn't Mom. Knowing that he grew up in the same house, I asked him next if *his* Mom and Dad—the grandparents who I never knew—planted them. No, he again replied. "But, Dad," I asked a third time. "Where'd they come from originally?" He shrugged and answered, "They've just been coming up forever."

What more do any of us need to know? Especially now. Especially at Eastertide. For isn't the dying and rising of Christ a time of eternal rebirth for all Christians? Isn't this the time our souls stir with the promise of Resurrection? At this very instant, I realize that Mom's favorite symbol of springtime somehow epitomizes everything we've come to believe about this holy season—the empty tomb and the joy of a faith blossomed fully alive. I've got nothing against the lily, but for my dollar, say hello to the simple and unassuming daffodil—Easter's newest poster flower.

Decades ago, the now late English poet Thomas Blackburn wrote these words, "Awake thou wintry earth—fling off thy sadness! Fair vernal flowers, laugh forth your ancient gladness, Christ is risen!" How he speaks my heart, albeit with considerably more passion and eloquence. Perhaps he—along with my past—even influenced my wife and me to plant our own daffodil bulbs alongside our house several years back. Excuse me for a second while I go take a look. . . . Hey, Mom. *The flowers are blooming!* But I guess you already knew that.

Writing the piece brought back a lot of Mom memories. I still carry one of those little funeral cards around with me—Mom's "Life

goes on, and it is good" message to the world after she passed away. Sometimes I pull it out and reread Mom's simple words. One of these sometimes was on the recent three-year anniversary of her death. It was a Monday, and I was attending morning Mass.

After Communion, I returned to my seat and fingered the already-torn-and-starting-to-yellow funeral card. In a very short period of time, I remembered many things. I thought about the phone call I got at work from my wife telling me that Mom had died. I thought about my being in a state of disbelief during the entire car ride back to Streator. I thought about how pretty the flowers looked at Elias Funeral Home, but how they smelled of death. And I thought about the way Dad leaned over and kissed Mom's cold forehead just before they closed the casket for its journey to the church, and ultimately, into the ground.

I must admit that it was a sad minute or two, but Father Tom snapped me out of it with his after-Communion reflection, a short piece entitled, "Smiles Breaking Through Tears," taken from *Bread for the Journey*, a collection of daily thoughts by noted Catholic author Henri Nouwen. The passage for the day, March 30, tells us that even though losing a loved one is like watching a sailboat disappear over a distant horizon, we must trust that someone is waiting for the same boat on a faraway shore. "Death is a painful loss," Father Tom went on, reciting Nouwen's words, "But when we think about the One standing at the other shore eagerly waiting to welcome our beloved friend into a new home, a smile can break through our tears."

I don't know what prompted the author to write these particular words for the day's reflection, and I don't know what prompted Father Tom to choose a reading from Henri Nouwen's book. All I know is that I heard exactly what I needed to hear, exactly when I needed to hear it. And now, at Eastertime, I appreciate the message even more. In his classic story *Moby Dick*, Herman Melville ponders, "Where lies the final harbor, whence we unmoor no more?" Mr. Nouwen has reminded me of the answer, at the same time reinforcing Mom's wisdom of the ages: "Life goes on, and it is good." From one shore to another. And upon all the placid or stormy waters in-between.

It's time for Pop's first medicine hit. Last night was a feverous night. Hopefully, the dawn will be cool.

[25]

From bad to worse. My father fell and broke his right hip a few evenings ago. It happened very quickly.

I HAD WHEELED POP into his bedroom a little before 8:00 P.M. to get him into his pajamas. Following our routine, I next stepped out of the room to throw his clothes into the laundry pile, which is on the landing going into the basement. After the drop, I was returning to the bedroom when I heard a dull thud. In truth, I thought the noise had come from upstairs, where Sarah and Paul were cleaning their room. Rushing past Dad's door on my way to a second-floor rescue, however, I saw out of the corner of my eye that his wheelchair was empty. I found Pop on the floor two steps away, and he was looking up at me with a confused look on his face. I'm sure I returned the same.

I called for Gail and together, we got Pop back into the chair. He couldn't say why he was trying to get up, and I knew better than to demand an answer. It wasn't Pop's fault that he fell. It was mine for leaving him alone, I guess, even for a few moments. Pop said he was fine and I hoped that he was right, but I didn't really think so, especially when I tried to stand him up to change him. I saw him wince. I felt the hesitation in his body as I supported him from the backside. I eased him back into the chair and called 911.

The ambulance people came and got him again, and like before, I went along for the ride.

The medical types in the emergency room received Pop as graciously as they had before. They impress me, these people—the doctors, the nurses, the paramedics. Especially the ones who work in emergency settings. They have to be forceful and calm at the same time. I thank God for the work they do. Now more than ever.

Surprisingly, Pop did pretty well that night. They got him onto an emergency room bed. We waited a long time for the x-rays to be taken, but in the meantime, he didn't seem to be in much pain. And I told Gail that the one thing I noticed was that Pop almost seemed to be enjoying himself. I'm sure that's the wrong word, but Pop's room was right in the middle of the emergency area. Doctors and nurses and x-ray technicians were in and out every so often asking him—and me—questions. The activity out in the hallway was pretty fast-paced, too, and Pop seemed to fancy all of the commotion. He was lucid and speaking atypically well. And that's when I told him directly that I was sorry for letting him fall. He looked at me in disbelief and said that he shouldn't have gotten up out of the chair. My wife said it better than both of us the next day when I was sharing my guilt with her. "Accident's happen," she said. I suppose they do.

As I share these thoughts with you, Dad is recovering in the hospital. The orthopedic surgeons tell me that the hip surgery went well, but his other medical concerns are now taking precedence over the broken bone. Currently, he's running a low-grade fever, he's weak, he's being given his medicines and his nutrition through a nasal feeding tube again, and he's battling aspiration pneumonia. "Trust in God." I keep telling myself. But sometimes, it's hard. Sometimes it's real hard. Please pray for Pop.

[26]

I got a nice call the other day from the pastor at one of the churches I write for. Father Kalas had read about Dad and his broken hip because I wrote a column about the whole business. He said he was just calling to see how I was doing.

THEN HE ASKED ME SOMETHING that I'm still grappling with—something that my wife and I have talked about plenty over the past few weeks. "You don't think that in any way this was your fault, do you?" he said. I told him no, but I keep hanging on to the notion that if I hadn't walked out of the room to throw Pop's laundry into the pile—if I had just taken care of his dirty clothes later and stayed with Dad—that he wouldn't have ditched the way he did.

A couple days out of surgery, Pop was showing some responsiveness, but not much. That's when the guilt came again, but it took a different form this time. A more damaging form. I began to see myself in some of the nurses and aides who came to care for Pop. And I didn't like what I saw. The harsh tones. The shaking heads. The lack of patience. I'm ten times worse on my poorer days with Dad, and he's paying me to treat him badly! It's become clearer to me now. How can I say, "I love you, Lord" every day when I can't even show love and kindness to my own father?

Along with talking to Mom in the mornings when I run, I also pray for Pop. Usually, I thank Jesus for watching over Dad day-to-day, then I ask him, if he's in the mood, for a "big-bang miracle." I ask Jesus to let Pop stand up and walk. These days, though, I pray simply that Dad recovers from the hip break. I pray this for Dad's sake, yes. But I pray it for my own sake, too, so that Pop can return home here and I can do a much better job of recognizing Jesus in the face of the old man I'm proud to call my father.

Pop spent about two weeks in the hospital, then was transferred to ManorCare for rehab. Mary and I have been going to see him every day. He pulled the feeding tube out again so Mary and I told the nursing home people to try feeding him by mouth. It's hit and miss on the meal front as well as the medicine front. He's actually coming off a couple of very bad days. He's weak and nearly inaudible, and he's not doing much in therapy even though the therapists are trying.

I called Jim and gave him all the news, and he sees Dad when he can. Mary and I try to make it to the nursing home twice a day—for lunch and dinner, basically—to encourage Pop to eat. Like before, we sometimes don't even know if he knows who we are. Mary and I have joked about this in the past, but it seems worse now. One of the doctors said that Pop's swallowing may shut down completely and that without the peg tube in his stomach, this could be the end for him. He even suggested that we consider hospice, or end-of-life care for Dad.

Maybe, and yet both Mary and I sense that Dad isn't ready to cash in his chips just yet. We sense—despite Pop's distance and nonresponsiveness—that he still wants to be in the game. For me, this feeling of hopefulness is still in the handshake every night at bedtime. Just like I did when Pop was at home, I bless him on the forehead, pray over him, and ask him to let me check the grip. Even on his weakest days, there is still strength in that goodnight handshake. Firm and reassuring, it tells me that the deal is still on.

My mother's legacy in my mind is her freshly baked pies. My father's is now and will forever be the strength of his grip.

Meanwhile, the get-well cards are pouring in. Uncle Russ and Aunt Phyl. Aunt Helen. Marge. Pop even got one from some school parents, Paul and Alison. They live down the block from us on the way to St. Constance. Once, when I had to pick up my son from somewhere and no one was here to watch Pop except for Sarah, I called Alison and asked if Sarah could call them if she needed any help with anything. Alison said sure, and I sense that she meant it. The card from them was a complete surprise, but in addition to telling Pop to get well soon, it also told me that they were in my corner.

Another card came from Aunt Dorothy, Pop's sister. Pop calls her "Dot." Pop and Dot. I never thought of that before. She's pushing ninety, this woman, but she's a doer. Her husband, my Uncle Irv, died over twenty years ago, and Aunt Dorothy still lives in the same house all by herself. She's slowing down these days herself, getting quite a bit of assistance from her daughter, my cousin Sis, but she's still pretty independent.

Anyway, Aunt Dorothy sent a card, too. Pop keeps all of the cards he's gotten from people over the past few years, and in putting them away after they fell from his shelf the other day, I realized that Aunt Dorothy has really connected with Pop the most throughout all of his ordeals. She calls every few months to say hello. She sends cards for Easter and Christmas and for Pop's birthday like everybody else. But she also sends little notes along for no reason, and she's a good writer, to boot. Here's what she wrote to Pop following his hip break:

Dear Jim,

Our thoughts are with you, hoping the pain will go away, and that very soon, you will feel a lot better. Why you have to have so many health problems, I just don't know. A person who is so kind, and so well liked. I have many people ask about you. So Jim, hang in there, that hip will be healed. Our thoughts and prayers are with you always.

Love, Dot.

Good old Aunt Dorothy. Good old Dot.

I would be remiss if I didn't tell you again how supportive my wife is through all of this. I can see a lot of women yelling at their husbands to get on with things, to get back to work, to make some money. That corporate life seems so far away, but at times, I long for it. The social worker at ManorCare told me today that they will be releasing Pop in a week or two because he's planing out in his therapy again. He's really not improving much at all. Then what? His new hip is virtually untested since he's been essentially in bed or sitting in a chair for weeks. Pop can't get up and down the stairs anymore, so we'll have to put in a lift or ramp or something.

And what if I *can't* deal with him physically anymore? Back to Topco? Switch careers? A regular job—be it at Topco or anywhere else—sounds very appealing in some respects. Paid benefits. Time off. A normal family life again. In other respects, though, it sounds very unappealing, primarily because I would be giving my writing a back seat instead of letting it sit up front. These are the conversations I have with Gail every day. She's understanding, calming, and as always, a good man in a storm.

Despite the long afternoons and evenings at ManorCare, we've had plenty of fun along the way. Mary and I have always been close, but our Pop care effort has drawn us even closer. We share family stories at Pop's bedside. She talks about John and Chris and Jeff. I talk about Gail and Sarah and Paul. We banter with the nurses and with the aides. We play the *guess the blood pressure game* when it's time for Pop's vital signs. And we were both laughing with Margaret, a hard-working and cheerful aide, a few days ago.

If someone were to ask me for a list of my ten all-time favorite movies, somewhere near the top would be *Cool Hand Luke*, the Paul Newman classic about a group of chain-gang prisoners and how they related to each other and to the "boss," their generic term for anybody and everybody in charge. A particularly annoying boss—the Captain—is played by Strother Martin, and one of his on-going lines throughout the film whenever the inmates get out of line is a menacing, "What we have here is a failure to communicate."

Fine. So Margaret was delivering the patients' lunches while Mary and I were sitting with Pop. Before long, our conversation was interrupted by loud voices coming from across the hall and one room down—Sig's room. Sig is ninety-six years old, he uses his feet to "walk" his wheelchair up and down the corridors at alarming speed, and he's a little hard of hearing. Margaret was trying to tell Sig that the main dish for the day was quiche. Sig apparently misunderstood, or was asking if it contained cheese, and this is how the conversation went down, all at about one hundred and ten decibels:

"Cheese?" Sig asked.

"Quiche," Margaret replied.

"Cheese?"

"Quiche!"

"*CHEESE?!?!*"

"*QUICHE!!!!*"

What we have here is a failure to communicate. . . . I think they finally got it all resolved, for silence reigned in a few moments, but it was fun while it lasted. At least for Mary and me. And by golly, Pop was laughing, too.

[27]

Dad continued to struggle at the nursing home for a few more weeks and was very nonresponsive to conversation.

IN TRUTH, THE NURSES and the therapists got more chatter out of him than Mary and I did. We were often jealous of his attention to strangers, and his apparent disregard for us. Once or twice on his better days, Dad said he wanted to return home with us, but only at my prompting, and there wasn't much force behind the words. I told Mary what I had said before—if Dad wanted to stay in the nursing home instead of coming home with us, it was okay by me. Mary said we should try it at home for a while—if we could indeed manage it now—and see how it goes. And soon enough, we got the word from the nursing home that they were going to be releasing him from therapy. Once again, we had to take Pop home or check him in as a resident.

At least that's how the conversation with the nursing home people ended up. The first time the social worker sat down with Mary and me to talk about our plans, she said upfront something like, "You'll be checking your father in here as a resident, correct?" I had to smile to myself, and Mary picked up on the same thing. The social worker had the file. She knew that I had cared for Dad at our place for two and a half years. Now, she thought that we thought it was finally nursing home time for Dad. I told her "No," but I was less than confident. I told her that we were going to care for Dad at home again.

Home. Several months ago, long before Pop fell and broke his hip, I caught him in the living room trying to take his shirt off—a routine that Mary tipped me off to and that I'd been trying to break him of ever since he moved in. I'd explained to him countless times that I didn't think it was appropriate for him to undress himself in this fashion, especially with Sarah and Paul running around. Whether he understood or acquiesced just to get me off his back I'm not sure, but the incidents became less frequent, and, until this latest episode, I thought they had abated completely.

I had to attend an evening meeting that night, leaving Gail in charge of readying Dad for bed. Shortly before 8:00 P.M., Gail wheeled Pop into his room and told him that he could take his shirt off. After tending to a few things, she came back moments later to find Dad sitting there without having attempted to remove his shirt. Gail told him once more that he could begin taking off his shirt, but upon returning a second time, she again found him with his buttons intact. She told him a third time that he could begin taking his shirt off to get ready for bed, but this time, Dad said he didn't think he should. When Gail asked him why not, Pop answered, "Because the director of the home doesn't want me to."

Gail found the answer humorous. I found it bittersweet when she shared it with me. After years of caring for Dad, I had been reduced in his eyes from the loving son to the Director of the Home, and I thought of this again two Fridays back when he returned here after the hip break. I was very concerned about his homecoming because he is markedly weaker now than before. It took four people—my neighbor Clarence and his friend and Mary and me—to carry him in his wheelchair up the front porch steps, and once in the house, it was harder than ever to transfer him into his chair. Come Saturday morning, though, after his first night back in his own bed, I was stunned to see that he was showing signs of improvement. He was definitely more communicative than he had been in over three weeks at the nursing home. By Sunday, he was standing unassisted with the walker for a few seconds. By mid-week, he was taking a few tentative steps.

I don't know what's going to happen down the road. Even with his short-term improvement, Dad's care has now risen to a new level, and I don't doubt that there's a time coming when I won't be able to physically care for him here anymore. With Gail's assistance and support, though, I'll deal with that problem when it arises. At this instant, all I know for certain is that Dad seems genuinely happy to be back, proving quite possibly that Dorothy was right all along. Trite though it may be, perhaps there really is no place like home. As Director, I couldn't be happier.

And I'm a better caregiver now than I was before. I've always done the mechanical stuff pretty well. I've been giving Pop his meds on time and exercising with him and keeping him clean ever since he got here. But now I'm much more positive and upbeat about it. Why? Because I saw myself in the harshness of some of the hospital nurses, and know I can do better in caring for my own father. Also, I read something on the bulletin board at ManorCare that caught my attention. It was part of their mission statement, I think, and it said that nurses and aides would greet each resident in the hallway as they encountered them. I can cheerfully do the same.

Primarily, though, I realized that one of these times—maybe next month, or maybe next year, or maybe five years from now— Pop is going to take ill or have another fall and not come back here after his hospital stay is finished. "Gather ye rosebuds while ye may / Old time is still a-flying / And this same flower that smiles today / tomorrow will be dying." Robert Herrick was onto something back in the 1600s. Dad is my rosebud, right here and right now. And it's time to treat him like the flower that he is— gently, not roughly. Gail and Father Tom still say I'm way too hard on myself. Perhaps. But I thank God for giving me this chance to care for Pop again, and this time, I pray, I'm going to do it better. Gotta go. Time to tend the roses.

[28]

I haven't written in so long now, but we've been busy at this end. Most importantly, Pop continues to do well.

SURPRISINGLY WELL, IN FACT. He did great at his most recent Dr. Stone visit, and his numbers were pretty good—weight, blood pressure, pulse. He is up and walking every day. He doesn't like doing his exercises, but he still does them with me. We do plenty of walking, but not as much as we did. It's just harder for Pop now after the hip break. He would probably be happiest, though, if we didn't do any walking at all. "Let's stretch those legs, Pop!" I said to him a few days ago. "We've already stretched them," he said in return. And he wasn't smiling when he said it.

He's developed some sores on his legs from wrapping them around the hospital bed rails and rubbing them there. He doesn't mean to do it, of course, but the sores still form. I've taken to tying a blanket around the bed rails so that he can't slip his legs through. It's not always effective, but things are better than they were, and the soars are healing. I tell people that I've been caring for Pop for going on three years now, but I still haven't figured out his routine. Like Pop, though, I'm still in the game, and happy to be here.

And one thing new since the last pneumonia bout? He takes more naps now—sometimes in the morning, but usually in the early to mid-afternoon. He often says he doesn't want to take them, but I can tell. When he's sluggish and doing poorly, I get him into bed anyway, and invariably, after he's rested for an hour or two, he does much better both physically and mentally. I remember how I always took naps in kindergarten back at Grant School in Streator. I even brought my own blanket to school.

You know, I always enjoyed those naps, but as I grew up into a man, naps definitely took a back seat. Naps became like afternoon tea. For old people. Well, you know what? I don't feel particularly old, but these days, like Pop, I often find myself enjoying a cup of tea in the afternoon. It's nice. And one of these days, after I put Pop down for a nap, I'm going to take a nap, too. It worked for me in kindergarten, and what goes around keeps coming around.

Anyway, we once again put Dad into ManorCare for two weeks in early August, then went family camping, this time to Michigan. We had a wonderful time, but like last year and the year before, one of the highlights of the trip actually occurred before we even left. It was when I dropped Pop off at the nursing home. He was in good spirits. He was just showered and just shaven. His grip was as strong as ever. About a year or so ago, I realized how useful it would be to have everything anyone might ever need to know about Pop—as far as health care is concerned—on a single page. I prepared such a page and gave it to the doctors when Dad fell last April. I updated it following Dad's fall and gave a copy to the admissions nurse, too. Here's a copy of it:

NOTES ON THE CARE OF JAMES REYNOLDS (born 5/18/21)

News of note—Fell and broke right hip last spring. Healed. Leg scars from rubbing against chair or bed rails.

Meds—*Sinemet 25/100*—1–1/2 tablet six times/day;
　　　Permax .25 mg—1 tablet three times/day

　　Schedule:　　7:00 A.M.—Sinemet (see Sleep patterns)
　　　　　　　　9:00 A.M.—Sinemet and Permax *together*

11:00 A.M.—Sinemet

1:30 P.M.—Sinemet and Permax *together*

4:00 P.M.—Sinemet

6:00 P.M.—Sinemet and Permax *together*

Note: Meds must be crushed and mixed with small amount of water/juice before serving. Monitor to be sure it is swallowed. Prefers to have a glass of water to go along with meds. Please do not mix meds with ice cream/yogurt due to possible negative effect of milk protein on meds absorption. (Reserve milk for late afternoon, evening snack/meals.)

Up/down times—Extremely variable. Usually worst shortly after meds. Best times typically in early morning and early afternoon. Even though we have air conditioning and run it constantly, he seems to do worse in summer and better in fall, winter and spring. High humidity typically drains him.

Internal temperature—He tends to run low—usually less than 98.0. Please monitor closely. Small increases can have a marked effect on mental/physical abilities.

Speech ability—Extremely soft-spoken. During down periods, cannot speak at all. During down times, has tendency to repeat words over and over, often something he's heard on TV.

Meals—Must be pureed unless easily broken down in mouth (cookies, donuts, bread, pancakes, etc.) Likes sweets. *Sometimes cannot swallow and food must be removed until he's feeling better.*

Typical schedule:	7:30 A.M.	breakfast
	10:00 A.M.	snack (cookies, donuts, cake)
	Noon	lunch
	3:00 P.M.	snack (same)
	6:15 P.M.	dinner

Continence—Generally incontinent during the day; always during the night.

Bowel movements—Usually every 5 or 6 days. Heavy. When less frequent, he loses physical strength. I give him one or two glasses of prune juice/day.

Constipation—More of a problem since his broken hip, probably due to decreased walking. If no bowel movement in 5 or 6 days, give him 4 tbsp milk of magnesia in a small milkshake. Repeat as necessary.

Sleep patterns—Retires early (around 8:00 P.M.). *Use bed rails.* May try to get out of bed (unlikely). May try to remove diaper and gown (also unlikely). *May have to be woken at 7:00 A.M. to give him the first med.*

Sitting in chair—Must be monitored during down times as he has tendency to scoot forward in chair and fall off or lean forward till his head is down in his lap. Occasionally lists to the right. Use belt to strap him in.

Mobility—When he's doing well, he can walk up to twenty-thirty feet with the walker. Stay with him! Use gait belt. Tires easily. When he's not doing well, mobile only by wheelchair.

Exercise—Typically, I have him do arm lifts in the morning and walk with the walker before breakfast and snack times. *Best to walk with him or exercise him when he's doing well, not at a set time.*

Naps—Typically he doesn't ask for a nap, but you can tell. When he takes them, typically around 9:30–11:00 A.M. or 1:30–3:00 P.M. On occasion longer. On occasion both A.M. and P.M. naps.

Showers/shampoos—I clean his bottom with soap and water every morning and give him a shower and shampoo once per week (on Fridays). If you can give him a few more—great!

Shaving—I shave him every third day or so.

Drooling—Sometimes nominal, sometimes heavy. Keep bibs handy.

Interests—ABC morning news and Oprah. A little socializing. Sitting outside for short periods. Snacks.

Dentures—Wears an upper plate only. Keeps it in over long periods (weeks).

Misc.—Likes to fold things. *Often has a nearly-impossible-to-unpry grip:* can make transfers difficult!

Doctors—Kim Stone (internist), Michael Rezak (neurologist), Gregory Fahrenbach (orthopedic surgeon).

The nurse was impressed. I'm not the best caregiver, as you well know. But I'm probably not the worst, either. Hopefully, little things like the Pop-care sheet indicate this to others. Anyway, after Pop settled in, Mary and I went out again for hot dogs and fries at Portillo's. Pop was in good hands, and I was on vacation!

We had a great two weeks, and Pop did well this time at the nursing home with no setbacks to speak of like last year. Pop actually met with Dr. Rezak just a week or so ago now. It was a routine visit. Mary once again met us there, and Dad was all smiles at the prospect of going out for donuts afterward. Pop did very well during the exam, and I think even the good doctor is impressed with Dad's ability to keep on stroking after all he's been through. The donuts, by the way, were delicious.

Back at home, Dad continues to be his courteous self. I put a bowl of oatmeal in front of him and he acts like it's gourmet fair. I give him cookies and a milkshake—often fortified with milk-of-magnesia—in the afternoon, and Pop acts as if it's caviar and champagne. Gail has said more than once that this arrangement wouldn't have worked as well as it has if Pop was cranky all the time. She's probably right. If anything, I'm the cranky one, but I've cleaned up my act, no question. Gail says I do a wonderful job with Pop, especially for being the one who's with him all of the time. I'm trying.

One thing about Pop is that he seems to float more mentally these days. Not all of the time, but more than before, it seems. Just before vacation I had him walk to the kitchen sink to do some exercises. I saw one of the therapists take him there once. It's a good place because Pop can hold onto the countertop where the sink is and kick his legs out to the right and left without interference. Anyway, we got to the sink and Pop just stood there for ten minutes or so, refusing to do any exercises whatsoever.

Finally, he said that he wanted to sit down. I don't always give in to this request, depending on how he's doing, but this time I said okay and positioned the wheelchair—which I had dragged along behind us during that walk—directly behind him. Then told Dad to go ahead and sit down. Immediately he started walking away. "Pop," I said. "I thought you wanted to sit down."

"Corn flakes," he said. Then he stopped and started going the other way. This time he said, "Cake." I told him that we were out of both cake and corn flakes, and he started grumbling. Sorry. And a couple of days later, when I took his ice cream bowl away after dinner, he smiled and said, "I sure like that steak and Susie!" Huh? I don't even try to understand sometimes. What is steak and Susie?

I'm still picking up freelance jobs from Catholic News Service, and my weekly (nonpaying) column for the church bulletins continues to garner positive feedback. Fortunately, so does the monthly column for *Senior Connection*, the Catholic newspaper I told you about. The *paying* Catholic newspaper. Paying or nonpaying, much of my column work has to do with Mom and Dad. How appropriate, for I still think I'm hooked up with both of them in the great scheme of things. One of my recent efforts involves my sister and the new ramp we had built to accommodate Dad's inability to navigate the stairs after the hip break:

RAMP LESSON

Things have changed in my father's life since he fell and broke his hip in mid-April. On a good day, he's still mobile with his walker and assistance, but while he used to be able to go twenty to thirty yards at a time before tiring, now it's twenty to thirty feet. He can no longer navigate the front porch stairs, so now we have a ramp to get him in and out. Transferring him from bed to chair and keeping him clean has also become increasingly difficult. "Max assist" is the term I heard the therapists use before he left the nursing home. And these days, as much as I don't like to do it, I use a gait belt to strap him into the wheelchair so he won't fall again while trying to stand unassisted. One broken hip, I figure, is one broken hip too many.

My sister came over a couple of weeks back to watch Dad so that I could spend a few hours away with Gail, Sarah, and Paul. Mary knew that I often secured Dad in his chair with the gait belt, but I didn't tell her that I'd recently started wrapping each end around a wheel spoke before fastening the buckle in the back (this prevented Dad from pulling the buckle toward him and undoing it). The weather was fair, so Mary decided to wheel Dad to the front porch. The gait belt, however, precluded the wheels from turning. She pushed the chair forward anyway, overcoming its friction against the floor by sheer power and determination. Difficult? Extremely.

I laughed when she told me her story, but I wasn't laughing just a few days later. I had run some errands with Dad and was preparing to get him back into the house by wheeling him up the ramp. The *steep* ramp. Upon beginning our great ascent, however, I found that the chair—like my old Dodge Duster—kept pulling to the left, and it wasn't until I was a third of the way up that I saw the problem. The left brake was still on. Realizing that I couldn't let go of the chair, I proceeded onward and upward anyway, over-coming the left wheel's friction against the ramp by sheer power and determination. Difficult? Extremely.

Later that evening—after my heavy breathing had subsided and I had gotten Dad into bed—I understood the simple lesson to be learned from these two mishaps. How many times do I let things prevent me from going forward? Or let things make the trip harder than it needs to be? My anger can do it. My pride, sometimes. My stubbornness. I need to let go of these things because I am convinced that Jesus envisions for me—for all of us—a joyful ride, a ride unencumbered by whatever it is that can make us, at times, grind bitterly to a stop. "Put your shoulder to the wheel!" Aesop told us long, long ago. Good. We've just all got to remember to release the brake.

And so the work continues on both fronts—writing and Pop care—and I say again, they're connected. I had a long talk with

Gail yesterday about life here with Pop. I wanted to be sure she was still okay with it. She said that she was. There are positives concerning our situation, no question. But there are negatives, too. Financially, it's taking its toll. The wolf is certainly not at our door, but our short-term savings are being used up. Gail says I should ask for a raise. I don't want to, although I probably will one of these years. I love the writing I'm doing, but it has to generate more income. With time, I believe it will.

Pop sneezed last night at bedtime and his dentures—or chops, as we call them—came flying out. Weird visual, you know? Anyway, it's time to put his cleaned plate back in, and do a few other things, too.

[29]

Holiday greetings from me to thee! Fast year, no? I don't want to get morbid or anything like that, but I can remember my mother telling me years ago—shortly after my grandmother Patches died—that one of the nice things about death must be the peaceful silence that it brings.

SHE WAS IRONING CLOTHES in the basement. Sensing it had a been a rough day for her, I tried to make her happy by singing the Our Father song that we had recently learned at St. Anthony's grade school. I don't remember if it worked, but I've always remembered our conversation.

And only recently have I begun to understand it. These days I'm home all day taking care of my father and—to a great extent when they're not at school—my children as well. Gone are my days of leaving the house at 7:00 A.M. and coming home at 6:00 P.M. looking for dinner. With my wife working a few days a week and being heavily involved beyond that with volunteer school and Girl Scout work, I'm often the person everyone turns to around here. I've taken to doing my running at 5:00 A.M. or earlier because I know that if I wait until people get up, my chance for some time alone will be gone.

Fortunately, I understand also—as Mom did, too, of course—that we don't have to go to the grave to get our share of silence. A walk alone. A room alone. A Silent Night. . . . Coming into the Christmas season, we had a fairly heavy snowfall, and snow has a way of quieting things down. All of this inspired my Christmas message, and I share it now with you once more:

Quietly the snow falls,
    calling the world to hush.
But the rush of the holidays has already begun
    and we cannot help but get caught up in its noisy run.
We hear the soft harmony of carols
    as well as the brash clanging of bells.
We hear holiday greetings at every turn
    as well as the churn of shoppers hurrying this way and that.
We hear the laughter of children and department store Santas
    as well as the sometimes frantic banter
        between customer and clerk.

The sounds of the season surround us, of course,
    but behind them. . .
Oh, behind them lies a silence delicious and deep,
    keeping us focused on the magic of this blessed time.
For we know, don't we?
We know that Christmas cannot be spoken
    or negotiated or blasted from a car radio.
No, this is the season of dreams—
    of a red-suited man in a silver sleigh;
    of an infant child in a manger—
        and we know that its truest essence has no sound at all.
Instead, it lies in that quietest of spots where the heart runs warm,
    where it beats silently and simply,
        "I believe. . . ."

May the sounds of the holiday make you smile.

May the silence of the holy day bring you joy.

All is well this holiday season. Pop had a great fall (as in autumn) and I am still amazed at how well he responded to coming back here after his preceding great fall (as in hip break). In some ways, life is easier for me now, because Dad is less inclined to go out and less inclined to exercise. In other ways, his care has gone up a notch, particularly on the transfer front. He has lost much of his ability to help himself in transfers from bed to chair, from chair to shower bench, from chair to commode, etc. I am essentially lifting him these days instead of guiding him. I helped a friend move recently, and she said that I was strong. I don't feel particularly strong, but lifting my father several times a day has probably done my upper-body strength some good.

Also, I learned from the nursing home people when I brought Dad back here that whenever I transfer him, I should lead with his good, or unbroken, hip. They said it had something to do with the bone healing properly—that leading with his good hip puts less of a strain on the healing fracture than leading with his broken hip. I didn't argue; I just adapted all of my transfer situations to fit the requirement. It's been several months now, so I think the danger period has probably passed. I'm still leading Pop with his good hip, though. I don't want to take any chances.

[30]

I've got a few moments and I thought I'd share this with you:

ON SEARCHING, AND A NEW YEAR'S TOAST

Considering the good time / bad time Parkinsonian swings my father goes through on a daily basis, one of the best things about having him living here with us is that I can keep an eye on him—like Mom used to before she died—and help him to take advantage of the good times. When he's doing poorly, there's not much anybody can do. But when he's doing well—when he's "on," to use his neurologist's language—I can get him into the shower or ask him to do a few exercises or help him along with the walker or just sit with him for a while on the front porch as his mood and the weather allows.

I could tell by the way he was carrying himself in the wheel-chair a few weeks back that he was doing okay. Still, something wasn't right, and I had seen the look several times before. The straining neck. The leaning forward at the waist. The peering over the eyeglasses. He was looking for something. Usually these matters are resolved quickly, but this time, the pencil by the phone or the towel on the wheelchair arm or the stack of old mail on his bookshelf didn't do it for him. Not wanting to lose the moment, I helped Dad to stand and encouraged him to at least walk while he was doing his looking. And walk he did. Much more than usual, in fact. He walked over to my computer desk. He walked to the front windows. He walked to the television table. He walked to his bedroom. And the entire time, he kept straining, leaning, and peering. And opening every drawer he could get his hands on.

In truth, I didn't really care what he was after. I was just happy to have him up and moving so well for so long a stretch. But I was with him every step of the way, and after a while, I grew impatient and wanted to bring the session to a close. "What are you looking for, Dad?" I asked at last. "It's hidden," he said. "*What* is?" I asked. "I don't know," he said. "Then how will you know when you find it?" I asked. "I'll just know," he said.

Eventually he was satisfied and asked to sit back down, though I cannot tell you now (nor could I have told you then) what it was that he found. I can only tell you that at seventy-seven, my father is still teaching me a thing or two. For how many times over the years have I been looking for something and just couldn't put my finger on it? Perhaps an answer to a difficult problem. Perhaps the right path to take. Like a rose in winter, the New Year is blossoming all around us, and since we couldn't be together on New Year's Eve, let us raise our glasses now. Here's to our collective tomorrows—with God's help, may we all find what we are looking for. And even if we don't know what it is at this particular moment, may my father's counsel for each of us ring ever true: May we all know what it is when we see it.

[31]

I didn't think spring would ever get here, but things are finally turning green again. I bet I shoveled ten times over the first few days of the year.

As BLIZZARDS GO, THIS WASN'T 1967—according to the meteorologist types on TV, it was worse. At least as far as total snowfall goes. Every time I turned around, it seems, Pop was asking me where I was going. "Out to shovel," I said. Usually, he asked if he could go out and help me. I couldn't help but smile. I always suggested that he stay inside where it was warm, and told him that when I got back, I'd make us both some hot chocolate. "Oh, boy" was his typical response. Oh, boy, indeed!

My son Paul—or the Meister, as we often call him—is loving the snow, as is his sister Sarah. I'm big on snow, too, but I've got to be honest with you. I've enjoyed it less and less these past few years, and having to push my father around in his wheelchair through it has had a direct effect on my attraction to the stuff. This year, I didn't have to worry about it for a while, because it snowed so much so quickly just into the New Year that Pop wasn't going anywhere. I eventually got the ramp shoveled so that Dad could make it to his late-January appointment with Dr. Rezak, but before I did, Sarah and Paul used the ramp as a sledding hill. I joined them on it quite a bit, in fact. Sometimes, we all have to go looking for fun. Sometimes, fun just plops down on our front porches.

I am happy to tell you once more that Dad is doing well. The guy's amazing. Even Dad's neurologist says so. I theorized to Dr. Rezak that maybe Pop's been doing so well because it's been so cold and the humidity's been low. I don't know how heat and humidity affect other Parkinson's patients, but they are not my father's friends. Dr. Rezak said that without question the weather can play a part in a patient's performance. He also said that Dad was doing well because of the care he is being given. We're trying.

Sarah has been taking ice skating lessons for a couple of years now, and she skated in an ice show sponsored by the rink not long ago. She skated great, as did everyone, and I enjoyed watching them all. Mostly though, I enjoyed Dad's reaction to the event. We had a great view, Pop and me, because they put us in the wheelchair seats: the first row, right behind the hockey glass. I sat in a folding chair next to Pop to keep an eye on him. He did well, and I'll long remember what he did during the big production number.

There must have been fifty skaters on the rink at one time. Some of them were very good. Some of them were beginner types. But they filled the ice as they went through their well-choreographed number, and about halfway through, Pop took off the white baseball cap which he always wears whenever he goes out and extended it toward the ice. He was doffing his hat in recognition of the skaters. He also wore a huge grin on his face. I don't know if any of the skaters saw him, and even if they did, I don't know if they knew what Dad was saying by this old-fashioned gesture. But I knew. It was cold sitting there just feet away from the ice for nearly two hours, but when Pop grinned and doffed his cap, I felt warm all over. And I think he did, too.

My writing continues. I have now finished several more columns and received a nice freelance assignment from a large bulletin publisher in the Chicago area. And I've read magazine articles and seen stories on the news about something called the sandwich generation—folks my age who are busy juggling the demands of children, sick and aging parents, and work all at the same time. I'm doing it, too, I guess. But from a different perspective. My work is my father, but it is also—or at least I sense that it can be someday—the writing that I do. I told Dad thanks again just the other day for letting me work on the words. He said that I was doing a great job. Then I asked him if he thought Mom would like what I was doing. He smiled and said, "I think so." I hope so.

I'm not out of words, but Pop is banging his wedding ring on the bed rail again. I'm sure Mom had no idea when she slipped the thing on his hand nearly fifty years ago how he would end up using it. As always, it's funny how things go. For now, I go as well.

[32]

I want to tell you a pretty amazing Pop story.
At least I think it was pretty amazing.

As CERTAINLY MUST BE THE CASE in many households around the neighborhood and around the world, 7:00 A.M. to 8:00 A.M. can be a crazy hour. And I'm embarrassed to tell you that at our place, we could win an award for it. Craziness, I mean. Since I try to be on the streets running before dawn, I'm typically showered and breakfasted when the storm hits, but even so—and even though I know it's coming—the fray can still leave me spinning.

It's the time when Sarah and Paul come bounding down from upstairs—Sarah (generally) promptly, if not several minutes early; Paul (generally) only with considerable resistance. It's the time they ready their books and backpacks for the day. It's the time they tend to their morning chores: taking out the trash, emptying the dishwasher, feeding the animals. Or at least it's when they're supposed to do all these things. It's also the time I make breakfast, pack lunches, and let Phantom out. Then in. Then out. Then in. . . .

And as you know, my primary assignment in the morning is taking care of Pop. The 7:00 A.M. hour, actually, is prime-time Pop care. He doesn't always rise and shine then, but unless he's in a deep sleep, it's when I give him his first medicines of the day and clean him up with soap and water. And if he's up to it, it's when I get him out of bed, encourage him through his exercises, get him dressed, and head him out of the bedroom for his morning coffee. And in the midst of all the confusion a couple of mornings ago, Pop said something that stopped me in my tracks.

I had spilled some water in his room and was cleaning it up when Dad spoke slowly, clearly, and atypically forcefully, "This is a holy place." He sounded like Moses! I asked him to repeat it just to make sure I heard it right. Often his responses change but this one didn't, and "This is a holy place" came through a second time. Thinking I was on the verge of some great epiphany moment, I tried to get Dad to elaborate. *Holy* in what way? Holy how? But my father was quickly out of the zone and returned my questions with confusion, silence, and blank stares.

I keep pondering the words. To anyone observing this household in action during the 7:00 A.M. hour, it would appear to be anything but holy. But perhaps Dad was on to something. Because despite the chaos and all of the trials, this is a family in love, and maybe love—even hectic love—covers "holy" just as well or better than candlelight, incense, and hands folded in prayer. Indeed, maybe one man's burning bush is another man's spilled water on the floor. In this household and in countless households around the neighborhood and around the world, holy comes to call during the 7:00 A.M. hour. I don't always recognize it, of course. But apparently, my father does.

The other thing I want to tell you about was the physical exam I took the other day. There's a Pop connection. Isn't there always? The set-up, unfortunately, has to do with Dad's bowel movements. Hang with me here, okay? Anyway, Pop has been a little more constipated since he broke his hip. The hip doctor told me this might happen—as did Dr. Rezak—because Dad's been walking a little less post-hip than pre-hip. I never thought of it before, but I guess walking and exercise help to keep the bowel movements moving along their intestinal track. Makes sense.

And even before the hip break, I noticed that if Dad hadn't had a BM for several days, he started doing poorly both mentally and physically. I give him two glasses of prune juice a day, but when that isn't enough, I slip him a milk of magnesia milk shake, and usually within a day or, two, Pop is regular again. At least until the next blockage.

Trouble is, sometimes I lose track of when his last bowel movement was, so I found myself giving him a M-O-M shake a day or two, or even several days, after I should have. So shortly after the broken hip, I began recording his bowel movements along with his temperature in the book I told you about earlier. SBM=Small Bowel Movement. MBM=Medium Bowel Movement. LBM=Large Bowl Movement. It's not a very complicated system, but it serves its purpose. Sometimes I even get clever with the entries, as in, "loose," "pasty," "just right," or "Jabba the Hut." I often joke with my sister and my wife that they're the only people I know with whom I can speak openly about my father's bowel movements. Looks like you're another one of the lucky souls. Sorry.

Anyway, so I go to the physical and before the actual exam begins, the doctor is asking me a bunch of questions about my medical history and my lifestyle. Do I exercise? Do I smoke? Do I drink much caffeine? These sorts of things. I have pretty good answers for everything she throws my way. I'm even enjoying myself, to a certain extent. Then she lobs a question that I had never really thought of before. She asks me how frequently I have bowel movements.

The question stops me cold. "I don't know," I say.

"Once a day?" she prompts. "Twice a day?"

I think for a moment and nothing comes to me. Then, knowing that she doesn't know the whole Pop routine, I smile and say, "Actually, I can give you a much better accounting of my father's bowel movements than I can of my own." She just looks at me funny. I guess you had to be there.

[33]

Greetings from the home front. We got home a month ago from our annual family road trip. This year we hit Jamestown, Williamsburg, and Washington, D.C.

It WAS A WHIRLWIND ADVENTURE, with many late nights and early mornings. Especially the D.C. part. The touring was great, though, and I even got the chance to meet my editor from Catholic News Service, who I've been doing some work for over the past few years. Sarah's in seventh grade this year, Paul is in fifth, and Pop is still plugging along.

We put him into ManorCare for the two weeks we were gone, just as in previous years, and we picked him up when we returned. Mary said he did okay there, but he seemed pretty lethargic his first several days back. Like all of us, he needs a little adjustment back into the routine, I suppose. He had his regular appointment with Dr. Rezak just before we left, and he was doing fine then. Dr. Rezak said he saw no need to adjust Pop's medications and he told me to just keep doing what I was doing.

Pop makes it easy. I put a plate of meatloaf in front of him the other night, along with some chopped-up green beans and some little pieces of homemade, buttered bread. Pop just lit up and said,

"This is a wonderful place!" The next morning, about an hour after I had given him his regular breakfast, he said, "Would you please get me a bowl of cereal at your convenience?" I'd be happy to, Pop. I'm glad you're enjoying yourself.

It's been a good year, all told, and I'm really digging the ebb and flow of family life here. Pop ebbs and flows, too, of course. Some days good. Some days bad. On the bad days I call Mary and Jim and put them on "hospital alert," letting them know that Pop isn't doing well and that I might take him in. Mary usually talks me though these episodes, and I'm really appreciative of her support. I'm appreciative of Gail's support in the same way. And I heard a commotion out by Pop's chair the other day only to find Sarah and Paul playing beach ball volleyball with Pop in his wheelchair. Pop was grinning from ear to ear as the brightly colored ball flew back and forth among the three of them. Without everyone involved with this—without the kids, Gail, Mary, the neighbors, the folks at St. Constance, even Jim, in his distant way—none of this would be happening. I may be strong enough to lift Pop out of bed in the morning, but I'm not strong enough to carry the burden of caring for him alone.

I got a call from the *Chicago Tribune* the other day. I sent them an essay on ice skating and the Pop connection about two months ago, and they were calling to say that they were accepting it. I've been on cloud nine ever since. The piece won't run until the weather turns cold, but just knowing that the editor there liked my work made my day/month/year. And they're paying me for it, as well! Depending on the weather, it may not make the paper until after Christmas, but maybe they won't mind if I share a copy of it with you now:

ON SKATING WITH DAD AND SARAH

Marilla Park. Even the name of the place was wonderful, and when I was a boy growing up in Streator, Illinois I spent a lot of my time there. I haven't been out that way in quite a while—not since long before my mom died a few years ago—but then it was a hilly, roughly developed tract of land north and east of town with a running stream, a small lake, and some picnic tables. I didn't go there for picnics, though. My time at Marilla was the winter. It was there that I got my first taste of sledding, downhill skiing, and what has proven to be one of my favorite participation sports, winter or otherwise—ice skating.

With my father doing most of the work, I strapped on a pair of double-runner skates long ago and glided onto the ice. But even with four strips of metal beneath me, I was like Paul Simon before the song came out—just slip-slidin' away. Dad was always there for me, however, holding me up as I held on. And as I got bigger and better, Dad taught me an arm-in-arm duet skating maneuver that I took to right away, so much so that when Miss Lucky showed our third-grade class a similar dance step in the St. Anthony School gymnasium, I was already way ahead of her. She asked me where I had learned it. Proudly, I told her about Dad and Marilla Park.

Streator didn't have any indoor rinks or Zamboni machines, but even if it did, Marilla would have still had my heart, especially at night with a light snow falling. I loved the whole outdoor skating scene—from putting on my boots in the frosty air to the occasional creaks in the ice that echoed like cannons going off in the darkness to the warming fire which seemed to be forever smoldering in the old trash can on the northern shore of the pond to the cup of steamy hot chocolate that Mom always had waiting for me when I got home. Life then was delicious. With whipped cream.

But life's flavors change. I went to college, moved away from Streator, took a job in Chicago, married my best friend, and a few years later, we started a family of our own. When our daughter Sarah was born over thirteen years back, I can't say that I was really thinking about getting her out onto the ice, but with time, that's where we ended up, and suddenly, I was the Dad lacing up the boots and guiding a little one along. I took Sarah to Skate-on-State for her first time out with a light snow falling and the lights of the city all around. It was magical. It was Marilla Park all over again.

Sarah wanted to go skating a second time and a third and a fourth. Gladly I took her, and it soon became apparent she had an interest in the sport that went beyond what I could teach her, Miss Lucky's dance step notwithstanding. Next up—the McFetridge Indoor Ice Arena on Chicago's northwest side. McFetridge—not quite as lyrical-sounding as Marilla Park. And any snow falling wouldn't make it to the tips of our tongues there. But it had smooth ice and professional instructors who were as friendly as they were talented. Sarah began her lessons with nervous anticipation, and nearly three years later, she's still at it, passing from level to level with only one or two setbacks. Whenever I could along the way, I would sit in the shadows and watch her, applaud her, pull for her, and before long, she was helping me out with crossovers and t-stops and maneuvers I had never heard of before. Thus the student becomes the teacher and the teacher becomes the student.

For my forty-fifth birthday, my wife signed me up for lessons at McFetridge. It's funny, for often now, when she can, Sarah is sitting in the shadows watching *me*, applauding *me*, pulling for *me*. Recently, we were both scheduled to be tested at our respective levels on the same day at roughly the same time. She was nervous. I was nervous. She passed to Freestyle II. I passed to a ranking considerably below that. We high-fived each other, and as we went out for coffee cake to celebrate, I couldn't help but think about how I had grown from holding my father's hands on the ice to following in my daughter's footsteps. Or at least in her figure eights.

I stopped going to Marilla Park years ago, but I believe that a portion of who I am was formed there under a starry sky with skates on my feet and with my breath curling up toward heaven.

My father, who has Parkinson's disease, came to live with us not too long after Mom's funeral. Dad has good days and bad days, but when he's doing well, he likes to hear about my time and Sarah's time on the ice. I was talking with him about skating just the other day, as a matter of fact. We reminisced about our Marilla Park adventures, and he told me that he was never really all that good of a skater. That's not how I remember it, of course, but even if it's true, he was certainly a gifted teacher. As is his granddaughter some forty years later. And in the cosmic scheme of things, I'm the lucky student in between.

I read it to Pop before I sent it off and he thought it was wonderful. And when I told him about the paycheck coming my way, he was flabbergasted. I've been writing columns akin to this one every week for years, and now I'm going to get a paycheck for one of them. I used to make an equal amount at Topco barely batting an eye. Now I make it by spending hours and hours on an essay, rewriting the thing four or five times, sending it off, and waiting for weeks to get a reply. Oddly, this is where the joy lives.

I guess that's all for now. Pop has had a rough couple of days. Maybe today will be better. I put Mary and Jim on hospital alert not long ago, but Pop snapped out of it and strung some good days back to back.

[34]

Pop had another visit with his neurologist in late October, and Dad once again came through with flying colors.

I MENTIONED TO DR. REZAK that Pop had been drooling a little more than usual for the weeks preceding the appointment. This has come and gone and come and gone with Pop since he's been here. Dr. Rezak suggested something he called Botox, which are injections of some sort, designed, I think, to minimize saliva production in the mouth.

This would help Pop's drooling problem, true, but I'm not sure what it would do for a guy who has a hard time swallowing. Seems to me that saliva might help that process along. Mary agreed with me. Dr. Rezak said we could take it or leave it for Pop. The poor guy is on enough medications already if you ask me. And I guess Dr. Rezak was asking me. So I told him no, but thanks, and said that I would keep the towels at the ready. Overall, Pop is doing fine. Overall, it's been a pretty good year.

But just when you think there isn't a cloud in sight, it starts pouring. First, I fell and broke my cheekbone in a skating accident. I was showing off a hockey stop for Sarah and her friend when both of my edges went out from under me. I fell on the right side of my face—Yow! And x-rays the next day confirmed the break.

The oral surgeon told me that it will heal with time, but on the short term, it hurt like hell. Maybe I'll be one of those guys who can predict the weather when I'm Pop's age because of this. I also hurt my arm and shoulder, and am told it will take a long time, plus maybe some therapy, to get it back up to speed. But all of this is nothing compared to what happened to Pop just before Thanksgiving. That's when he stopped breathing again.

It was dinnertime, like before. He wasn't doing well, so I had taken his food—a chopped spinach salad—away from him. Again we heard those horrible sucking sounds. Again we called 911. Pop had actually come out of it on his own—and much more quickly than before—when the medical types showed up. They said they should take him in just to be safe. Gail and I said okay. I went with Pop to the hospital again in the front seat of the ambulance.

Upon reaching the Emergency area at Resurrection, I hopped out and was waiting when the paramedics swung the back ambulance door open. There was Dad. He was hooked up to an IV, he was wearing an oxygen mask, and his eyes were working the crowd. And when he saw me—when he really saw me—do you know what he did? He reached up his left arm and waved to me. He was okay, and I'm telling you true, I almost cried right there on the spot!

I shook his hand and asked how he was doing when the paramedics had gotten him out of the ambulance. He said he was fine, and he looked it. He saw all of the commotion going on as they brought him into one of the emergency rooms. I hung with him every step of the way. At one point he looked at me and asked, "What should I be doing?" I had to laugh. This poor man was at death's door just minutes ago, and now he's asking what he can do. My father has been carrying his load for nearly eighty years. He'll carry it until the day he dies. And thank God, it wasn't that day shortly before Thanksgiving.

They kept Pop there until nearly 11:00 P.M. By then, they had run all of the tests and called all of the specialists. The doctors at the hospital said that he showed no signs of heart attack or stroke. They once again couldn't account for whatever caused his breathing to stop, but I'm still hanging on to my wife's theory from the first go-round. Pop gets congested often, and several times since he's been with us, he's sneezed, and like a gallon—okay, maybe a pint—of phlegm has come up. It's pretty messy, but I always thought it was harmless. I've been wrong before. Maybe he's getting these mucous plugs that occasionally block his windpipe. That's Gail's story, anyhow, and I'm sticking to it.

Gail came and got us around 11:30 that night, and by midnight, Pop was back in his own bed and resting comfortably. Two days later, he was smiling and asking when the turkey would be ready. I have plenty to be thankful for every day of the year. I have my wife. I have my children. I have my friends. I have my writing. And on this past Thanksgiving especially, I had my father. For all of the smiles he has brought to this household, thank you, Lord. For all of the laughter, thank you, Lord. Even for all of the tears and anguish, thank you, Lord. I have been given a great gift, this opportunity to care for Pop. Truly, I am blessed beyond all measure.

Oh, and not long after these two incidents, Gail had to take Paul to the hospital for a possible broken nose following a rough-housing accident with Sarah. It wasn't broken, as things turned out, but we've had better stretches. When I started buying my own insurance after Pop came, I took a really high deductible to keep my premiums low. It worked for the first three years. I'm paying for it now.

[35]

ON A SILENT NIGHT, they say, He came . . .
and after two thousand years,
the peoples of the earth still remember Him.
We remember His birth, obscure and unheralded
despite the star,
despite the angels,
despite the prophecies riding sublimely upon the wind.
And at this time of year especially,
we remember the things He taught us.
His was a message of peace,
and now we embrace it with all our hearts.
His was a message of joy,
and now we sing it for all who would care to hear.
And His was a message of love,
and now we bring it to one another; indeed, to the entire world.
This is Christmas . . .
Beyond the glitter and silver and gold,
this is the story and the glory it holds . . .
It is as simple as it is divinely profound.
And these twenty centuries haven't lessened its awe and wonder.
History brings us to the third millennium of His gentle message,
but almost mysteriously, it remains as fresh now
as it did when He first spoke it—
when He first lived it—
—so long, long ago.
And with our every breath this holy season,
we wish it now for you and for everyone you hold dear:
His Peace . . . His Joy . . . His Love. . . .

[36]

I'm writing with petroleum jelly and Band-Aids spread over almost all of my knuckles. They tend to splinter and crack during the winter anyway, but since Pop's been here, it's been worse.

TRYING TO MINIMIZE the likelihood of germ transfer from me to him, I wash and dry my hands probably five to ten times a day, usually after I handle Pop in some fashion and often before I do. It must be especially dry in the house these days, for my knuckles have never looked—or felt—worse. They're cracked and bleeding all the time, it seems. Gail tells me to use cream on them, and sometimes I do. It helps, but mostly, I forget to use it. Cracked and bleeding knuckles. Pop should be so lucky.

I noticed something weird with Dad the other day. First thing in the morning, or when he's doing poorly and absolutely can't stand, I change him in bed by rocking him back and forth and fitting the diaper beneath him. I learned this technique from the aides in the nursing home, and I've learned that it's not a bad system. When Pop is able, though, I prefer changing him when he's standing up. He holds on to the walker. I drop his pants from behind him, remove the old diaper, clean him, then swing on the new diaper. While going through this routine the other day, however, I noticed some bulges in the front of his abdomen, below the belt line, one on either side.

I didn't say anything about them to Pop because I wasn't even sure what I saw. This all happened when Pop's legs were giving way and I was once again trying to support him on my lap, so I thought it just may have been the way he was standing. Or not standing, as the case may be. Later that day I had occasion to change him in bed after one of his afternoon naps, and I saw no sign of the bulges. In truth, I sort of forgot about them because the next few times I changed Pop, he was in bed.

A day or two later I changed him again when he was standing up, and as before, the bulges reappeared. I asked Pop about them, but I didn't know if he could even see them. Whatever the problem was, Pop said it wasn't bothering him and he felt no pain or discomfort from the come-again-go-again bulges. Even when I poked them. And I poked several times. I called Mary and told her about them, describing them as the size of a walnut on either side of his front abdominal area. Mary said that without seeing them, she didn't know what to tell me. But the next time Gail was home when I was changing Pop in the standing position, I called her in to see the walnut bulges. Do we have fun in this household or what?

Anyway, Gail suggested that I call Dr. Stone. I did, and she told us to bring Pop in. "Bilateral inguinal hernias." That was the diagnosis. I've always heard of hernias, but I never knew exactly what they were. Seems they're protrusions of an organ or tissue through an abnormal opening. I always thought that hernias were caused by heavy lifting, but I guess they can also be caused by excessive straining during a bowel movement. This is probably what happened to Pop. Regardless of how they got there, though, the bulges went away when Pop was laying down because every-thing settled back into place. The bulges came back when Pop stood up, essentially because of gravity.

Hernias are fixable through surgery, but since Pop is in no pain, Dr. Stone suggested that we just take a wait-and-see approach. She said to watch him closely and to let her know if they start bothering him. She said that we could come up with a plan if and when we have to cross that bridge, but for now, Dad was doing fine and she wanted to leave well enough alone. I used to always subscribe to the philosophy, "If it's not broken, don't fix it," but after the medical advice I received following my broken cheek-bone, and now Pop's wait-and-see status, I'm buying into a new philosophy: sometimes, even if it is broken, don't fix it!

Pop also had a trace of blood in his stool the other day. I told Dr. Stone about this, too, and she wanted to do a CBC on him—some sort of blood work that they can compare to previous tests to see if he is losing any blood. I said okay, and we're waiting to hear the results. Pop smiled through it all, and only winced a little when the needle hit. I'm remembering that card Aunt Dorothy sent him a few years ago, when she said that Pop was too good a guy for all of these bad things to be happening to him. And Gail's mom once told me that old age isn't for sissies. I'm with you, Dot, and you, too, Shirley-Mom. And I'm also with my elderly neighbor Peggy, who, when I gave her the hernia news, shook her head and said, "Whatcha gonna do, John?"

What we're going to do is stay the course. We're going to keep taking care of Pop as best we can. And me personally? I'm going to keep walking with him and exercising with him. I'm going to keep getting him into the shower. I'm going to keep pureeing his food and crushing his meds. I'm going to keep monitoring his tempera-ture and his bowel movements. I'm going to keep slipping him milk of magnesia shakes with water on the side. I'm going to keep taking him out of the house when he's able and the weather is accommodating. I'm going to keep hauling him off to Mass on Sunday. And most especially, I am going to keep blessing him on the forehead every night and telling him that I love him.

Dad had another Dr. Rezak visit toward the end of February, and he did fine. Day-to-day he's hanging in there, even after all he's been through. But there's no question that over the course of his four and a half years here, he's declined both physically and mentally. Still, every time we see Dr. Rezak and Dr. Stone, they say that Mary and I and the rest of my family are doing a great job with Pop.

It's nice to get the news, but all of us—the doctors, Gail and I, Mary—know that Pop's going south, not north. Damned Parkinson's. Oh, maybe some days he goes north a few steps. Maybe some days he goes north quite a few steps, in fact. And when he smiles over a bowl of oatmeal or one of Mary's cookies, his eyes sparkle like sunlight on snowflakes. These are the days I cherish. But like maple leaves in autumn, he's dying all the same. I asked Gail the other day where she thought we'd be in five years. I didn't expect the bluntness of her answer. She said that Pop would be dead and I'd be writing for a living. Hmmm. . . .

[37]

*I turned forty-six back in February. Forty-six!
Like, how did that happen? Doesn't seem that
long ago that I was climbing in my folks'
cherry trees back in Streator and delivering the
Times-Press.*

I'VE TOLD GAIL THAT OFTENTIMES I feel like I'm still in high school. And truly I do. But forty-six makes me realize that I'm far removed from those glorious days. Hopefully, I'm a good forty-six, though. Despite my recent skating accident, hopefully, I have some good years left.

I've been keeping a journal since Pop came to stay with us. I don't write in it everyday, but I write in it enough to keep up with things. Jim sent me a card and a check. Nice. And one of my favorite birthday gifts was a new journal that Sarah put together for me. I'm always telling her that homemade gifts are best. The journal she got me was store-bought—a basic black cardboard cover with a spiral-bound spine. Sarah spruced it up, though, by applying some cutout designs on the front cover. It's a series of purple and aqua open rectangles in decreasing sizes, and at the center of them on a white background is a series of hearts cut out from the same paper. She even wrote me a poem on the front inside page. It's Pulitzer material, no question:

Daddy,
Do you remember days of yore
When you were not so very sore
With broken cheekbone, hurting shoulder,
Dry bleeding hands from so much water?

I love you just the way you are
(Graying hair and beard and all . . .).

Dear Daddio, though forty-six,
You still have much more time
I hope in which we can still
Go skating, bowling, and more.
In this journal, Daddy dear,
Write down whatever you may feel.
Record this birthday, strong and clear
To remember those days of yore.

So happy birthday one more time,
You may think you're getting old,
But remember Mary's forty-nine!

I called Mary after I read the last line. I've been zinging her about being a few years older than me for the past fifteen years. Now Sarah is doing it, too. Like father, like daughter!

As Mary and I and Jim and Carol went through Pop's house several times over the years following Mom's death to get it ready for selling, we came across bags and bags of old photographs. Many of them weren't marked and must have been family members from long ago, but many of them we recognized. In the commotion of cleaning up the house, we threw all of them into a single large bag that has been sitting in the corner of Pop's room for over a year now. I finally called Jim and asked if I could bring them over to him so that he could go through it first. He said okay and I headed out.

It would have been a long drive and even longer day for Pop, so he stayed here with Gail. When I got to Jim's, I suggested that he take out whatever pictures he wanted, then just return the rest to us. He said he would. We chatted for a while. Did lunch. I asked him about his life, and he told me about his work status and Carol's, and about house stuff.

I gave him a complete Pop report. I also tried to talk with him about his anger with me for watching Dad. Like before, he didn't want to talk about it. Then I asked him if he was at least okay with how I am physically caring for Pop. He said that he was. Good. As long as Pop is doing well, I guess I don't really care what's bothering Jim. Still. He is my brother. Jesus says to reconcile with our brother before bringing our gifts to the altar. I don't know if it's possible to reconcile with Jim right now, but I like to think that someday we'll get beyond all of this. Gail says it won't happen unless he has his own epiphany moment. She's probably right, but for now, I'm happy to know that Jim's satisfied with my day-to-day care for Dad. It's not full support, but it's something, and I'll hang on to it for a long time. Even, I suspect, after the Pop thing is over.

[38]

The Chicago Tribune finally ran my ice-skating piece just into the New Year, and they even accepted and ran another piece later on in the spring about wildflowers and a place back home called Spring Lake. It's really about Dad, though. He liked it a lot. Hope you do, too:

ON SPRING LAKE AND WILDFLOWERS

With the ice gone away and the wildflowers finding their color, there was no finer place on earth when I was a boy than Spring Lake in springtime. More pond than lake, it was a small, unmarked patch of Streator-owned country not too far west of town that my parents introduced me to when I was a child. As I grew older, I would go out there on my own—behind the high-school football field, down the tracks, across the catwalk spanning the Vermilion River. It was the kind of journey that many parents wouldn't let their kids take these days. But thirty years ago, the world was a little gentler, perhaps, a little kinder, a little more forgiving.

Skipping stones was one of my favorite things to do there; I was good, and to quote an old Walter Brennan character, "No brag, just fact." But the place had much, much more to offer. It was also where I picnicked with my family, hiked, picked red raspberries, saw the dead bloated sheep that I will never, ever forget, swam, ran, fished, and helped construct some wooden park structures as part of a Key Club service project in high school. And even though the work was subsequently destroyed by people who didn't love the area as much as I did, Spring Lake was still a place of beauty to me.

I savor my Spring Lake memories because I almost never had them. It was before the time that my parents let me go there alone. My sister was nine or ten or so; my brother, a year older. I can't remember what everyone was doing that day. Perhaps Mary and Jim were pulling up algae from the flat shale rocks at the beginning of the mini-rapids leading into the mini-falls. Perhaps Mom was preparing lunch. Perhaps Dad was dozing in the sunshine or skipping stones himself or daydreaming about his work at the local bank.

But I know what I was doing. I was sitting on the boulder at the top of the falls. It was a warm day in early spring, and because of the recent melting of the winter snows, the water was like the pitches I would never be able to hit in midget league—high and fast. As I recall it, the rush of the water crashing into the tiny lake below was deafening. It was the sound of thunder that never ended. It was the sound of twenty strikes being rolled all at once and over and over and over again at Streator's Bowl-Mor Lanes.

I cannot tell you how I came to be in the water. But I can tell you that it was cold. And I can tell you that the undertow didn't look kindly on young boys who should have known better. Quickly, Dad was above me on solid ground, and like a hand-crank crane at the city park carnival, he lowered his arm down to the water and came up with the prize. Meet my father James— personal banker, personal hero.

Time took us all away from Spring Lake. Mom and Dad stopped going eventually. Jim, too, after a while. Mary went a few times with her husband and young boys, but those visits faded away as well. But I kept going, even after I moved away to college and ultimately bought a home in Chicago. I took my wife-to-be there. I took my children there, too, with my daughter Sarah becoming especially fond of the place. And right up until my mother died and I stopped going to Streator regularly, any trip home to see my folks was more special if I could make it to that small, unmarked patch of country not too far west of town.

It was on one such visit several years ago that Gail and I dug up wildflowers from Spring Lake and transplanted them into our front flowerbed. And every springtime, with no maintenance whatsoever, they come back to say hello. Long diagnosed with Parkinson's disease, my dad lives with us now. He hasn't plucked me from any turbulent water recently, but he is life-giving in many other ways, and it is my sincerest hope each day that I am somehow returning the favor. We occasionally sit on the porch when the weather is fair. I've told him that some of the wildflowers are Streator's own, but sometimes, the significance appears to be lost on him. But for now at least, it isn't lost on me; nor, perhaps, on my son Paul, who awoke on a sunny morning last year after a warm evening shower, and said, "Hey! It smells like Streator outside."

My home may now be situated under an O'Hare International flight path, but in springtime, anyway, I have yellow buttercups that speak to me of a quiet place I will always hold dear. The Kennedy Expressway may now be only a skipping-stone's throw away, but in springtime, anyway, I have lilies-of-the-field to fragrance my world and slow it down a bit. And I may live now in one of the finest cities in the world, but in springtime, anyway, I have forget-me-nots to help me remember the world-class city I came from; and that in many ways I'm just a kid again, Dad's still day-dreaming at my side, and Spring Lake is just outside my window.

To a writer, the daily mail can be either a friend or an unwanted intruder. I put the intruders in a file upstairs. The rejection file. It holds all of the letters that editors around the country (or around the block) have sent me saying, in essence, see you later. "Dear Mr. Reynolds: Thank you for letting us review your work. We regret to inform you that it does not meet our editorial needs at the present time. . . ." By comparison, the friends I embrace with a separate file all their own right here on the main floor. These are the acceptance letters. And every now and then, I get letters out of the blue from strangers that simply touch my heart.

Such a letter came just the other day, in fact, sliding through the mail slot along with the bills and the assorted fliers. It didn't carry a return address so I couldn't tell who it was from, but it was the only piece of mail that was addressed to me by hand and not by computer. Naturally, I went for it first, and it didn't disappoint. It turned out to be from a Tom and Mary Purcell—Streator folk—who had read the *Tribune* pieces and who were writing to say that they enjoyed them. Supportive words are gold to most writers. These words were no exception to me.

But touching me more than the compliment was the remainder of their letter. They shared with me some of their own stories of life back home, and they sent warmest regards to my father. Before he retired, Dad worked at one of the two banks in town—the Streator National Bank—while Mr. Purcell worked at the other, the Union National. Mrs. Purcell wrote that her husband had great respect for Dad, "always a gentleman." She also wrote of memories they both had of my mother when Mom used to work at Bryant's, a small neighborhood grocery. The words brought a wistful smile. Tom and Mary's last sentence, though, is the one that touched me most. "Thanks again for sharing your memories," they said, "but most of all, for remembering your roots."

I chased down their address and sent a brief note back to the Purcells explaining that of the many things my parents gave me, one of the dearest to me is my Streator roots. Yes, I moved away. Yes, I bought a house in Chicago and yes, I'm raising my children here. But there is something of Streator that will always be inside of me. Mom put it there. Dad put it there. The city itself put it there. And I am the better for it.

Pop has been doing pretty well these days, but he gave us a little scare in early April. He's been sleeping later and later, it seems, which is fine with me. If he's tossing and turning, I now give him his first Sinemet dose around 7:00 A.M. right in bed after I clean him and change him. If he's sleeping really soundly, I won't even wake him. Then I let him sleep until nine. Then I wake him, give him his first meds, and adjust the schedule through the rest of the day. It seems to be working, but for a stretch there beginning in late March, he was doing noticeably worse than he had been doing up to that point.

On April first, he was a sleeping fool, because even after waking him at nine for his first med, he fell back asleep and didn't wake up on his own until 11:00 a.m. Gail kidded him about it when I called her into Pop's room so that she could say good morning to him. Pop laughed. The non-laughing matter at hand though, was that his temperature was 99.4. I don't normally take it in the morning because generally that's the coolest reading of the day. But Pop felt warm to the touch, and he had been sluggish for a few days prior. I suspected that something was probably going on with him that wasn't good, so I spoke with Gail, called Mary, gave Pop two crushed tablets of 325 mg. acetaminophen, and said I would keep a close eye on him.

I checked his temperature several more times throughout the day, and he was doing okay: 97.5, 96.0, 95.6, 95.5. But he was 99.1 at bedtime so I gave him two more acetaminophen and put Mary and Jim on hospital alert. The next two days were the same without the high temperature reading in the morning—Pop was okay early and got feverish as the days went on. On April 3, though, he was sluggish all day, so I called Dr. Stone's office. They directed me to an immediate care clinic. Mary met us there; good old Mary.

The doctor there gave Pop a mini-physical. She said his vitals were good, and his breathing—which can be indicative of aspiration pneumonia if wet and broken-sounding—was pretty good, too. She ordered a chest x-ray just to play it safe and said that it didn't really show a pneumonia problem. Mary and I had occasion to see the negative and I couldn't help but recall with Mary a story that happened a few years ago.

It was during another of Pop's visits to the hospital for a chest x-ray in conjunction with a suspected case of aspiration pneumonia. When the film came back, the doctor put it up on the screen, looked at it briefly, than went on to other matters. Mary and I were waiting in an adjacent room with Pop, and we could both see the x-ray as well. The picture meant nothing to me, but Mary said, "Uh oh, he's got it."

"Got what?" I said.

"Pneumonia," she said.

"You know how to read x-rays for pneumonia?" I said.

"I do," she said, adding that she had seen the x-ray years before on the occasion of one of Dad's earlier bouts. Impressed, I asked her what about the negative tipped her off to Dad having the pneumonia. She pointed to a whitish portion of the film that was low and off to the side. I told her that I was truly impressed at her medical knowledge and we both braced ourselves for the news that Pop would have to spend the night there.

Shortly thereafter, though, the doctor came back and told us that Pop's x-ray was clean. Mary and I were both thrilled to hear it, but I was confused. The x-ray was still hanging on the lighted board only a few feet away. Not wanting to incriminate Mary completely, but very curious, I asked the doctor if she could explain the picture for me. Specifically, I asked her what the white area was. Nonchalantly, she said, "the heart." I thanked her and she walked away. Then I turned to my sister and said, "My God, Mary, he has a heart!" Mary was not amused.

Anyway, the doctor at the care clinic gave Pop a prescription for an antibiotic. I had it filled after I had gotten Pop home for the night, but it was en route that Dad said something I hope I'll never forget. I explained to him that he was okay, and that he didn't have to go to the hospital. I explained that the x-ray looked pretty good, and that the doctor was just prescribing an antibiotic to be on the safe side, considering Pop's past history with aspiration pneumonia. I told him that I was taking him home, then I would go out, get the medication, and give him his first dosage that evening at bedtime. That's when Pop turned to me and said, "I don't know what I'd do without you."

And I don't know what I'd do without Pop. Guess it works both ways.

[39]

Pop is pretty much recovered from his non-descript problems of several weeks ago. The antibiotics seemed to do the trick, and his temperature has been holding steady as of late.

A RECENT WEEK'S CHART shows steady temps along with four tablespoons of milk of magnesia in a milk shake. The very next day, LBM! Yea, Pop is doing okay, but as I've been telling Mary more and more lately, he's not doing okay with authority like he's done in the past. This year is not as good as last year for him. And last year wasn't as good as the year before.

Mary continues to come over to watch Pop so I can go out with Gail and the kids every so often. Shirley-Mom is still a big help, too. Had lunch with Howard a while back, too. Gail stayed home with Pop. This care-giving gig wouldn't have lasted nearly as long as it has were it not for all these folks coming to my rescue. Even Howard, unknowingly, has played a major role in all of this. As simple as lunch with an old boss-turned-friend may seem, I look forward to these get-togethers from one date to the next. I've always known that caregivers are supposed to take time for themselves. Even before I ever dreamed that I'd be taking care of Dad, the notion made sense. But now that I'm living the life, I appreciate the notion—and the time off—so much more.

We celebrated Father's Day a few weeks back. Nothing special. I made barbecued chicken, cole slaw, and fresh bread for dinner, one of my favorite meals. Played catch in the alley with Sarah and Paul. They'll be going into eighth grade and sixth grade in the fall, and their throwing arms are both developing nicely. Had some Squirt soda to drink. It all seemed to fit, per the enclosed *Senior Connection* column, my Father's Day piece:

"THREE SQUIRTS FOR THE THREE SQUIRTS"

The pop selection at our place is pretty basic. A cola type. A lemon lime type. Maybe a ginger ale. That's why my son Paul and my daughter Sarah were thrilled to see me come back from the local Jewel store a few nights ago with one six-pack each of Cherry Seven-Up, Country Time Lemonade, A&W Sparkling Vanilla Cream Soda, and Squirt. I had purchased them begrudgingly because they were $2.99 each and I knew that I could get a full case of a single flavor for less than five bucks on sale. But Paul needed four of those plastic ring things that hold six-pack cans together for an art project at school, and what's a father to do? The next day, however, the sting of the purchase faded and I was actually glad I bought the stuff, for as I looked at the cans on the kitchen counter, I recalled the long-ago history I had with one of the flavors, and appreciated its story once more.

Going out to eat was a real treat when my brother and sister and I were small and growing up in Streator. It's not that our family was poor, but we weren't rich, either. Our father worked at the local bank and our mother put in a part-time week at Bryant's Grocery, a neighborhood corner market. Whatever money they made, it was enough to keep Jim and Mary and me in Catholic grade school for eight years each and food on the table. Mostly, Mom stretched ground chuck and noodles to feed us, but every now and then, Dad herded us into the family car and took us to the 820 Club, a restaurant/bar across the street from the Owens, Illinois glass factory, for dinner out.

As I recall, our folks usually went for the chicken while we kids pulled in with the burger and fries. It was always good eatin' there, but what I remember most about our 820 Club outings—beyond the food or the low-hanging smoke or the shimmering beer signs behind the bar—is Dad ordering the drinks for us. Every time we went it was the same, and every time we went I loved to hear it: "Three Squirts for the three squirts."

How appropriate as Father's Day approaches that something I did for my son brings me back to something my father did for me when I was a boy. These days, I am privileged as a father to care for my children and to watch them grow strong and true. I am also privileged as a son to care for my father, whose struggle with Parkinson's disease is as humbling to watch as it is inspiring. I would never be so presumptuous to assume that my wife and children have anything planned for me for Father's Day, but should we find ourselves gathered for dinner as a family on June 18th—even if it's just around our dining room table—the drinks are on me. Two Squirts for the two squirts. And one Squirt for my dad—the biggest man I know. Happy Father's Day.

So, I'm standing at the seafood counter of the same local Jewel store when a guy who I've never seen before asks me if I'm John Reynolds. Suspicious, I tell him yes. Then he asks me if I'm the John Reynolds who writes the bulletin column and who has occasional essays published in the *Chicago Tribune*. I tell him yes again. Turns out he goes to my church. Seems he always reads the weekly column, but didn't know who I was. Then he saw my picture a few times in the *Tribune* and remembered the face when he saw me standing in line. He said the column should be national.

My motivation for moving on the man's words was actually prompted by a recent conversation between my brother-in-law Greg—a dentist—and my sister, which Mary later shared with me. Mary said that she and Greg were talking about my writing—about my column in particular. Mary, who asks for a hard copy of everything I write, said that the work was very good. Greg had read a handful of the weekly pieces, too, and he agreed, but added that I could never make it financially writing a weekly column.

When Mary told me all of this, I think I knew instinctively that Greg was right. But I thought about it for a long time one morning during a long run, and I thought that maybe it could work after all. One or two churches is nothing, as Greg said. But how about a lot of churches? Gail said we'd have to sit down and work through some numbers, but it had potential. Mary thought a self-syndicated column could work, too. And when I shared the notion with Pop, he thought it was a great idea.

Between Pop care and household duties, I began working on a cover letter. Gail helped me nail it down. Over the past several weeks, I've sent it off with sample columns to each of forty different parish pastors here in the Archdiocese of Chicago. Then I held my breath (but not tightly) and waited. Surprisingly, three churches called and signed up a few weeks later—just over the last couple of days, in fact—and that's what prompted this letter. I had to tell a good friend the good news.

And, they sent their checks in. Paid work. What a concept. I showed the checks to Dad, and he was amazed. In truth, I'm a little amazed myself. I told Dad thanks again for letting me take care of him. In one of my sample columns, Dad was once again the star player:

ON COLLECTION BASKETS AND GIFTS TO GIVE

When I was a young child attending Sunday Mass, my folks would often give me a coin or two to put into the collection basket, and I always relished making the drop. Ironically, shortly after he came to live with us and we began taking him to Sunday Mass about forty years later, my father would sometimes ask me for a dollar to put into the basket as the usher brought it around. For a while I tried giving him the money before we arrived at church, but invariably, he would put it in his front shirt pocket and forget about it by the Offertory. Now, I check his attentiveness and give it to him shortly before the ushers start doing their thing. Usually, Dad is alert and gives up the dollar without any hesitation. Sometimes, though, he gets confused and still slips it back into his pocket, then the usher—none the wiser—passes him by. Sometimes, he makes the dollar disappear by wrapping his entire hand around it and the usher—again, none the wiser—passes him by. Last weekend, however, Dad threw us all a curve.

I asked him as the collection began if he wanted a dollar for the basket. He told me yes. I folded the bill in half and handed it to him, and he held it clearly visible in his left hand. He seemed pretty alert so I wasn't thinking much about it until the usher slid the basket in front of my family and me. My son Paul dropped his envelope into the basket per usual, and I did the same with ours. Dad appeared to look right at the basket, but he kept holding on to the dollar. Clearly, the usher expected Dad to drop the bill into the basket—as did I—so he paused there for a few seconds. I nudged my father, who was sitting immediately to my right in his wheelchair, and said, "Dad, the basket." He didn't respond, so I got into his line of vision and said, "Dad, do you want to put the dollar in the basket?" I expected a positive response and a quick drop. Instead, I got a rather thoughtful, "No."

Smiling to myself, I signaled the usher to move along, but later I realized how I can be so like my father in such regards. I cannot recall ever refusing to drop my donation into the basket, but how many times have I refused to give the gifts and talents with which God has graced me because it was just too much bother to do otherwise? Similarly, how many times have I refused to gift my neighbor with kindness or understanding when given the opportunity to reach out my hand? James tells us that every good gift comes from above. When we give of ourselves, therefore, we are really giving back to God. Perhaps that's something we should all keep in mind, for when it comes to giving freely of our gifts, the buck ultimately stops which each and every one of us. Or with my father, depending on the day.

I was thrilled with the orders. Gail was too, but she put things in perspective. I'm charging $156 for fifty-two columns, so "Let's see . . ." she said. "Now we're up to nine dollars per week?" I'll need nearly two hundred parishes more to make ends meet without Pop care money coming in—which is my goal—but I'm smiling nonetheless. And why not? My father is hanging in there, it's summertime, and I've got a little writing money in the bank. "Life goes on, and it is good."

[40]

Pop's been struggling these past few days. It may be the humidity. Even with the air conditioning turned on almost all summer long, he still has his bad times. Dr. Rezak told me once that the air conditioning helps, but some Parkinson's patients are adversely affected by the barometric pressure as well, even if they are in a climate-controlled environment. So it may be with Pop.

WE'RE LEAVING IN A COUPLE OF DAYS for the family camping trip. We're heading north this year—to Minnesota, ultimately—where Sarah and her team are skating in a precision figure ice-skating competition. I'm actually skating, too. They have a big production number this year. The same sort of thing they had a few years ago when Pop doffed his hat to the skaters. I wasn't going to do it, but Sarah liked the idea of my skating with the group this year. I told her I'd do it if Wendell did it. Wendell is another skating Dad. As misfortune would have it, Wendell signed up, so I did, too. Wish us all luck!

Mary made the arrangements again this year to put Pop in a nursing home while we're gone. She was considering a new place this time, a place a little closer to her so that she could get over to visit him in less time. I told her that would be fine, but suggested that she consider returning Pop to ManorCare instead. I explained that he knew people there, and that he might be more comfortable there.

My words were true enough. But I had another reason for suggesting ManorCare, a selfish one. Pop is doing okay, and I like taking him to ManorCare to let the staffers see how well he is faring. It makes me feel good. I want Jane and Becky and the whole crew to see that I am still doing it—that I am still taking care of Pop and that he is doing well because of it. The people at the new nursing home, the one Mary suggested, don't know me or the history I have with Pop. The people at ManorCare do. And I want to hear them say what a great job I'm doing. As my friend Bob at Topco would say, "It doesn't make you a bad guy." Or does it?

[41]

We're home, and the kids are already back in school—eighth grade for Sarah and sixth grade for Paul. Amazing.

SARAH'S SYNCHRONIZED SKATING TEAM got first place and our production number team claimed second in the skating competition, but we cut the trip short because Pop took ill. We had been camping all the way, and since we don't have a cell phone, we were basically unreachable. I caught up with Mary by pay phone when we hit Minneapolis the day before the events, though, and she gave me the news. Seems that Pop had another swallowing spell—or nonswallowing spell—a few days after I dropped him off at ManorCare. Mary said they rushed him over to the hospital across the street thinking that he had some sort of heart attack or stroke or something. She said she told Jim the news as well.

Mary said he was stable, but not doing all that well. She said that we didn't have to cut the trip short, but what else could we do? Earlier in our trip, Gail and I and Sarah and Paul attended the Old Log Theater in Excelsior, Minnesota for an evening performance of "Over the River and Through the Woods," a play about a young man leaving New York to take a job in Seattle and trying to say good-bye to his grandparents on both sides with whom he's had Sunday dinner for years.

It was funny, touching, and thought-provoking. The phrase one of the grandparents used often was *tengo familia,* which, literally translated from Italian, means something akin to "I am a family man." Liberally translated, it means much more. We have so many choices in our lives. Which ones win out? Which ones lose out? I told Gail that as much as I wanted to spend another week with the family camping in Minnesota, we needed to return home to be with Pop. She agreed. Tengo familia.

Dad was sent back to the nursing home after a three-day hospital stay, but this time for rehabilitation instead of R&R. He's still there. Pop remained pretty shaky for the next two weeks—primarily, we think, because of a medication mix-up which occurred at the hospital and which didn't come to light until several days later. And during that time frame especially, Mary and I made a point to visit Dad at least once a day, usually twice. Even though it often seemed as if he didn't know who we were, we again thought it was important for us to be there.

Dad was distant per usual on one such visit. Kara, the occupational therapist, was trying to get him to play catch with a ball—something he enjoys doing when he is up to it—but he wasn't up to it at the moment. Kara turned her back for a few seconds to tend to something else and I was standing several feet to the side when Mary positioned herself with the ball directly in front of Dad. In her ever-cheerful, ever-smiling, and ever-enthusiastic fashion, she encouraged him to catch it. Dad had a different idea, though, and voiced it when he politely told my sister—his only daughter—to "Go away."

Good old Pop. He's had a rough go of it since the onset of Parkinson's disease, and it's not letting up any. On top of the disease complications, his glasses and dentures were lost somewhere along the way. The nursing home is blaming the hospital and the hospital is blaming the nursing home. I finally got the nursing home people to say that they would pay for the dentures, that I should just send them the bill and they would see what they could do for us. It's something.

And in the meantime, Pop is just trying to get along. He is very weak. He is eating somewhat, but not with authority. Likewise with his exercising. The nursing home people told me they would be releasing him in a week or so. We'll see how it goes at home. I called Jim and told him I'd be bringing Dad back here. When Pop came back here after the hip break two years ago, he perked up like nobody's business. Maybe it will happen again. I pray it will happen again.

Part Four

End-of-Life Care

Many years ago, I had occasion to visit someone in the hospital who was quite literally on his deathbed.

I DIDN'T KNOW THE PERSON, and I didn't know the circumstances. I was just visiting parishioners from my church to tell them that the parish-at-large was thinking of them. Many of these little pastoral conversations lasted fifteen to twenty minutes, and when I left the respective rooms, both the patients and I were usually smiling. Things didn't work out this way on the day in question.

For on the day in question, I encountered a death-watch upon entering the patient's room. The patient's family was there en masse, and sorrow hung in that place like a dark cloud. I introduced myself to one of the family members and then found that I had nothing much to say. I think I muttered something about how there are no answers at times like this. Insightful, no?

After sharing my condolences with them all, I prayed for the patient, blessed him, then walked away in silence.

End-of-life care. I have since come to learn that it goes far beyond deathbed care, as certainly that family learned in the days, weeks, and perhaps months and years leading up to their loved one's death. Not always, but sometimes, we are blessed with the opportunity to prepare for the loss of someone dear to us. Of course, I was blessed with no such opportunity when Mom died. She was alive and apparently healthy one minute, and the very next minute, she was gone. But when we know what's coming, we are wise to act accordingly.

Even saying this, I know that I can do better with my father, because I knew what was coming for him on the day he moved in. Mom often joked that Dad would live longer than she would, and it's proven to be the case. In similar fashion, especially after the first few years when Dad was doing so well here, my sister would often joke the same way—that Pop would outlast both of us.

When we care for anyone in Pop's condition, we need to keep in the back of our heads the notion that every little cough, every little cold, every little medical setback might very well be the patient's last. Ailments and infections that are barely noticeable to a healthy person can be the beginning of the end for the immuno-compromised individual. End-of-life care is about paying attention to the details, and keeping in mind that the details begin to matter long before the family gathers to await the final breath.

[42]

Pop came home—sans eyeglasses and dentures—in late September. Without his chops, it's hard to understand him, even on his good days. And his good days are nothing like his good days before the camping trip.

HE'S SHOWN SOME IMPROVEMENT over his nursing home days, but he's still weak. Mary and I took him to an optometrist the other day to have his eyes checked. The doctor said that Dad had some cataracts going on, and suggested that maybe we should see an ophthalmologist about having them removed. She said it would improve his quality of vision.

We thanked her and said okay, but both Mary and I were thinking that the last thing Pop needs at this point in his life is another surgery. Afterward, we went out to lunch with Pop in the food court of a nearby mall. Just for fun, I asked Pop if he could read the writing on one of the storefront windows twenty feet away. Between bites of his McDonald's hamburger, he read it to me word for word.

As for the chops, Gail's mom is a denture technician—the whole family is into dentistry—and she said she would come over and work with Pop to make a new upper plate. She's been busy, though, and I haven't heard anything from her after she said she would do the work. I asked Gail to remind her. It would be nice to give Pop his chops back. He looks so good with them in, and then we could all understand him a little better.

I'm worried about Dad. I've been caring for him for over five years now, and I think I know him pretty well. I know how he gets through his days, and he's not getting through them at all like he used to. Which is not to say that he hasn't had some good days since coming back here. He has. He's had several, in fact. But I'm beginning to see the weakness in him. I'm beginning to see the frailty in him. I remember when I first started writing how Mom said Pop was slowing down. Well, he's slowing down again. And as I much as I don't want to admit it, this may be for the last time. Mary knows all about Pop's status. I called Jim to tell him my concerns. He said that Pop has always rallied in the past. I hope he's right.

Pop's swallowing is as weak as it's ever been, though. As in the past when he was going through hard times, I've taken to giving him those Ensure-type drinks, the fortified, flavored milky things that are supposed to be loaded with vitamins and minerals. I know they're not meant to replace a well-balanced diet, and that's not my intention. But if I can get a can into Pop each day along with a meal or part of a meal, maybe it will be enough. As Howard told me during a recent get-together for lunch, it's not like Pop is expending a lot of calories day to day. He's not, and he's sleeping a lot more, besides.

Just after Pop's broken hip, one of the doctors told Mary and me that we should consider hospice care for Dad. Mary and I knew that he wasn't even close to needing that end-of-life sort of assistance. Shortly thereafter, Sue—Dr. Rezak's nurse, who sold us an old wheelchair after Pop's chair collapsed one day and a loaner chair I got from Howard didn't meet Pop's needs—told us that we would know when hospice care was warranted. Albeit more quickly than I had expected, I am beginning to understand what she meant.

[43]

Pop's had a few more good days over the last two weeks, but mostly poor days—days when he stays in bed until the late morning, gets up for a while, eats a little, then goes back to bed in the early evening.

HE'S HAD DAYS LIKE THIS in the past, but they've come and gone, like he was fighting a forty-eight-hour bug or something. This time around, they're a little too frequent for my liking. Probably for Pop's liking, too, although he smiles when he can.

It's Sunday night, and I'm worried. Two nights ago I was worried, too, but not as much. In fact, I was so not-as-much-worried that I went out with Gail to our parish dinner dance. It's always a nice time, and we had purchased our tickets weeks earlier, so why not? With Sarah in eighth grade now, I feel a little more comfortable in leaving her alone with Pop sometimes. Two nights ago, I went with Gail to the dance at 6:30 P.M., leaving Sarah in charge of Pop and Paul. Then I left Gail there at our table and returned here a little before 8:00 to get Pop ready for bed.

I had him stand with the walker and when I took off his diaper, I noticed that he had soiled it slightly. This was a good sign, because his last significant bowel movement had been several days earlier, and I had given him a milk of magnesia shake the day before. I positioned the commode beneath him and waited for the BM to happen. But as I was waiting, I noticed something, I swear, for the very first time. As he sat there wearing his open-backed hospital gown, I noticed how there was almost nothing left to him. I noticed that he looked as if he could be blown away by a strong November wind. Or even a summer gale.

I just stood behind him for a moment or two and let the realization sweep over me that my father—the person of strength, the bank vice president, the guy who fixed roofs and unclogged drains and worked all of those auction sales and told me I was old enough to marry Gail—was a frail, old man. Even when I gave him his shower last week, I didn't notice how thin he had become, perhaps because I was worried as usual about transferring him onto the shower chair and then off again, and getting him quickly into his clothes. Last night, though, as we both waited for the BM to drop, it hit me what a difficult road Pop has been on. And how much it's taken its toll.

The BM was large and firm—usually a good sign—and before I went about cleaning it up and getting Pop into bed, I called Shirley-Mom in keeping with the plans for the evening. I had no problems in leaving Sarah in charge for an hour and a half, but I didn't want to leave her in charge for the entire night. Gail and I planned on being home by midnight, but I wanted an adult to Pop-sit for the balance of the evening. Shirley-Mom said she was available—as she has been so many times over the past five years for us—so we asked her if she would watch Pop this time around, too. Mary was happy about this as well, because it saved her a trip; Mary lives half an hour away; Shirley-Mom is a stone's throw.

I returned to the dance after Shirley-Mom showed up and we had a wonderful time. Gail had saved me a seat. Several people asked how Pop was doing. Not wanting to get into the BM and frailty issues, I said he was having a rough go of it and left it at that. In my heart, I knew that it was only a half-truth.

Pop had an iffy day on Saturday, at least according to Gail, who was with him most of the day. I got him out of bed earlier than he wanted to get up, I think, because I was selling some of my Christmas cards at a craft show and I needed to get the table set up within the proper time frame. Pop was a little groggy, but not too bad. I put some waffles in front of him before I left, along with some prune juice and a cup of coffee. He said thanks as he always does, shook my hand as firmly as ever, and wished me luck with the sale. Thanks, Pop! Then I loaded up the car, kissed Gail good-bye, and hit the bricks.

I sold a couple of hundred dollars worth of cards at the show, and had a great time in the process. I read somewhere once that no work of writing is complete—really complete—until it connects with the reader. I connected with a lot of readers Saturday afternoon, and it made me feel good. Several of the people reading the cards were moved to tears. High praise, indeed.

I got home mid to late afternoon on an adrenaline rush and I wasn't too disappointed to find Dad in bed. It gave me a little more time to relax before shifting back into my Pop mode again. I shared the good news of the show with Gail and she shared with me the bad news that Pop didn't eat well for lunch, and that he seemed pretty out of it so she got him into bed for an early afternoon nap. I got Pop out of bed in time for dinner, and he did fine, eating an entire plateful of chopped-up chicken burrito. I settled him into bed at the usual time, and wondered what the next day would bring.

The next day—today—has not been a good one. Pop has been in bed for essentially all of it. He hasn't really eaten anything, and he's very tired. If this was another time—last month, last year, even last week—I wouldn't be surprised to find his temperature readings on the rise and maybe pneumonia setting in again. But

I've been checking his temperature all along. The readings are true. He's not sick. He's just lifeless.

Somebody forwarded something to me on the Internet a while back. It was a list of ways you can tell you're getting old. I don't remember any of the entries except one, and it went something like this: "You can tell you're getting old if when you're sleeping, people look at you and think that you might be dead." It's humorous, perhaps, only if you don't have an infirm and elderly parent living in your house. For there have been a lot of mornings when that's exactly how I've checked in on Pop, especially after his rough nights. There have been a lot of mornings when I watched for the rise and fall of his chest under the hospital gown. I've even said those little prayers people say, "Please, Lord, please let him still be alive." As if the Lord doesn't have bigger matters to tend to than an old man with Parkinson's disease and his care-giving son.

[44]

The last three days have been a blur.
Pop was, in fact, breathing on Monday
morning, just as he's been breathing each of
these days since, but I can't say much more
about his state of well-being than that.

MONDAY WAS A BAD DAY, perhaps the worst of the three. He didn't get out of bed at all, and I saw no need to try to rouse him. Mostly I sat with him. I've been doing a lot of that lately. Makes me wonder why I didn't sit with him more when he was doing okay.

Anyway, he was hit and miss with the medicines. He just lay there, propped up on the pillows. Sleeping mostly, but sometimes awake. And when he was awake, very noncommunicative. Sometimes over the past five years, Pop has been noncommunicative because he's been mad at me. Too many exercises, usually. But this time, he couldn't say hello if he wanted to. And I sensed that he wanted to.

I held his hand and checked his grip once or twice. It was as weak as it's ever been, and that's what really frightened me. I've always said that Pop's grip was my barometer as to how he was doing, and for the first time since he moved in, the barometer was falling. At one point, though, when Pop showed a moment or two of lucidity, I asked him if he wanted to go the hospital, or if he wanted to stay here at home. He spoke his response slowly, but he spoke it clearly. "I want to stay here," he said. No matter what happens in the minutes or hours or days ahead, I'm going to hang on to those words. And take comfort in them.

Later on in the morning, Pop's breathing—which had been heavy and labored—got very shallow very quickly. I thought he was going to die. I cried a lot of tears that morning, and, since I had told both Gail and Mary that they should go about with their days and that I would call them if I needed them, I cried all those tears alone. I wonder if Pop heard my sobbing. I wonder if he felt the hot tears falling down my cheeks and upon our clasped hands.

After the scare had passed, I called Gail and told her that I was going to call Father Tom to see if he could send someone over to give Pop the Sacrament of the Anointing of the Sick. Gail said it was a good idea. Like always, she was a good man in the storm. The Church used to call this ritual the Last Rites, remember? Seems it's not just for the dying anymore. Somehow, that made me feel better in asking for it. Requesting the Sacrament of the Anointing of the Sick for your failing father is a lot easier to swallow than asking for the Last Rites.

I made the call from a portable phone in Dad's bedroom, punching the rectory's number with the thumb of my right hand while holding my father's hand in my left. My words didn't come easy, but Father Tom was patient with me, and said that he could be here in about ten minutes. I had dried my eyes and was still holding Dad's hand when he stirred for the first time in hours shortly after I hung up the phone. And when he looked around and said in a very weak yet audible voice that he was hungry, I couldn't help but smile; even the mere mention of a priest coming seemed to perk him up.

Dad was not very responsive when the good pastor arrived minutes later, but he was more responsive than he had been, so after the anointing, I shared with Father Tom a story that came to mind with Dad's unmistakable—albeit feeble—resurgence. Years ago as a minister of care, I was visiting a hospital patient who was also frail and weak. When I walked into the room and introduced myself, she summoned all of her strength, propped herself up on her elbows, and asked, "Which priest are you?" I told her that I wasn't a priest. She immediately slumped back into the bed. We had chatted for several minutes when she summoned her strength and propped herself up again and asked, "Which deacon are you?" I told her that I wasn't a deacon, either. That's when she slumped back into the bed again and spoke the doleful words, "You're not even a *deacon?*"

Father Tom liked the story. He's been great through all of this, and I'm not just talking about the sacramental stuff. He's always gone out of his way to see Pop and to shake his hand after Mass on Sunday. Father Tom often jokes that Pop gets more attention than he does as the pastor. I don't know about that, but I have to admit that the people of St. Constance have taken to Pop in kind fashion. They adopted him from the very beginning, and it often brings me near to tears to see how they come around his chair and shake his hand and offer to get him a cup of coffee at the fellowship gatherings we often have after the liturgies. And Dad sits there grinning. Pop has blue-gray eyes—handsome ones, apparently—for a lady told me once as she was fawning over Dad that a woman could get lost in those eyes. I smiled, and thought of Mom.

After the anointing and the story, Father Tom stayed a little while longer there in Pop's room with me, praying silently. I found comfort in his presence. I silently recalled that time that Pop announced—from this same bedroom—that this was a holy place. That was in the commotion of the preschool hour. Now, in the stillness of perhaps a deathwatch, I felt a sense of holiness, too. Despite Dad's claim that he was hungry, he didn't really eat anything as the day dragged on. C'mon, Pop. C'mon.

Before long, Gail surprised me by coming home from work. She said she would have come sooner, but she had to get someone to cover her desk. Shortly after again, Mary showed up. Father Tom said his hellos and good-byes to my new support, and after he left, Gail and Mary joined me in sitting with Pop, and that's pretty much where I've stayed for the past few days. I'm not a priest like Father Tom, of course. Heck, I'm not even a deacon. But I'm hoping my father doesn't mind.

Thanksgiving is next week, so Mary brought Pop a little plush turkey that gobbles when you squeeze it. Mom always liked stuff like this, too. Maybe it's an inherited trait. It can go with the Furby sitting out on the bookcase by Pop's chair. Mary brought us that thing a few years ago. I guess we're supposed to talk to it and teach it sounds. Nobody talks to it but Mary, though. So in she comes with this gobbling turkey and shows it to Pop, saying how cute the thing is. Of course, she's only trying to get a rise out of Pop—anything—for she knows from my phone reports that he's not doing well. Gail told Mary, "If you ever bring me a gobbling turkey on my deathbed, I'll kill you." Not funny. But funny, you know?

I called Jim the other night to tell him about what was going on, but I got his answering machine. I told him how poorly Pop was doing.

Dr. Rezak's nurse said that we'd know when the time was right for hospice care, and the time seems right now. A nurse, Tracy, from Rainbow Hospice came over Monday night. Gail found their number in the phone book because we just needed to talk to someone about Pop. Tracy came in the evening after dinner, and she was very nice. She checked Dad over first when she arrived, and all of his vital signs were good. I had been monitoring his temperature all along and was finding nothing out of the ordinary. He didn't seem sick to me, like I said before, just lifeless.

I told all of this to Tracy. She explained that Dad actually looked pretty good, but that when the body is ready to go, it often just shuts down. She said that it's a very natural thing, and many times, people try to prolong a loved one's life by extraordinary means when it's really time to let that life go. She said it is a hard thing to do, but that it can be a very loving thing to do as well. She explained that hospice care was all about the dignity of the patient, and it was focused on keeping the patient comfortable and well cared for through the final stages of life. After hearing Dad's history, she said that we were doing good by Pop, and it was comforting to me, Gail, and Mary to hear the words.

I found comfort in some other words that night, too. Comfort that came to me when I least expected it. We were sitting around the table talking with Tracy when the phone rang. It was Irene, a lady from church. She was planning the Christmas party for the ministers of care, and she was calling to see if I would bring one of my famous lemon meringue pies to the gathering. "Famous" was her word, not mine. I had brought a lemon meringue pie to a church gathering about a year earlier. Mom always made a great lemon meringue pie, and once again, I was trying to follow in her footsteps. The pie must have been a hit, because there was Irene asking me to bake another one for the December gig.

Irene didn't know that when she called, I was talking with a hospice nurse about my father's possible death. She didn't know that Tracy had given me a phone number to call as soon as Dad died so that someone from Rainbow could be with us. It's not that she made it sound like Dad's death was imminent. But days, weeks, or, if Pop rallied, maybe even years down the road, the day would come, and Tracy was preparing me for it. When I got the news that Mom had died, my knees nearly buckled beneath me. Tracy was trying to strengthen my knees, I guess. And in the middle of it all, Irene wants me to bake a pie.

In truth, her phone call lifted my spirits in untold measure. Mom took care of Dad like nobody else ever could, as much as I've been trying to these past five years. And as I've told you before, if one thing describes Mom's love for life, it was in the way she could make a pie. Dad loved her pies, and he's enjoyed all of my attempts to match them. Since my first pie-making effort shortly after Mom died, I've felt that she was living on through the work of my hands. Even as Dad slips away, pie making is something I can hang on to for my family and me. Mostly for me. I didn't tell Irene about Dad or the hospice nurse. I told her I'd be happy to make the pie.

Another nurse, Maria, came yesterday. She didn't stay long, but she told me the same thing that Tracy did relative to Pop's state of health. I knew that his temperature was good because I've been checking it and recording it all along: 93.8, 96.9, 97.0, 96.1, and 96.9. Whatever's got Pop, it's not aspiration pneumonia. He just looks like he's shutting down. And like Tracy said, it's natural. Maria said that the rest of his vital signs were good, too, and that we should just keep doing what we're doing.

Pop hasn't really eaten anything in a couple of days now. I've gotten most of his medicine into him, but that's about it. He perked up a bit yesterday so I raced down to the local drugstore and bought him some raspberry sherbet. It's ice water, basically, with flavoring, and since Pop was swallowing ever so slightly, I thought it might do some good. Pop took several swallows, then he shut down again. It's funny what you grab on to at moments like this. Gail went back to work for the day, but Mary came over again. We sat by Pop all day long. I think he knows we were there.

Mary came over again today. Pop is still struggling. A few swallows of soda and sherbet. He's lost so much weight. The tears come freely to me now, more so than I thought they would. Perhaps taking care of someone for five years can have that result. Pop had another hospice care visitor today, this time a home health aid named Madeline. She gave Pop a thorough sponge bath there in bed and I must say, he looked pretty spiffy when she was finished.

I clean Pop's bottom every morning with soap and water, but I haven't given him a full body sponge bath in a long time. If ever, now that I think about it. I give him showers, though. Lots of them, in fact. As I see Pop lying there in his bed so weak and frail, it's hard for me to imagine that I gave him a shower just last week. His decline has been gradual from the get go. Such is Parkinson's disease. It was more pronounced but still slow since he came back here after getting sick when we were in Minnesota. From last Sunday to today, however—just four days—it's been dramatic.

Mary spent the day here again. Gail and Sarah and Paul, too, have been terrific with Pop from the very beginning. And they are no less terrific now. I don't know how much Sarah and Paul are grasping all of this, but they are old enough—especially Sarah—to know that Pop is going through a very difficult time right now. I was telling them both just last night that Pop was doing poorly, and that I wanted them to know how much it meant to their grandfather—and to me—to see how supportive they have been through it all. I cried as I spoke the words. Gail lifted me up. I love this family.

Jim returned my call this evening. I told him that Pop was not doing well and that as much as I hoped he was going to rally, I couldn't be so sure this time around. I asked him for his work telephone number so that I could call him there about Dad if I needed to. He told me to call him at home and leave a message.

[45]

Pop passed away tonight, a little after 6:00 P.M. Dinnertime. Pop's favorite time of the day. He had another rough one. Or perhaps it was me who had it rough.

DAD DIDN'T SEEM TOO TROUBLED by anything; in fact, he was nonresponsive and sleepy for the most part. The hospice people recommended that I keep an oxygen tank in the room for Pop if he needed it. We've had it in place for a couple of days, now. I'd given him oxygen through a thin plastic tube that slips just into his nostrils, but I don't know how much good it did. The hospice nurses said his oxygen level was okay, but it would be nice to have the tank on hand. And so we did, but as far as I could tell right up until the end, Pop wasn't in any discomfort. He was just fading away.

Following Madeline's lead, I gave him a full-body sponge bath this morning before Mary came over again. He looked pretty spiffy once more. Gail was home from work most of the day today, and it was nice having her. Mary and I sat there with Dad the entire day. Gail came in sometimes, but she was often busy with household matters, not to mention Sarah and Paul. They both came in to see Dad when they came home from school. "Hi, Pop!" they said in turn, like they've done so many hundreds of times before. But this time it was different, and I think they knew it.

Several times before they got home, Pop would slip into his shallow breathing mode. Then, I always called Gail to join us in case his breathing stopped altogether. I would have called Jim at work, but I didn't have his number.

Sarah and Paul were scheduled to go to the circus that night with their Auntie Sunny. Sunny was picking them up around 5:00 P.M. or so. Gail and I thought they should go. I called them both in to say good-bye to Pop before they left. Only Sarah, I think, had an inkling that it might be the last good-bye to the old man she fell in love with in the little kitchen back in Streator so many years ago. Sarah didn't say the words, but I could tell that she was reluctant to leave for the evening. Gail and I kissed her and told her to have a good time.

Pop died about an hour later. Shortly before his final breath, Dad looked up to the ceiling with a look of wonder on his face. I likened it at the time to the look on a child's face upon seeing fireworks for the first time. My sister and I both glanced up, too. Mary asked Dad what he was looking at, but he couldn't respond. She then asked me if I thought he was hallucinating. I told her no, that hallucinating implies the seeing of something that isn't real. I am convinced that whatever Dad saw that night was real indeed. And wonderful. Maybe he saw angels. Maybe he saw Mom. Maybe he saw Christ himself with outstretched arms.

That's when I called Gail into the room. I wanted her to be there with us. I needed her to be there with us. She stood over me as I sat on one side of Pop's bed holding his left hand. Mary sat on the other side of Pop's bed holding his right hand. Pop's breathing became regular again, and in the moment of calm, Mary told Pop that he could go home to Mom now. Then, as if she misspoke, she quickly followed her words with, "Or, you can stay, if you want to." Humor finds a way.

Moments later, he took his final breath, and as he did so, I reached up and blessed him on the forehead as I've done so many times before and told him that we loved him. Mary repeated her earlier words about going home to Mom, and he was gone. I was still holding his left hand, Mary was still holding his right, and Gail was behind me. I was in the delivery room with Gail when she gave birth to Sarah. I was there when she gave birth to Paul. Holy moments, both. But Pop's death, at the other end of the circle of life, was a holy moment, too. And Pop knows all about holy.

Our first call was to the hospice people as we had been instructed. Gail placed it, and Kathy arrived shortly thereafter. She confirmed the death, comforted us, and spoke to us about Pop's passing. I told her that I couldn't believe how quickly the color left Pop's face and arms. Just before he died, his color was a gentle pinkish peach, the color kids try to reproduce with crayons when they are in first grade. Seconds after his death, the body was ashen and gray. And I realized all the more that this wasn't Pop; that this was indeed just a shell, and that the essence—the colorfulness—of my father had moved on.

Gail had called the local funeral home, Muzyka's, a few days earlier to tell them that Pop was doing poorly and that when the time came, we wanted to make the funeral arrangements through them. Muzyka's is not far from here, and over the years, they have been very supportive of our parish. I've seen their ads in our bulletin. I've received probably a dozen Muzyka calendars through St. Constance since we joined there. Instinctively, I told Gail to call them when she asked about the plans we would have to make. Gail said they were nice over the phone, and they proved nice in person, too.

When the representatives arrived that night, they were cordial and professional. Kathy spoke with them. I think she knew them. Previous gigs, perhaps. Kathy and the funeral home people suggested that we step into the kitchen when they removed Pop from the bedroom because it can be a hard thing to watch. We did as they suggested, but I caught a peek of Dad's body being carried out on the gurney. Kathy and the funeral home people were right. Before the Muzyka folks left, we scheduled a meeting at their place for the following afternoon. Just like we met at Elias's when Mom died. Here we go again.

Kathy left then, too, and I started making phone calls to relatives and friends. Everyone was sympathetic. I told them I'd get back to them with details of the arrangements after we made them the next day. I called Jim, too, but nobody was home. I left a message.

A few hours later, Auntie Sunny brought our children home. We shared the news with them. Sarah cried a little. Paul did, too. A little while ago Gail and I agreed that if we had to plan my father's death, we probably couldn't have done it any better, especially with Sarah and Paul being gone when they took Pop's body away. Our children have done great by Dad, but Sarah's only in eighth grade and Paul's only in sixth. They didn't need to see their grandfather die.

It seemed to hit Sarah the hardest. I think she felt a little bad—maybe even a little guilty—that she wasn't here for Pop at the end. But she was here for Pop every day for the previous five years, bringing him his tea in the afternoon sometimes, skating for him at her ice shows, playing beachball volleyball with him. And Paul? Often at bedtime he made Dad smile by shaking Pop's hand. Two firm grips locked in a manly embrace of love. No, my kids didn't need to be with their grandfather when he died, and do you know why? Because they were with him—really with him—when he lived.

I hadn't heard back from Jim as the evening wore on, so I called him again. He was home this time. I told him the details of Pop's passing and asked him if he could join us at the meeting with the funeral home people tomorrow. He said he'd try to make it. I also told him the general arrangements that we had planned—a wake visitation at Muzyka's, and then a funeral Mass back in Streator. He seemed okay with it.

It's been a long day. I'm going to bed. No medicines to crush tonight.

Part Five

From Life, to Death, to Life Again

Caregivers are a special breed. I didn't recognize this when Mom was taking care of Dad—even though I should have—because I was always on the outside looking in.

I'VE COME TO KNOW THIS after spending these past five years in my mother's shoes. Only now do I realize that the caregiver's work is sacred work. I got down on myself, and often, on how I did with Dad. Now that he's gone, I'll probably be celebrating my good days and remembering my bad days for a long time to come.

But this is not uncommon. I've read enough newsletters and magazine articles on care-giving and I've surfed enough websites dealing with the subject to know that I'm not alone. The credentialed experts tell us that it is normal to feel a wide array of emotions while care-giving day to day—joy, sadness, self-satisfaction, frustration, anger. I have felt them all, often within the same day, if not the same hour. Over the course of Dad's stay here, I've had occasion to speak with other caregivers, and now I know who the real experts are. They are the people who put time in on the care-giving front, who know from the inside looking out what it's like to angrily clean up food from the floor one minute and to warm to our loved one's smile the next.

Care-giving—if done well—is life giving, too, which leads to an interesting dilemma upon the passing of those in our care. I've spent five years of my life caring for my father. Care-giving has defined me for all this time. But now Dad's gone, and my care-giving identity goes with him. What am I now? *Who* am I now? Just as my father is dead, a portion of my very self is now dead, too. From life giving to death giving, in a sense. Strange. So again I turn to the experts, credentialed and/or experienced. They tell me that time will help; that time will tell; and that life wins in the end. I believe them. In many ways, the journey is over. In other ways, it is barely begun.

[46]

It's funny. When Pop was doing well for all those years, I found that I wrote early in the mornings. Now I write late in the evening.

Yesterday was a numbing experience for the most part. I went to 8:00 A.M. Mass. Sat in the back row. Father Tom had the service. Afterward, I approached him before he had a chance to walk into the sacristy to tell him about Dad. He was surprised to hear that Dad passed away so quickly since the anointing on Monday. I told him how grateful I was to him for coming to see Pop, but also for being so kind to him over the years. I started to cry through it all. He told me to sit down, which I did. Together we sat there in the nearly empty church. He in silence; me in tears.

He asked me about the arrangements. I told him that we were meeting with the Muzyka people later that day but that we planned to have something up here and something back in Streator. He said that the Muzyka folks were nice and that they would take good care of us. He also said that St. Constance would have a prayer service for Pop on the night of the wake, whatever it turned out to be. I told him I would keep him posted. He said thanks. I never expected the tears to come so readily.

We had to ready a burial outfit for Pop. I've helped him get dressed for the past five years. I guess I'd be helping him one last time, to a certain degree. He had a suit that he'd worn once or twice for special occasions after he came here. We packed it up to take to Muzyka's. Funerals, I guess, are special occasions. We had a clip-on tie that Mary had gotten him a while back. That went, too. As did the shirt off my back. Literally. All of Pop's shirts had some degree of Sinemet staining on them. Pop-spots, we called them. The stuff just didn't come out in the wash. But I was wearing a white button-down collar casual shirt that day. Mary had gotten it for me for Christmas the year prior. I wore it often, and just as often, Pop said he liked it. Well, here you go, Pop. It's yours now.

Everyone met here before heading over to Muzyka's. Then, as soon as we sat down with the funeral home guy, Jim said he had a problem with us having a wake service up here in Chicago and just a short visitation at the church before the burial in Streator. Jim said that Pop grew up in Streator, that his brother and sister were there, and that we should have more of a service in Streator. He said that he didn't even know why we were having a service up here in Chicago. I asked the funeral home guy if he could leave us alone for a few minutes. He said okay.

Jim proceeded to repeat his case. In truth, his idea to have a longer visitation period at St. Anthony's back in Streator was a good one, and I told him so. Then I told him that we needed to talk this thing through as a family. In the end we agreed—at least, Mary and I agreed—to have the wake at Muzyka's on Sunday. Jim was satisfied with an extended visitation at St. Anthony's on Monday prior to the funeral Mass there, but I think he still has a problem with the service up here. Yes, Pop was born and raised in Streator and yes, he has family and friends there. But he lived here for five years, and he has family and friends here, too. The people at St. Constance have embraced Pop since the beginning. Shouldn't they have a chance to say good-bye to him as well?

Next we had to pick out the little saying for the back of Pop's funeral card. No words of Pop's own wisdom for this one. He had shared many of them with me over the years, but I wasn't in the frame of mind to recall any of them. Nor was Jim or Mary, apparently. We went with the Serenity Prayer this time. It seemed more fitting for Dad than for Mom anyway: "God, grant me the Serenity to accept the things I cannot change, Courage to change the things I can, and Wisdom to know the difference."

Finally, we picked out the coffin. It was just as weird as picking out the coffin for Mom. Like before, we went with something less expensive than more expensive. Muzyka's said they would send the obituary notice to the local papers, and to the *Times Press* back in Streator. It was the paper that Jim and I delivered when we were kids. Dad had his name in print a few times for something or another—usually bank related—over the years. Now he'd be making it in again.

I called Father Tom after everything was nailed down. He said that the St. Constance wake team would hold a brief prayer service at 7:00 P.M. on Sunday. He said he would be there for it and asked if I wanted to say a few words at the conclusion of the service. I hadn't really thought about it, but I told him yes. I asked Mary if she wanted to say anything too. She said no. I asked Jim the same thing. He said no, too. Finally, Father Tom asked if I would mind if he went to the funeral Mass in Streator at St. Anthony's on Monday. Streator is two hours away. I told him that I would be honored to have him there, and asked if he would say a few words on my father's behalf. He said that he would. I was—and have long been—touched by his kindness.

I started getting phone calls from the relatives back home telling me that the obituary notice didn't run in the *Times Press* on Saturday as it was supposed to. Great. I called Muzyka's and they said they sent it across. The *Times Press* people had already gone home for the day, so I called WIZZ, the radio station back in Streator. I told them what had happened and asked them—if I faxed them something—if they could read it on the air either on Sunday night or first thing Monday morning. They said they could if I got it to them quickly. I spent the next half-hour putting together a modified obituary notice from the *Tribune* copy and faxing it off to the radio station.

Later that night, I cried in bed, and made love to my wife. I felt warm in her arms, and she felt warm in mine. During this time of death, I guess I just wanted to feel alive, and our togetherness has never felt more right. The wake is tomorrow.

[47]

*I knew that Pop had friends here, but I never
expected the show of support we received
from the neighbors and from the people of
St. Constance.*

FROM THE BEGINNING of the wake until the end, there was a
steady stream of people passing through to share their condolences, and at 7:00 P.M. the place was packed. SRO. Carol and Jim,
who had prepared a beautiful tribute to Dad with the pictures I
had given him earlier, spent most of the afternoon and evening
down in the funeral home basement with Carol's sister and her
husband. People handle grief in different ways.

I spoke with many people in Muzyka's "B" parlor. I don't now
remember even half of them. But I remember their kindness. I'll
always remember their kindness. Toward the beginning of the
evening, one of the nuns from the parish came up to Gail and me.
Sister Marion. A couple of years ago on the Feast of the Holy
Family, Sister Marion did the readings at Sunday Mass. The first
reading was from the book of Sirach, and in part, it went like this:
"My son, take care of your father when he is old; grieve him not as
long as he lives. Even if his mind fail, be considerate with him;

revile him not in the fullness of your strength. For kindness to a father will not be forgotten, it will serve as a sin offering; it will take lasting root."

The words brought tears to my eyes even then, for so many times, I had, indeed, grieved Pop as he lived, and reviled him in the fullness of my strength. When I was angry with him, or frustrated that he couldn't stand, I would sometimes lift him roughly off the floor from behind and, I swear, I did it just because I could. God, forgive me. But just the same, I told Pop I loved him every night, and a few days before he died, I asked him if he forgave me for all the times I let him down. He said that he did. Why can't I believe it sometimes?

Anyway, Sister Marion told me after the Mass that when she was doing the reading from Sirach, she was talking directly to me. I sensed it, so I felt a certain connection to her when I saw her in the funeral home tonight. And there, she said two things to make me smile. To my wife—who had gotten her hair cut a few days before Pop died—she said, "Off the record: nice hair." And to me she said, "When you pray to your Mom and Dad, pray big."

Toward the end of the service, someone who I didn't know impacted me a great deal, too. She came up to me after viewing Pop in the coffin shortly before 9:00 P.M. The funeral home was essentially empty, and she said to me in the silence, "Even in death, you can tell a man of character." Like no one else could that day, she nailed it. She absolutely nailed it.

Father Tom and Sister Marie Ellen led the prayer service which started around 7:00 P.M. It was very nice with kind words about Dad and kind words of support for the family. It's funny, I never did get Pop registered at St. Constance, and no, he never had church envelopes. But he was as much a parishioner there as anyone. In an odd way, this evening proved it to me. And when it came time for me to share a few words about my father, I turned to some notes I had written down. Roughly, this is what I said:

When Gail called me over five years ago with the news that my mother had died suddenly, the first thing to enter my mind took me by surprise: *Why couldn't it have been my Dad?* What kind of life did he have, after all, with his advanced Parkinson's disease? But when he came to live with us and right up until the day he died, he has been changing my opinion. He's taught me that a life less than perfect can still be a remarkably wonderful one.

I like to think that for the past five years my family and I have done something positive for Dad. But I know that for the past five years he has done something positive for us. He's given us things to think about. He's made us laugh. He's brought us to tears. Dad was a gentle man, and a gracious one. We usually positioned his chair in the living room near the front door, and when visitors came to call, they could expect two things from my father—a very firm handshake and a smile. If we put a bowl of oatmeal in front of him in the morning or a pureed taco for dinner, more often than not he'd just light up and say, "Oh, boy!" And if we cleaned his hands after supper or untangled his legs from the hospital bed bars, his first words were often, "Thank you."

What I want to do tonight is take my father's thank-you's and extend them on to you. To everyone who has ever shaken my father's hand or kissed him on the cheek and wished him well, thank you. To everyone who has ever nodded or smiled in my father's direction, thank you. To everyone who has ever asked me how he was doing, thank you. To everyone who has ever just once thought of our father in a caring regard, thank you. To Gail, Sarah, Meister, you're so good. And to my entire family who has rallied around this effort, thank you all. My memory runs long, and I'll not forget the kindness you have shown this man.

At my mother's wake, a well-meaning but somewhat misdi-rected woman who I didn't even know told me how sorry she was to hear of my loss. But then she added something that I've been hanging on to ever since: "Don't be surprised if you lose your father soon, too." In the cosmic scheme of things, I suppose she was right. Still, five years is five years, and I know that they have not only mattered, that they have not only been meaningful, I'm convinced that they have been touched by the hand of God. Thanks, Dad. I wouldn't have missed them for the world.

It was all I could do to get the words out. Gail hugged me for a long, long time, just as she did in Pop's room on the night he died. We're home again now. The funeral is tomorrow, and we'll be leaving for Streator first thing in the morning.

[48]

We put Pop in the ground today. It was a cold day. The visitation at the church was nice.

MY HIGH-SCHOOL BUDDY MARK was there, embracing me just as he did when Mom passed away. And several people whom I remember from the old days stopped by to extend their condolences, too. Many of them were retired bank employees telling me how great it was to work for my father. One woman said something that I'll remember for a long time. She stood in front of the open casket in the back vestibule of the church for a few moments. Then she walked away, came over to me, and said almost with a sigh, that if my father had one fault, it was that he was too good for his own good.

Mom used to tell me the same thing—that Dad was always helping people he barely knew. And somebody sent Dad an electric carving knife as a thank-you for his banking services once. Dad said he didn't think it was right that we use it. He said he was just doing his job and he didn't want to compromise his position by taking an expensive gift. Accordingly, it sat unopened in the cabinet on the back porch for years. It was probably sold in the house auction a few years ago. Dad's actions have always had an impact on me. And I suspect they always will.

At the funeral Mass, Father Ham said some nice words about Pop, just like he said some nice words about Mom five years earlier. But it was Father Tom who really touched me that day, for he knew my father. Father Tom had seen Dad in church Sunday after Sunday for a long time now. He said that Pop was loved, and that he taught all of us how to love by his cheerfulness in the midst of adversity. And he joked again that Pop was more popular in the parish than the pastor. If Pop heard the words—and I think he did—I'm sure he enjoyed them.

And if he heard the words, I hoped he liked the poem I read following Father Tom's testimony. I explained that I had actually written it for Pop as a Father's Day gift several years ago. I didn't tell the people gathered at St. Anthony's that when my mother read it for the first time, she cried.

> His is a gentle reflection . . .
>   taking its direction from a quiet heart and quieter soul.
> Sometimes I can't see it even when I am looking for it.
> Sometimes I can, even when I am overlooking it.
> And if I mistook it for my own,
>   now that I'm grown,
>   would anyone really mind?
> Surely I'll find not,
>   for although it is unkempt and windswept,
>   I believe that it fits me like no glove ever can or will.
>
> I work hard because he has taught me to work hard.
> I laugh because he has taught me to laugh.
> I cry because he has taught me to cry.
> And in a way I do not fully understand,
>   I love my wife because he cherishes my mother.
>
> Something terrible has slowed his step over sunsets past,
>   and I hurt to see him hurt.
> But the mirror of his goodness will never desert
>   him . . . or me.

And the nearer I get, the clearer the image becomes.
I am my father's reflection.
I am my father's son.

We went to St. Anthony's cemetery following the Mass to lay Pop next to Mom. We drove there via Ottercreek Street back home, and as the funeral procession of maybe five to ten cars rolled along, two cars going in the opposite direction pulled off to the side of the road and stopped to let us pass. This struck me, for I have never seen such a thing happen up here in Chicago. Indeed, I've drummed my fingertips on the wheel impatiently as I've waited for funeral processions to get by. And here, two cars pull aside and stop to show their respect. Seemed small-town to me. And I remembered that I had seen my father do the same thing when I was a kid.

It was rough at the cemetery. We gathered around the vault as the cold wind swirled about. I can't speak for the others, but it cut me to the bone. Father Ham said some more nice words about my father. The really touching element of the service, though, was provided by the Navy color guard. Stationed in Guam during World War II, Pop never talked about the war, and for years I never thought to ask him. I tried discussing it with him when he came to live with us after Mom's death, but he didn't have much to say about a lot of things by then. And now that he's gone, our conversation has dried up altogether.

I may have missed the details, but I got the big picture at Dad's grave site today when the Navy personnel who waited for us there folded the flag covering my father's casket, presented the colors to my brother on behalf of the President of the United States and the U.S. Navy, and sounded taps as Dad's body was lowered into the ground. Tears fell, and for another quiet soldier, day is done.

The hearse drove away as we all got back into our cars to do the same, and in a sweeping instant, I gained great insight into the death business. I never thought about it at all until Mom died. Then I realized how important the funeral industry is and what a great service those employed by it offer the mourning family members left behind. Our dealings with the Muzyka Funeral Home people solidified my feeling in this regard, but when I saw the hearse pull away, it hit me that beyond the compassion and professionalism that everyone there showed me, this is still a business like any other—a cereal manufacturer, perhaps—that delivers its product then returns to the plant for another load.

Pop's body, in essence, was a raw material, as was the casket and the flowers and the funeral cards. The finished product was Dad, embalmed, laying in the less-than-more-coffin, just like Mom before him. And when the product was delivered—into the ground, in this scenario—the truck, or hearse, returned to the factory, or funeral home, to get another shipment. Strange.

Seconds later, a much different thought consumed me. One of the Naval officers had gotten into the car to drive away, but the other one stood at attention by the side of the one-lane gravel road there in St. Anthony's Cemetery, waiting for all of our vehicles to pass. I was in the lead car, but I asked my wife, who was driving, to hold for a moment; then I got out and hurried over to the man. I told him how meaningful it was to have him there, and I thanked him for everything he and his fellow officer had done. That's when he gave me the five-word response I hope I'll never forget—"It was an honor, sir," he said.

This is how I hope to always remember these past five years of taking care of my father. For all of my shortcomings and failures, I pray I did good sometimes, too. My father was a good and decent man, a man who I always respected and who I came to love. St. James? No, but in the end, he was a man of character, just as the lady at the funeral home described him. And in the end, it was an honor to take care of him over the final years of his life.

At the funeral home the other night, we saw one of those relaxation fountains sitting on a parlor end table. It was there when we arrived, and I thought that it was just another funeral home fixture, like a lamp or a plant stand. It wasn't until my wife told me that it was a gift that I looked at it closely and saw the card tucked away at its base. "Peace to all of you . . ." it read, and it was signed by our friends Bob and Thelma and their fifth-grade daughter Elizabeth. Their thoughtfulness touched me that night, and it continues to touch me now, long after the sympathy cards have been opened and all the flowers have withered away.

I used to keep Dad's Parkinson's disease meds—his 25/100 Sinemet and his .25 mg. Permax—on the kitchen counter along with the mortar and pestle I used to crush them. Twelve pills a day, every day for the five years he lived here after Mom's death. But with Dad's funeral Mass and the burial now behind us, I've gotten rid of the medicines and put the fountain on the kitchen counter instead. Before, when I looked at the spot, I saw my father's infirmity. Now when I look at the spot, I see—and hear—some of the peacefulness that our friends extended to us on that sad, sad Sunday evening.

As a memorial gift, it seems to fit better at our place than it did at the funeral home anyway, probably because this is where Dad ate, slept, and sat on the porch in the springtime. This is where he played beachball catch with my children and joked with my wife. This is where he died, yes, but this is also where he lived. I know that Bob and Thelma and Elizabeth's gift is just copper piping and so many stones. Still. It has a living voice, for when the household quiets down now, it speaks to me not only of a life that once was. It speaks to me, too, of a life that flows on and on, gently, forever.

[49]

It's been a couple of weeks now since Pop's funeral,
but I still find myself walking toward his door
at night sometimes to see how he's doing.

I FINISHED A CALLIGRAPHY project today—something I wrote for Pop. And I cried a lot today as I went through the sympathy cards again. It's going to take a while. And now, what to do? Back to Topco? Keep writing? Writing is the easy part. The hard part is making enough money to keep the family going. Gail is still supportive— as are my children—as I try to find my place in the world.

I'm spending hours and hours responding to the sympathy notes people have sent our way. Both up here and down in Streator, everyone has been so kind, and I feel compelled to answer each one personally and in some degree of detail regarding their connection either to Dad or to my family over these past five years. Mary has come over a couple of times to help me with the task, which seems overwhelming at times. I'm sure no one would mind if I just signed my name on behalf of the entire family, but I can't bring myself to do it, so the job goes on.

A central theme, which I refer to again and again, is not so much the kindness of the sender upon the occasion of Dad's death. This, in truth, means little to me, and is almost expected. What means so much to me is the kindness that these people have shown Dad over the past five years and before, going back to his Streator days. Long before his death was imminent, these people were asking about him, calling to see how he was doing, shaking his hand at Mass, bringing him coffee and cookies in the church hall. Kindness at the time of loss is nothing special to me. Kindness over the run of days and months and years is extraordinary, just as my father was extraordinary.

A former school secretary, Marcia, sent a touching card, which was inscribed with an aborigine philosophy that really hit home: "We are all visitors to this time, this place. We are just passing through. Our purpose here is to observe, to learn, to grow, to love . . . and then we return home." Marcia is a Bohemian type, and both my wife and I feel closely connected to her, even though we rarely see her these days. The tears were flowing as I responded to card after card after card when Gail, thanks to Marcia—provided me with a little relief. Gail came across the card first, and she said to me, "Of all the people we know, who would be most likely to send us a sympathy card based on aborigine philosophy?" I thought for a few moments and responded, "Uh, Marcia?" Gail smiled and gave me the card. I read it and smiled, too.

An old friend, Doug, did a nice thing. He e-mailed several of the people I used to deal with back in my corporate days and who are now part of a quality assurance organization to which I belonged before leaving to take care of Dad. Doug told them about Dad's passing, and they sent their condolences, too. And one person in particular, Scott—who I didn't even know all that well—sent me something via an e-mail message that I have already committed to memory and that I hope to hang on to for a long time. Scott said the words were spoken by a Jim Elliot, the first Christian martyr of the Alliance Church, and this is what he said: "He is no fool who gives up what he cannot keep in order to gain what he cannot lose." Thanks, Scott. Wherever you are.

Maribeth, a school mom over at St. Constance, sent another endearing note. She surprised me when she told me that she wanted to attend the funeral Mass down in Streator with Father Tom. I told her that her presence there—while certainly not expected—would mean much to me. Following the funeral, she sent me these words, which I keep in my journal and to which I have often already referred:

> Dear John, Gail, Sarah, and Paul,
>
> I know that this has been a very long and difficult week. Continue to remember that you and your father/grandfather are in my thoughts and prayers. I would like to thank you for allowing me to come to the services in Streator. I hope that in some small way, my presence lightened your sadness. It was very important for me to be there. I felt like I knew your father/grandfather. I knew him through each of you. I've had the pleasure of being introduced to him on a few occasions. I respected him and admired him for he was a man of dignity. I've seen his gentleness and love. I pray for him to be at peace.

Every time I read Maribeth's message, it brings tears to my eyes. Good tears, though. Mom and Dad told me for years and years as I was growing up that I came from good stock. Now that they're both gone, the words ring truer than they ever did. They ring true, and they make me warm.

I look at death differently now in regards to my children. When Mom and Dad were alive, they were the buffers between death and my children. Now, strangely, Gail and I are the buffers. Now there is only one generation separating them from the grave. I know that kids die early sometimes and old people can live to be one hundred. Still, Mom and Dad are gone, and now it's up to Gail and me to keep death away from Sarah and Paul.

And besides their words of sympathy and praise for Pop, several people sent Mass intentions to us on my father's behalf. I remember that Mom got a lot of these, too. I don't know how much prayer for the deceased helps, but I figure it can't hurt. We also got quite a bit of money and it all ended up here. Over three hundred dollars in total. With it, I made a fairly large contribution to the American Parkinson's Disease Association, and I sent a check in a lesser amount to Rainbow Hospice to help them in the work they do.

I also contributed to the St. Constance Parish Educational Endowment Fund. The fund was established within the past few months with an eye to the future of St. Constance School. Pop was well known within school family circles, as we always took him to the family Masses and then to the socials in Borowczyk Hall. Once I took Pop Christmas caroling with the Home and School Association. I drove around the block with Pop in the car as the carolers went door to door. I took Pop to various school events like our breakfast with the Easter bunny. I took him to the pet blessings in the school parking lot. I took him to school for an open house or two, and into one of the classrooms a few years ago for a "Rainbows for All God's Children" presentation. In my note to the principal with the check, I said that Pop's memory would linger around her hallways for a long, long time. Mrs. Panczyk told me that she agreed, and on the school's behalf, she said deeply and sincerely, "Thank you."

Mary was okay with all of this. I called Jim to tell him about it, too, but no one was home. I left the message on his machine and asked him to call me back if he had any problems with what I was doing with the money. He never got back to me, so I guess he's okay with all of my donations. I did get through to Jim the other day to invite him over for Christmas, but he said that he didn't want to get together with either Mary or me. Sad. Dear Lord, please soften my brother's heart toward me and the rest of the family. And please soften my heart toward him.

I had another interesting conversation the other day, too. Howard called to offer me a job. He said it was a good position back in the lab—back in Quality Assurance—but that I needed to react to his offer right away because they needed to fill the slot quickly. It was the phone call I was dreading in some ways, but looking forward to in some ways, as well. It all sounded pretty appealing. A regular paycheck. Paid insurance. Paid vacation. Security again. Yes, it all sounded terrific.

I told Howard no. My head had a hard time saying the word, but my heart had less of a struggle. I never grew up dreaming of being a food technologist or a middle manager in the corporate world. I grew up dreaming of being a writer. It's how I saw myself. But just as Dad was too good for his own good, I was too smart for my own good. I figured that everybody could write; I thought I had to do something else. I absolutely backed into my foods career. Thanks to people like Howard and Bob and Barbara, I learned a lot in the process, but from nearly the beginning, I sensed that it wasn't my true calling in the world.

Going back to work now—right now—would be a step backward for me. Not in terms of my salary or my position within the company. Topco is a great company, and I was always proud to call it my home. Indeed, I am convinced that if Dad had been the person who died five years ago—not Mom—I would still be there. Maybe I'll even be there again someday. But if I go back to the corporate world now, the dreamer takes a back seat to the practical man. And right now, it's the dreamer's time.

I told all of this to my friend Casey a few nights ago at a holiday gathering of our parish pastoral council. Casey is a special person and a dear friend. She has been supportive of my writing work for as long as I've been doing it. Shortly after I brought Dad into our home, in fact, she got me an assignment rewriting her company's corporate literature. In the great scheme of things, it was a small assignment, but it earned me several hundred dollars and it made my "writer" title a bit more meaningful.

Anyway, Casey was supportive once more that night. She hugged me and told me that not going back to work and writing instead was a good decision. I can't tell you how warm her words made me feel. For just as when I quit work to take care of Dad in the first place, I can feel the negative vibes sometimes when I tell people—and I've told a few now—that I'm going to write full-time instead of returning to a traditional, corporate environment. Many people I've told seem skeptical. But, oddly enough, not Howard.

Even as I was turning his job offer down, he was supportive of what I was trying to do.

And Casey gave me a book that night. It has a lot of blank pages in it and the idea, I guess, is to journal my feelings now that Dad is gone. Essentially, the book is a guided tour though the grieving process. I'm supposed to supply most of the text, and along the way, a picture of a barren tree becomes alive again with each passage. I may or may not take the journey on its pages. But I will continue to write in my own way, and I do not doubt that I will find healing there. But whether I use the book or not, I'll long remember Casey for offering it to me, and for telling me that it is okay to take the road less traveled.

Mom and Dad both liked my writing. I'm still writing my weekly column. I've even sold it to a few more parishes, and much of the text has turned to my father. I read Dad many of the finished pieces before they went to print. He didn't get the chance to hear my column for the first Sunday of Advent. I offer it now to you. And to him.

ON ADVENT, DAD, AND CELESTIAL CELEBRATIONS

There is a whisper of sadness in the Reynolds' household this first Sunday of Advent, for my father James is no longer with us to help us celebrate the season. He died here at home in his own bed a few weeks ago after having gifted us with his presence for just over five years. I was holding his left hand when he passed; my sister was holding his right; and my wife was there, too, somehow holding all of us—Dad, Mary, and me—in her heart.

Tears flowed that Thursday evening, and we didn't try to stop them. They weren't tears for my father, of course, for we knew that he had gone on to a better place. Instead, they were tears for ourselves, for one another, and, I suppose, for the rest of the family and friends who would soon be getting the word. As the days slip away, though, the tears are becoming less and the smiles more. And the smiles came fuller force still when I read a recent e-mail message from an old friend who had heard the news of Dad's passing.

Mike opened his note with words of sympathy for our loss and followed them with words of support for our effort in caring for Dad these past five years. He also told me that he would keep us in his prayers. But it was the last thing he wrote that gave me pause and brought the grins, because I had never really thought of it before, and Mike was the first to bring it home to me: "How wonderful it will be," he wrote, "for your dad to be part of the celestial celebration of Christ's birth!"

It brought me great joy to think of Dad kicking around paradise with Mom and the rest of the saints and angels in preparation for Christmas. And as I was envisioning the scene, it hit me that such a heavenly party would be nothing new for Dad—not really—because the man celebrated the event every single day. It's not that he never took the mistletoe down from the archway, the lights from the porch, or even the crèche from the mantlepiece. He kept Christmas by embracing the season's message of peace on earth and good will to all. It wasn't just a holiday phrase with him; Dad lived the Kingdom.

Shortly before the funeral Mass back in Streator, a woman told me that if my father had one fault, it was that he was too good for his own good. In truth, I remember Mom alluding to the same thing as I was growing up. She said that he went way too far out of his way to help people, often people he barely knew. Well, if Dad was too good for his own good, then it's a fault we might all do well to aspire to, especially as Advent comes and goes. For what better way to ready a place for Jesus in our hearts than to live our lives with caring and love like my father lived his? That celestial celebration Mike referred to is just getting cranked up. Let's all bring our best to the party.

And speaking of Christmas, I didn't get the new Christmas card out this year. A twelve-year tradition gone away. In truth, I had written the text of this year's message a few months ago, and I had planned to hand-letter it into card format in early November. But early November had different plans for us all. Hopefully, I'll get the card finished and send it out next Christmas to family and friends, but now I send it to you:

> Christmas cards.
> They fly like snow around the holidays,
>> but unlike a December snow that melts away,
>>> may this one linger warmly in your heart.
> We do not ask that you remember
>> the printed words upon the page.
> We do not ask that you remember the pattern or the design.
> Instead, we ask this Christmastime
>> and throughout the year that you recall on occasion
>>> why we send this card your way . . .
>
> We send it because you are Christmas to us.
> In one way or another,
>> you are a light in the darkness;
>> you are shelter from the wind;
>> you are silence when the whole world is screaming;
>> you are a connection from across the miles;
>> you are a smile when we need it most;
>> you are a gift.
> You uplift us in the truest spirit of this joyful season,
>> for in you we see the Child.
>
> We do not send this card lightly, you see.
> Quite the opposite,
>> we send it with much thought and caring,
>>> for who you are and what you mean to us
>>>> have great bearing in our life.
> During this time of sharing and always,
>> even if no words are spoken between us,
>>> we share the Holy Day with you and yours.
> Christmas cards.
> They fly like snow around the holidays . . .
>> but unlike a December snow that melts away,
>>> may this one linger warmly in your heart.

[50]

Dad is gone, but he isn't. Mom is gone, but she isn't either. They sneak up on me at the weirdest times. Often, they make me smile as I remember something they did or said.

JUST AS OFTEN, I FIND MYSELF reduced to tears, even when I'm sure there are no more to give. When Mom died so suddenly, several people told me it was better that way. When Dad faded away after years of struggle, several people told me it was better that way. So what's better? What's the better way?

The ramp is still up in front of the house. Sarah and Paul sledded down it again this winter, and I even joined them once or twice. And when people are coming to our home for the first time, I include the ramp in the directions: "It's the two-storey yellow bungalow with a ramp off the front porch." How many times I wheeled Pop up the thing! How many times I scolded him to let go of the railing as we went backward down it!

I had a superstition when I was a kid. I never went up or down wheelchair ramps, opting for the stairs instead. In my head I was thinking that I can walk, and I didn't want to use a ramp reserved for people who can't. I know it was stupid, but I've outgrown it now. I'm not afraid of ramps anymore, because my father and I have traveled them together. And for now at least, our ramp remains.

It's our intention to find a home for the hospital bed, the portable commode, the wheelchair, and the walker, and then turn Pop's room into my den, but Gail and I haven't really done anything yet. Just like we didn't really touch Pop's house for several months after Mom died. Actually, I did go in Pop's room a while back to ready it for Gail's Mom who was coming over for a few days following eye surgery. I cleaned out a portion of Pop's closet in the process, and the tears came again—hot and unending. "Is this shirt okay, Pop?" Or, "How about a sweater, today?" Mary and I talk almost every day and carry each other through it all. We even got together for lunch once. It felt weird without having Pop there, without having Pop slam his feet down and say that he's in the market for another shirt. She tells me that she's doing okay, but I can see it in her eyes, and I'm sure she can see it in mine. The sadness. The loss. The pain.

But I would be lying if I didn't say that in my eyes, at least, there is relief, too. Five years is a long time, and it's over. It's over! I hope it's okay to feel this way. I sense that it is. Years ago, not long after Pop came, Gail asked me how I liked being home and writing more. I told her I loved it. I also told her that it would be nice someday to be home and not be taking care of Pop. I didn't say the words then, nor did she, but the meaning was clear. It would be nice to be home and writing with Pop not here. After Pop passed away, I guess. It wasn't my wish, but now it is my reality, and it is bittersweet.

Gail—as she has always been—is supportive once more. Far from insisting that I go out and get a job, she thinks that the syndicated column could work, as long as I keep coming up with ideas and we can get the word out to other parishes. And she even seems to still enjoy having me around. Sarah and Paul are the same way. I mentioned the possibility of my returning to the traditional workforce to Sarah, and she said she liked having me home. I like it too, Princess, and for now, that's the plan.

Support and love don't pay the rent, of course, as I have quickly discovered. When Dad was alive, I had money coming in every month as his paid caregiver. Dad is gone. The money has stopped. But the bills haven't. If I can make it work at all, it's going to take some time to get the column off the ground, and how do we pay the mortgage in the meantime? Fortunately, Gail and I have long been good savers. We've joked for the past twenty years, in fact, that we saved big money on her wedding dress. We both forget the details, but we got the dress on some sort of discount, and almost every time we've made a nonessential purchase since— a purchase that cost a bit more than we wanted to spend—we dredge up the time-honored rationalization, "But we saved two hundred bucks on the wedding dress."

Beyond that two hundred, we'd been putting a little money away every month since we bought the house right up until Dad came. We don't have lot of cash in the bank, but it will last us several months even if we drew exclusively from it, and we aren't. Gail's working a few days a week as a dental office manager for her brother Greg, and I've got some money coming in from the weekly column, some freelance work, a weekly Catholic News Service gig, and a monthly column for *Senior Connection*. Many years ago I would have looked at this income if not as pocket change, then as "mad money," as Mom called her little stash from working over at the factory in Pontiac when Jim and Mary were in college. But it's not mad money any longer. Now it pays the kids' tuition and it puts food on the table.

Unfortunately, it doesn't stretch to the mortgage or the utility bills or the insurance or everything else that makes life so expensive. Why does everything cost so much? Dad's savings were far from depleted by the time of his death, thanks, in part, to the money he saved by being here. What's left will be split three ways between Mary and Jim and me. The inheritance, coupled with our own savings, won't last a long time, but it will last long enough for me to try this writing game for a few years. So many times when Pop was alive, I thanked him for letting me care for him and to work on the words. So many times he responded that he wasn't doing anything. Even in his death, he continues to gift my family and me.

Gail got me a book for Christmas, Stephen King's *On Writing: A Memoir of the Craft*. I read it in a couple of days, and I'm sure I'll read it many times again. The mere fact that she thought of me in this regard means the world to me. The book is a good read regardless of circumstance, and in my circumstance, it's a particularly encouraging read as well. We write much differently, Mr. King and I, and for different audiences, perhaps. But we're both still just writers, getting along one word at a time as best we can and trying to connect with the reader, whoever it happens to be. He says that he writes with his wife in mind. I write with Gail in mind. And tied up in that mindset is the notion that I write every column as if it were a letter to an old friend.

Toward the conclusion of his text, King writes that in the end, writing is about "enriching the lives of those who will read your work, and enriching your own life as well. . . ." This is what I want to do. I am who I am because of Mom and Dad and Patches and the other grandparents I never knew. And somewhere along the way, one of them—or all of them—put it in me to write. So it's not my fault that I've put all this down in letters. It's theirs. Blame them. Blame them all.

I had another *Tribune* essay accepted the other day. Once again, it's Pop-related.

ON USED CARS, AND KNOWING THE PREVIOUS OWNER

I'm forty-seven years old, and I've never bought new a new car. Not once. I bought my first used one, though, a red, '66 Volkswagen Beetle, back in Streator when I was about twenty, and I've bought four used cars from there since. Always got a great deal. Never felt the need to have the local mechanic check them out, either. And I had good luck with them, too. Now—as I'm looking for another pre-owned vehicle to replace my last Streator purchase—I'm thinking that all of my used car success has been as simple as knowing the previous owner. I bought each one from my dad.

It's not that I came knocking on his door. With every car after the Volkswagen, if fact, it was more the other way around. But I had my eye on Dad's Bug from the start. I had already driven it plenty around town. Repainted it, too. And I had the oil changed for him every three months or three thousand miles, just like he told me. Then, when my college ride dried up, I suggested to Dad that I buy his Beetle. Perhaps figuring I'd make it home from Champaign more if I had my own wheels, he said yes. And even with the great price he gave me, he told me to just pay him back a little at a time, whenever I could. Man, I wish somebody would tell me that again.

The Volkswagen gave way to a '72 Plymouth Duster (the car Dad bought for himself when he sold me the Bug). I drove that until it died, then he offered me his '77 Chevette, and after that, his '81 Horizon. All of these cars served me well, and I was happy to have them. Somewhere along the line, though, I started wanting something a little sportier, something a little more daring, something a Midwestern small-town banker probably wouldn't drive back and forth to work every day. I wanted a Jeep Wrangler. A red one.

When I shared this news with my folks, they seemed concerned. Maybe they just couldn't picture me in a vehicle with a roll bar. Or maybe they thought I should be saving my money for more important things—like college educations for Sarah and Paul, their two newest grandchildren. Either way, there was Dad again—keys in hand—offering me the car that I am only just now looking to replace—his 1985 Dodge 600.

282

It's a four-door, white sedan, about as anti-flashy, anti-sporty, and anti-daring as they come. I didn't want it. I wanted a red Jeep. But Dad was excited about me taking it, and, after he made me another great offer, I shook his hand like I had done four times before and said, "Sold!" Still stinging from my uninspiring purchase, I was walking into work one day when I asked Peter, a polite, young coworker of Middle European descent who was walking in at the same time, what he thought of my new wheels. "Nice car for a family man, sir." he said. A knife couldn't have cut me any deeper.

I've come to realize, though, that Peter's words were high praise. My father, the greatest family man I've ever known, died this past November—here at home, in his own bed—after living with us here for just over five years. Before the end came—and when he could, with assistance—Dad would hobble with his walker over to the front window. He'd lower his head and look outside, and he'd see my car—*his* car—the Dodge 600 parked on the street. "Car looks good, John," he'd always say, even when it hadn't been washed in months, and even as its nearly fifteen-year-old underbelly was rusting away. "Car looks good."

God, how I wish I could hear him say it again. Sometimes, I think I almost can. He wasn't a man who drove flashy cars, my dad, but besides the importance of regular oil changes, this is what he taught me: to work hard and to try to do what's right, even if it's not the easiest or most popular thing. He taught me, too, in his quiet and unassuming way, to cherish my wife and to love my children. And if I can say with my final breath that I have done these things just a fraction as well as my father did, then I'll rate my life as one terrific ride, regardless of the wheels beneath me over the course of it all.

I knew it was time for another car a few months ago when I offered a ride to a homeless person. She climbed into my 600, saw the sagging roof fabric, and said, "Whoa, you've got a problem here!" Since then, all of the potential deals I've found have fallen through; buying used cars was a lot easier when Dad brought them to me. Something will turn up, of course, but until it does, I guess I'll just have to keep the Dodge loping along, buoyed by Peter's words and by my father's memory. Nice car for a family man.

Long ago, in one of the first letters I wrote about taking care of Pop, I quoted a passage from the poet John Donne, and I'd like to quote it again: "Sir, more than kisses, letters mingle souls / For, thus friends absent speak." Written over four hundred years ago, the words have never been truer. I have written much over these years, but does it not seem like just a few days or weeks at most? So it is between friends—the years fall away when they get together. I will rest now, and I will write again on the subject one final time, for I feel that one more letter will finish my father's story. And this part of my own.

[51]

It is spring time now, and the harshness of winter is slipping away. Indeed, the coldness is leaving me, although I know that it can return at any moment to chill me and make me feel alone. I haven't found that car yet, but I'm still looking. I haven't found my place in the world yet, but I'm still looking for that, too. And Mom and Dad, I think, are helping me along the way.

I RECEIVED ANOTHER SYMPATHY NOTE not long ago. It came in well after the hundreds that arrived in late November, but the handwritten message inside explained much about the card's sense of timing. It was written by an old grade-school buddy, Kenny, who—like several of my grade-school and high-school buddies—spent many hours in my parents' home there on Van Buren Street. Those were good days—the best days of our lives, my mother always told me. She may have been right, but these days are good, too. And I am reminded by Kenny that long-ago days can play an important role in a distant and unforeseen future. This is what he wrote:

> John, It's not that I forgot to send this, but more that I wasn't sure of what I wanted to say. After listening to your poem at St.

Anthony's, I took the opportunity to reflect on the closing line, "I am my father's son." I may not be your father's son, but as he influenced you, I, too, can say that a little bit of your dad rubbed off on all of us. His quiet, yet confident demeanor, along with his faith, are attributes that I took from your dad. Hopefully, I can pass them along to my sons as well. Visiting your home was truly an enjoyable occasion, thanks to the role models of your parents."

Indeed, my mom and dad have touched many on their walks through life. Kenny. The rest of my friends. The people at the bank. The people at St. Anthony's and St. Constance Church. Their doctors and nurses. Their children. . . . I miss them both, as does Mary and Jim, I'm sure. But hopefully, as Kenny says, my parents' example may lead many of us who are left behind. It may even lead Jim and me back together again. I think Mom and Dad would like that.

If the path really is revealed in the treading as I read somewhere long ago, I am treading it now, looking every day to see where it will lead. And somewhere along the path, I believe, are the words. Easter will soon be here, and I just finished my column for the Great Sunday. It speaks of both Mom and Dad, and it seems a good way to bring this letter to a close. I cried when I wrote it, but as I reread it now, it brings me joy:

ON MOM AND DAD, AND EASTER SUNDAY

My mother and father had been married for nearly fifty years when Mom died very suddenly a few weeks shy of Easter about six years ago. It was a sad day. Unless Dad was working at the bank—which he did plenty—they were always together, those two. I remember Mom telling me often that Dad followed her around like a little, lost puppy dog. She said it in a whining kind of way, with something of *I-wish-he'd-just-leave-me-alone* behind the words, but I sensed that she liked all of his attention nonetheless.

All I know for sure, though, is that I grew up with them side-by-each. They did the dishes together. They walked to daily Mass together. They went to McDonald's for coffee. Or to Weaver's for fried chicken. And when it got hard for Dad to get around, Mom would stay at home with him. Or maybe she'd drive him up to see us between our visits there. I called them "Mom" and "Dad," of course, but the rest of the world knew them by their given names. Jean and Jim. Jean and Jim. Jean and Jim. You couldn't say one with out saying the other. They were like Romeo and Juliet, maybe. Or at least like ham and eggs. They just went together, and they fit each other like gloves.

Which is probably why the woman said what she did. I didn't even know who she was. I was standing near the casket at Mom's wake service on that gray March day. Several people offered their condolences, as did the woman in question. But beyond telling me how sad she was for me, she added something that I hung on to for the next five years—actually, until I was standing near Dad's casket last November. With every intention of sympathy, I'm sure, she said, "Don't be surprised if you lose your father soon, too."

I just wanted to throttle her. But I knew that she was well-intentioned, so I thanked her for her caring and let the moment pass. I remembered her words often, though, and at Dad's wake service, I recalled them once more, understanding that, in the great scheme of things, she was right. Still, five years was five years, I reasoned, and I knew then, as I know now, that the time my family and I spent caring for Dad was a sacred time for us all.

As our father took his final breath, I blessed him on his forehead and told him that we loved him. My sister, meanwhile, told him that he could go home to Mom now. And so he did. This will be our first Easter without them, but it will be their first Easter side-by-each again in a long time. On this joyous commemoration of Christ's rising, the Apostle Paul's poetic message rings as boldly as ever: "Where, O death, is your victory? Where, O death, is your sting?" I miss Mom and Dad. But today, especially, I celebrate what I know to be true. Jean and Jim. Together again, and still fitting each other like gloves.